to Renée

DAVID QUAMMEN

✵

THE
BOILERPLATE
RHINO

✵

NATURE IN THE EYE OF THE BEHOLDER

SCRIBNER

New York London Toronto Sydney

SCRIBNER
1230 Avenue of the Americas
New York, NY 10020

SCRIBNER and design are trademarks of
Macmillan Library Reference USA, Inc., used under license
by Simon & Schuster, the publisher of this work.

For information about special discounts for bulk purchases,
please contact Simon & Schuster Special Sales:
1-800-456-6798 or business@simonandschuster.com.

Designed by Brooke Koven
Set in MT Sabon
Manufactured in the United States of America

5   7   9   10   8   6

The Library of Congress has cataloged the Scribner edition as follows:
Quammen, David, date.
The boilerplate rhino : nature in the eye of the beholder / David Quammen.
p.   cm.
Includes bibliographical references (p.).
1. Natural history. 2. Nature. I. Title.
QH81 .Q17 2000
508—dc21   99-056894
ISBN-13: 978-0-684-83728-4
ISBN-10:   0-684-83728-5
ISBN-13: 978-0-7432-0032-5 (Pbk)
ISBN-10:   0-7432-0032-2 (Pbk)

FIRST PUBLICATION

EACH ESSAY was originally published in the column "Natural Acts," *Outside* magazine, dated as follows: "Rattlesnake Passion," January 1991; "The Narcotic of Empire," June 1994; "Hard Parts," March 1995; "Certainty and Doubt in Baja," October 1989; "Phobia and Philia," September 1994; "Who Swims with the Tuna," December 1990; "Tropical Passengers," August 1992; "Spatula Theory," July 1993; "The Great Stinking Clue," February 1993; "The Dope on Eggs," February 1988; "The Cats That Fly by Themselves," January 1994; "Local Bird Makes Good," January 1995; "One Man's Meat," August 1989; "Either or Neither," May 1995; "Beast in the Mirror," October 1993; "Palpating the Tumor," January 1993; "Rethinking the Lawn," July 1994; "Half-Blinded Poets and Birds," January 1990; "Time-and-Motion Study," December 1988; "The Boilerplate Rhino," June 1993; "Limelight," July 1995; "Gardening on Mars," February 1989; "Impersonating Henry Thoreau," July 1988; "God's Weakness for Beetles," June 1988; "Limits of Vision," October 1991.

The author gratefully acknowledges permission to reprint from:

Incantations: Poems 1966–1968, copyright © 1968 by Robert Penn Warren; *Audubon: A Vision*, copyright © 1969 by Robert Penn Warren; and *New and Selected Poems, 1923–1985*, copyright © 1985 by Robert Penn Warren. Reprinted by permission of William Morris Agency, Inc., on behalf of the author.

The Rock: A Pageant Play Book by T. S. Eliot, copyright 1934 by Harcourt, Inc. and renewed 1962 by T. S. Eliot, reprinted by permission of the publisher.

"The Rock" in *Collected Poems 1909–1962 by T. S. Eliot,* published by Faber and Faber Ltd. Reprinted by permission of Faber and Faber Ltd.

"Cobra" and "Counting Birds" in *The Theory & Practise of Rivers and New Poems,* copyright © 1989 by Jim Harrison. Reprinted by permission of Jim Harrison.

CONTENTS

IV. NEAR SIGHT

V. TRICKS OF THE LIGHT

INTRODUCTION

For fifteen years it was my job to think about the natural world, and about human relationships with that world, in a way that would interest the 500,000 readers of a certain magazine. Most of those readers were people who neither knew nor cared much about the difference between a barnacle and a limpet, the difference between a meadow and a savanna, the difference between an ecosystem and "the environment" (that vague, misguided locution), or the difference between Henry Thoreau the man and Henry David Thoreau the literary icon. The magazine was *Outside*, an admirable publication dedicated largely to travel, adventure, and outdoor sports such as climbing, kayaking, bicycling, ski mountaineering, triathlon, sailing, spelunking, scuba diving, parachuting off tall buildings, Rollerblading through tough neighborhoods, and grappling catfish bare-handed out of Louisiana bayous. I was one of its columnists, charged with filling a space each month with an essay of roughly three thousand words that dealt, at least tenuously, with science or nature.

The column was called "Natural Acts." It had been conceived under that title by the magazine's founding editors and written for the first four years (1977 to 1981) by an able essayist named Janet Hopson. I took over in mid-1981, putting my own voice, perspective, and set of concerns into it for the next decade and a half. When I accepted the invitation to begin writing this column, I thought I might have ideas and energy enough to carry through one or two years. But the ideas kept coming, and the time flew.

During that period, the saintly editors of *Outside* (notably John Rasmus, Mark Bryant, David Schonauer, and Greg Cliburn) allowed me unimaginable freedom to explore a wide range of peculiar theories, remote places, bizarre facts, and unpopular opinions, and to depart distantly from conventional nature writing, of which I have never much cared to be either a reader or an author. The editors, for their part, didn't want conventional nature writing either—no sensitive descriptions of wildflowers or babbling brooks, no sylvan dithyrambs, no hushed piety in the presence of Mr. Woodchuck and Mrs. Deer. They let me monger scandal about the secret life of spoon worms. They let me say tasteless things about bedbugs. They let me digress into history and culture. They let me discuss the latest scientific thinking on monogamy, earthquake prediction, and (these were three separate topics, by the way, not a logical triad) penises. They let me dabble in literary criticism, deliver eulogies when I felt moved to, rant about the end of life as we know it. They let me be silly one month and Jeremiah the next. The only stipulated requirements (well, implicitly stipulated) were that each essay, no matter how aberrant, should contain at least passing mention of an animal, a scientist, or a tree; and that I meet each monthly deadline with *something*. My first "Natural Acts" column, a contemplation of the redeeming merits of mosquitoes, titled "Sympathy for the Devil," ran in June 1981. My final column, a look at the evolutionary history and minatory significance of city pigeons, titled "Superdove on 46th Street," appeared in March 1996. (Neither of those essays is included here, since they've been reprinted in previous books.) Between the devil and the doves, I produced about 150 other columns. I never got two sneezes ahead of the deadline schedule, and I seldom knew more than a few days in advance what subject I would dive into next. Once a month for fifteen years I became frantic.

For a writer prone to vagrant curiosities, intrigued by verminous creatures, with a hearty appetite for library research (especially in scientific journals) and field research (especially in rainforests, swamps, mountains, and deserts) but not for the sort of telephone research (calling experts for canned quotes, ugh) that too often serves as the staple of science journalism, this column was an ideal gig. It gave me occasion to write some essays that would have been too far beyond the fringe for a freelance journalist selling work piece by piece. It also gave me a strong sense of the sacred, enriching, mutualistic relationship between writer and audience.

I mention that sense of relationship because a column is, in my opinion, different from other sorts of magazine writing. Part of a columnist's special task is to turn oneself into an agreeable habit, yet to maintain an edge of surprise and challenge that prevents readers from letting the habit become somnolent rote. One way of doing that is to deliver outlandish material in a friendly, companionable voice. Speak to the readers as though you and they know each other—an illusion that becomes, increasingly over time, true. Although the facts and ideas change drastically from month to month, something remains constant: the relationship. I loved the particular audience to which *Outside* gave me access. (I still do, so long as I can address those readers at feature length, and no more than several times a year.) But eventually I wanted to break the habit, for the best interests of all concerned. I quit the column after fifteen years because I was tired, very tired, of producing such short essays month after month, and because I didn't want to start repeating or imitating myself.

Now the audience is you. This book is an assortment of some of the more durable (I hope) and closely interrelated pieces I wrote during my latter eight years as a columnist. Unlike the three earlier books that I've drawn from magazine work—*Natural Acts* (1985), *The Flight of the Iguana* (1988), and *Wild Thoughts from Wild Places* (1998)—this one consists solely of essays that appeared in the "Natural Acts" column, with no larding of longer work done for *Outside* or other magazines. That self-restriction is a matter of choice, not of empty file cabinets. I wanted to make a book that reflects the range and trajectory of notions explored over time by one columnist for one set of readers. Although magazine audiences tend to be much larger than the audience any book (except a best-seller) receives, the relationship between a magazine writer and the readers tends, in most circumstances, to be fleeting and shallow. In a book, on the other hand, a reader undertakes a sustained and serious connection with the writer. And the bond that grows between a columnist and a magazine readership over a period of years, I submit, is more like the situation with a book. Themes recur. Ideas are teased at, tested by time as well as by further delving, advanced in small stages. Hobbyhorses are ridden, stabled, and trotted out again later. Characters reappear. Inevitably the columnist commits small, incremental acts of self-revelation, becoming a character too. If the columnist isn't careful, in fact, he or she might realize after some long run of years that the installments collectively represent not just a manifesto but an autobiography. That too is part of the deal. A column can be the most conversational form of journalism, but to create the sense of a conversation with readers, the writer must consent to be a person, not just a pundit. Good writing sounds like talk, not oratory.

In deciding which essays to include here, I focused on one underpinning theme: How do humans, in all their variousness, regard and react to the natural world, in all its variousness? Hence the discussions of rattlesnake handlers as well as rattlesnakes, of arachnophobia as well as spiders, of fruit-bat chowder as well as fruit-bat conservation, of trilobite photography raised to an art form, of God's and Tom Lovejoy's fondness for beetles, and of the famous rhinoceros that Albrecht Dürer knew only by hearsay. Hence also the book's subtitle, *Nature in the Eye of the Beholder.* This focus on human perceptions and attitudes isn't airily epistemological, nor is it a cynical concession to the narcissism of audience. It's what interests me—and, I hope, you. Even a part-time misanthrope like myself has to admit that, of all the weird species that inhabit this planet, few are more richly and horrifically fascinating than *Homo sapiens.* Although I believe that humanity collectively represents a ruinous ecological outbreak population of unprecedented puissance, I would never deny that as individuals we live out some compelling stories. Shakespeare said it diplomatically: What a piece of work.

In addition to that theme, I've touched repeatedly on two others: 1) the limits of scientific knowledge, and 2) the truth (okay, it's a truism, but like some other truisms, it's too often forgotten) that reality tends always to be vastly more complicated than initial impressions or assumptions would suggest. Having had many chances to study scientists as they study nature, I've seen that science itself is a fallible human activity, not a conceptual machine-tool, and that while accuracy and precision can be easily achieved, validity and meaning cannot. The imperfections and constraints vitiating scientific knowledge stand as a warning about the limits of other sorts of knowledge—even shakier sorts—including that based on eyewitness experience. Moral: We live in a tricky universe, and it behooves us to be just a bit provisional about our convictions. Spending so much of my working life on short-term but intense spates of research into widely various subjects, I've also been schooled in the lesson that additional investigation generally leads toward increased complexity, ambivalence, even confusion, not toward increased certainty. These two themes are connected, and toward the end of the book, in the essay titled "God's Weakness for Beetles," I bundle them into the Parable of Coleoptera: unidentified Amazon beetles as tokens that nature is vastly complex, human knowledge small. Of course I didn't consciously choose to harp on that pair of points as I wrote my monthly miniatures—about nutmeg economics, chimpanzee genetics, lizard research in Baja, flying cats, giant faces shaped in the topography of Mars, egg ranching, bizarre tropical fruit, the whereabouts of *Tyrannosaurus rex,* and dark matter as viewed through binoculars—but there they are. Maybe their hold upon me represents a vestigial effect from my years of immersion in the novels of William Faulkner. The Parable of Coleoptera, after all, is not so different from the parable of Thomas Sutpen.

I should emphasize, though, that these three recurrent themes provide only a loose organizational schema for the book, not a rigid program. Many other ideas are explored, many other saws bowed, and each essay is intended to stand on its own. Also, while I'm at it, here's another advisory: Although the sequential order of the essays is in some ways progressive, there's no need for you to follow that order in reading them. Jump around as your whim dictates. To help guide your browsing, I've retained the magazine practice of supplying subtitles as well as titles.

The "Natural Acts" column was a great opportunity in my professional life, but it's a finished phase, and the reader-to-writer relationship that concerns me now is the one with you. Even while conducting my part of that earlier conversation, I knew that it might later yield a book. So I was writing for you, as well as for the dear climbers and cyclists and catfish grapplers who read *Outside.* In sifting through scores of uncollected essays and re-editing just twenty-five for inclusion here, I've omitted those that seemed stale, as well as those that had no place within my baggy thematic rubrics; and I've adjusted time references in a way that eases these twenty-five away from their original topical contexts but doesn't pretend to bring every one up to date. They were written when they were written. (For particulars, see "First Publication," page 4.) I offer them to you now as a bestiary of wondrous creatures, a catalog of indecorous notions, and a gallery of peering human faces. I offer them as a window and a mirror.

✿ I ✿

ROADKILL
ON THE
HIGHWAY OF TIME

Rattlesnake Passion

On the Highway of Time in the Heart of Texas

The world is a changeful place and Texas, despite what some folks might think, is part of the world. It was seventeen years since I'd set foot inside the snake farm at New Braunfels.

All I remembered was a turnstile and a row of cages, a pit full of diamondback rattlesnakes, a fellow named John Deck, and the shriveled carcass of a two-headed monkey. Probably the two-headed monkey was a figment, I'd begun to suspect, invented by my own brain in the course of telling and retelling a good story. It was too mythic. It was too precisely the sort of detail that a person would concoct for some ludicrous, gothic piece of fiction. This two-headed monkey in my mind's eye, this pitiful thing, was dried like a piece of jerky. And oh yes, there was also a vegetable scale—a tin pan beneath a spring gauge—hung up above the pit. I couldn't have told you whether the vegetable scale was an artifact of imagination or of memory. Memory, imagination, whichever, as I drove back into New Braunfels on a spring day not long ago, I had no expectation of finding it. I had no expectation of seeing a two-headed monkey. Probably, I thought, the snake farm itself would be gone.

I envisioned it long since foreclosed upon or lost in the pot of a poker game, fallen derelict, a sad nightmare of broken windows and ragged chickenwire and fading signs, done in by shifting values and new fashions in entertainment. I pictured it haunted by dozens of snakes that had suffered terminal neglect in their cages, left to starve so slowly that even they didn't notice the exact moment of death, dried by the Texas heat into pretzel shapes more pitifully macabre than even a two-headed monkey. I remembered it in vivid but unreal colors, like a fever dream or a horror-flick sequence shot in queasy sepia. I had to remind myself that there had indeed been a snake farm beside the highway at New Braunfels, Texas, and I had indeed spent time inside. Most likely, by now, it had been bulldozed to clear the lot. Most likely it had transmogrified into a Mini Mart or a video store. The world is a changeful place. Back in 1973, when I first stepped through the turnstile, a person could make a living of sorts, evidently, from a serpent menagerie on a dust-blown roadside. What's the scale for? I had asked John Deck.

Weighing rattlesnakes, he had told me. We buy them by the pound.

John Deck was a young man with a particular attitude toward snakes. In Texas, where venomous serpents still outnumber humans and cows and Japanese automobiles, you find quite a sampling of particular attitudes toward snakes. Some folks just plain hate them. With purblind passion they detest the poor animals from the depths of their tiny, sour hearts. The diamondback rattlesnake, *Crotalus atrox,* being common and large and modestly dangerous, is the bête noire of these people. Snake-haters kill diamondbacks for fun. They kill diamondbacks with a righteous zeal that they'd like to believe is somehow religious or patriotic or, at least, neighborly. They kill diamondbacks from habit. These people gather together annually in great civic festivals of cartoonish abuse, and slaughter, and ecstatic adolescent loathing, that go by the label of rattlesnake roundups. Often as not, for such an event, the local Jaycees serve as sponsor. Diamondback rattlesnakes are bought by the pound. Typically there's a cash prize for the longest snake; a prize for the most rattles; and a prize for the weightiest total delivery of snake flesh. Admission is charged, crowds gather, Coke and Dr Pepper and gobbets of fried diamondback are available at concession stands. Of course it's all high-minded and innocent, on the surface. It's a way to raise money for the hospital or the fire truck. Deeper down it's a pageant of hatred, wonderfully medieval, reflecting the same dire élan that might have stirred a Bavarian village during the early days of the Black Death. March is the favored month for such doings, notwithstanding what T. S. Eliot said about April. In March the snakes are still groggy from winter, they're loafing in underground dens, from which they can be conveniently flushed with infusions of gasoline. By April, they've likely dispersed. Or they might defend themselves.

Other people, a smaller minority of contrasting disposition, are what you might call snake fanciers. Snake fanciers buy and sell, they trade and collect. They view snakes as precious and transcendent commodities—same way another person, hardly more sane, might dote upon canceled stamps or antique Packards or the Pete Rose rookie baseball card. Snake fanciers know the blue-book value of any species at any given moment. The Mexican milk snake, *Lampropeltis triangulum annulata,* is smallish and nonvenomous but beautifully banded in yellow and red and black, a close mimic of the coral snake, and therefore it's highly prized. The Western coachwhip is a big matinee-idol of a snake, but too common to interest a fancier. The California kingsnake, not native to Texas, might go for fifty bucks as a hatchling. And amid fanciers, as amid roundups: Diamondback rattlesnakes are wholesaled by the pound. It's a matter of supply and demand.

JOHN DECK was a snake fancier. He had only been rattler-bit a few times. At an early age he'd had his own pit full of diamondbacks, a plywood affair out near the garage. Some of the snakes would scootch themselves up vertically along the boards and John, cocky lad, used to knock them back down with his own quick right hand, delivering a light tap to the back of a rattler's head, until one day he presumed against a snake that was readier than he was, and caught a palmload of fangs. At the end of his grunt time in Vietnam, he came back from over there with a bag full of cobras, which he'd collected while walking patrol, using the butt of his M-16 for a pinning stick. When I met John, he was a full-time professional attendant at the New Braunfels snake farm—like a boy's dream of the perfect job, yes?—and still snake-hunting on his own time to fill out his private collection. I was fascinated. Sure, he told me, come along if you want. We'll go on down there to Terrell County.

Terrell County was not chosen at random. This was the place to go, this was the scene, if you were a serious fancier of the Texas herpetofauna. Diamondbacks could be had anywhere, but down in the rolling hills and gullies of Terrell County you might find a mottled rock rattler, or a Mojave rattler, or a trans-Pecos copperhead, or that exceptionally prized rarity, a Blair's kingsnake. So we drove in John's pickup, all through one hot afternoon and warm evening, to reach this Elysian desert on the far side of the Pecos River, just northwest of a border town called Langtry. We provisioned ourselves with sardines and Vienna sausages from the Langtry store. We cruised up and down the dirt roads by night, scanning the shoulders with high beams, on the lookout for nocturnal snakes, and then, after a few hours' sleep, by daylight we climbed through the gullies.

At some point we shanghaied a tarantula, which John locked away in a brown paper bag and which cost me sleep in the back of the pickup (we shared the truck bed, that spider and I, while John slept on the ground among scorpions) with its tireless scratching for freedom. In the privacy of the cab, as we cruised, John gossiped with other snakers over the CB. He talked guardedly to me about Vietnam, a delightful country if you happened to like deadly snakes. He told me some rattlesnake stories—the one about getting bit on the palm, the more elaborately comical one about the excitable emergency-room nurse who ran and tripped and broke her arm when he walked in for help and spoke the word *snakebite,* though that particular bite turned out to be empty of venom and he was less badly hurt than she was. He explained which species were scarce, highly prized, and which weren't. At another moment John mashed the brakes and dove out to grab a yellowbelly racer, *Coluber constrictor flaviventris,* a nonvenomous species and probably one of the more common in Texas. Notwithstanding the rarity theory of value, this racer was big and pretty and he wanted it; too eager to use a pinning stick, he nearly got chewed on before subduing it clumsily by covering its head with his hat. John Deck had an unheedful passion for snakes, almost any snakes, that an ecology-minded person just couldn't sanction and a generous-minded person just couldn't hate.

He didn't kill them. He didn't fry them. He didn't abuse them before crowds to prove the octane of his testosterone. He kidnapped them out of their habitat, yes. Sometimes he sold them or traded them, yes. Mainly he just fancied them.

In his company I enjoyed two days of vivid lunacy. And our quest for herpetological jewels was rewarded. We caught a nice little specimen of mottled rock rattler. We caught a trans-Pecos copperhead, elegant with its russet and tan bands. In those days this foolishness was legal. It even seemed like a good idea. The Blair's kingsnake, happy to say, eluded us.

A month later I left Texas. Too dry and too hot, I decided, with not nearly enough trout. I never saw John Deck again. But who could forget him?

SOME OF the things you can witness at a rattlesnake roundup in Texas or Oklahoma:

You can see thousands of pounds of diamondback rattlesnakes being measured and weighed. "We had 5,000 pounds of snakes turned in before noon the first morning," a snake-weigher at the Sweetwater Rattlesnake Roundup told a reporter from *Time* after the 1988 event. "They're brought in U-Hauls so they don't freeze. We don't buy dead snakes." The total at Sweetwater that year was 11,709 pounds, and Sweetwater is just one roundup among dozens. Although dead snakes aren't bought, dying snakes are, and if you looked closely you might see that many are not in the pink of health. Some have suffered broken necks from rough handling with tongs. Some are starved and dehydrated, having been captured months earlier and stockpiled in anticipation of roundup day. One Texas herpetologist reckons that 95 percent of the rattlesnakes turned in at a given roundup have not been collected that weekend or in that vicinity. So much for the traditional notion of roundups—as festive occasions for desnaking the local countryside.

You can see an arts-and-crafts show. Among the items on sale, you're liable to find snakeskin belts, snakeskin gimme hats, plastic paperweights containing diamondback heads, earrings made from rattles, and perhaps the ultimate, a toilet seat of clear plastic within which are embedded baby diamondbacks. Whether the toilet seat (retail, around seventy-five dollars) qualifies in these towns as a piece of art, or merely a craft, is a question I'm not in position to answer.

You might see children, whole families, being photographed holding live diamondbacks—squeamish but grinning folks, secure in the knowledge that these particular animals have had their mouths sewn shut. You might see parents paying five dollars to buy a child the privilege of decapitating a rattlesnake with a hatchet. You can certainly see a sacking competition, wherein contestants race against a stopwatch to stuff ten diamondbacks into a sack, with a five-second penalty added each time the sacker gets bitten. The world rattlesnake-sacking record has been intermittently held by a Texan named Cotton Dillard—at least, that's the claim made by Mr. Dillard. He posted a time of 18.6 seconds at the town of Taylor in 1984. In a more recent year, Mr. Dillard slipped to 34 seconds, after a penalty.

You can see a club of dauntless fellows who call themselves the Heart of Texas Snake Handlers, based in Waco but on the road during roundup season, performing vainglorious antics in their matching T-shirts. You can see them do the Kung Fu Walk of Death, strutting bare-foot down a gauntlet of diamondbacks and kicking the snakes aside. You can see them stack coiled diamondbacks on their heads. You can see them lie still in sleeping bags filled with rattlesnakes, purportedly to make an educational point about safe camping. Some guys have motor-cycles; some guys have golf; some guys get drunk and beat people up with cue sticks on Friday night; the Heart of Texas Snake Handlers have snakes. You can see that these boys possess, in their own right, a very particular attitude.

Confession: Though I've snaked my way across Terrell County with John Deck, I've never attended a roundup. Occasionally over the years I've threatened myself with the notion, as a journalistic enterprise, but I was reluctant to contribute further to the atmosphere of manic, media-hungry persecution. Much of my information about them comes from a Texan named A. J. Seippel, a mild-mannered computer executive and amateur herpetologist, who has an attitude of his own. "If this were rabbits, or any other animal, it would have been stopped a long time ago," Seippel says. He and others are working to stop it now.

Sign-carrying and leaflet-distributing protesters, including Jim Seip-pel, have laid siege to the roundups. Conservationists, animal-rights groups, Earth First!ers, Humane Society chapters, reputable herpetolog-ical clubs—more than two dozen organizations have united to raise the long-overdue cry that rattlesnake roundups are retrograde and indecent. Jim Seippel is a persuasive spokesman. In dry tones tinged only slightly with outrage and sarcasm, he tells me about the stockpiling, the Kung Fu Walk of Death, the sewing-shut of mouths, the decapitations for fun ("What they're teaching kids is that wildlife can be abused"), and the lucrative harvest of gallbladders, which get pickled in whiskey and shipped to the Orient as aphrodisiacs. "Most of these people are really not interested in snakes," he says damningly. "They're interested in profit from them."

Seippel wears a blue pinstripe suit. He is stealing moments from work in order to meet with me, a generous act, since his group at IBM is debuting a new family of products this week. We're seated over spinach salads at a yuppie restaurant in Austin. Times have changed.

JIM SEIPPEL was the focus of my visit but of course I have to go back to New Braunfels. For company I recruit my sweet and respectable older sister, who has raised two toddlers to college age and begun a computer career herself since the last time I made this drive. Lo, the snake farm is still there. EXCITING EDUCATIONAL ENTERTAINING, says the sign. Open for business, though it turns out that we are the only customers. We pay, and pass by the counter where the dried snake heads and scorpion paperweights and snakeskin wallets are on sale. My sister browses the cages, while I struggle to steady myself in the space-time continuum.

"John Deck still work here, by any chance?"

No. The current attendant doesn't know John Deck. This attendant is an amiable, heavyset old boy in jeans and a white T-shirt. I admit to him that, long ago, Deck and I made an expedition to Terrell County.

"You still hunt?" he asks me.

"Uh. No. Not anymore."

I mention that we had been on the lookout for a Blair's kingsnake. Then again, I say, probably anyone who goes down to Terrell County is on the lookout for a Blair's. He informs me that the Blair's kingsnake no longer bears that name; "gray-banded kingsnake" is what the field guides now say. And here in one of the glass cages is a specimen, a gorgeous little snake banded with black and orange and white and gray, hiding shyly behind its water dish. "Those gray-bands, they're up to three hundred dollar now," says the attendant. "Me, I just can't get into the same ballpark as that myself." In central Texas, as anywhere, inflation is pricing the working stiff out of the luxury-goods market.

"What'd you catch, down there in Terrell?" he asks. "You and old Deck." Oh, we got a trans-Pecos copperhead, I say, and a little bitty rock rattler. I don't bother to wonder why I should remember such tiny details, after almost twenty years. Memory is memory and, like love, it knows no logic.

"Now, both of those snakes," he says. "They're just out of sight now. Very highly prized."

Maybe he thinks I'm a potential buyer for some precious creature he's got stashed out back. Maybe he thinks I'm an undercover man for the U.S. Fish and Wildlife Service, trying to entrap him into dealing a protected species. Most likely he's just an innocent, unsuspecting guy who's happy to chat snakes. Leaving my sister to carry the conversation, I wander off. I look for the big rattlesnake pit but find no sign of it. Could be that I imagined that part. No sign of a vegetable scale, either.

Turning down the back row of cages, I admire this world-class collection of unpopular beasts. There is an Ottoman viper, an emperor scorpion, an orange-kneed tarantula, a blue krait. There is a hefty arthropod identified only as a "bird-eating spider," presumably from some vine-draped Amazonian glade. There is an albino monocled cobra. A trans-Pecos rat snake, a Mexican kingsnake, a blacktail rattler. A speckled rattler, a Panamint rattler. A Sonoran sidewinder, which is also of course a rattlesnake. I find it hard to fathom how anyone could loathe and abuse such lovely animals. Surely that kind of twisted passion went out with the Black Death. Suddenly I raise my eyes to a dusty bell jar resting before me on a shelf.

Inside is the carcass of a two-headed monkey, dry as jerky. When things change, it's always surprising. And when they remain unchanged, it's astonishing.

The Narcotic
of Empire

Nutmeg Economics and the Bargain of Breda

The seascape of the southern Moluccas is big and dreamy and warm. The sunsets are epic, reflected in pink and peach tints across high cirrus canopies, and the dawns tend to be spooky and still. Islands are many and far between. Each one looks idyllic in its own characteristic way, and so a person tends to take notice. I had admired those islands before, from a low-flying plane, but now I was seeing them from a more traditional perspective—the deck of a Dutch-owned ship. About midmorning of our second day out of port, I spotted a small nub of land on the starboard horizon. It was distant and green, low as a pancake, garnished with palm forest, and at this range showed no sign of human presence. It was an island called Run. I had heard of it.

In all the long sorry annals of national hubris and imperial greed, otherwise known as political history, this Run occupies a special small place. Geographically, it lies toward the remote eastern end of what we now call Indonesia. Most proximally, it belongs to the Banda group, a tiny archipelago amid the deep Banda Sea, just west of New Guinea, just south of Seram, a day's boat journey north of nothing whatsoever. The Bandas, including Run, together with a few other lumps of exceptionally fertile terrain (notably Ternate, Tidore, and Ambon) in the Moluccan region, were known to earlier chroniclers as the Spice Islands. Christopher Columbus had made them his destination, only to be road-blocked by America. Magellan's expedition had circled the world in order to find them. They were as widely famed and mooned over, in those years, as wild little places could be. And Run itself, among the littlest of the little, held significance out of all proportion to its size. As an icon of international commerce and contention, it belongs to a select class of backwater sites that have assumed frontwater import on the strength of strategic resources—Joachimsthal in Czechoslovakia with its uranium mines, Rjukan in Norway with its heavy water, and the oil fields of Kuwait come to mind. On the island of Run, the resource at issue was nutmeg.

Nutmeg? Yes, but it's a fact that makes sense only within its historical and economic context. The geographical context is essential too—and that happened to be the context into which I had just sailed.

I caught the attention of Piet, a Dutch-born artist latterly resettled in Bali, whose unenviable task as tour guide on this ship entailed nursemaiding me and my fellow passengers across a great loop of Moluccan ocean. Pointing over the starboard rail, I asked Piet for an identification of the low green nub.

Ya ya, that's Run, he confirmed. Yellow-haired and lanky, Piet lives a hermetic life during the off-season and paints handsome abstract acrylics on silk. Though he seemed tirelessly amiable on shipboard, I suspected him of counting the hours to the off-season.

Are we going there? I wanted to know.

Maybe he was lost in artistic meditation, or maybe he was rehearsing in his mind the day's regimen of manic tourism, which he'd recently chalked onto the briefing board in the galley, as he would each morning throughout this endless voyage. *Snorkeling. Beach picnic. Port call at Bandaneira, followed by ceremonial canoe races, native dancing, and souvenir-buying opportunities. Followed by snorkeling.* Who could blame Piet, amid three weeks of such nonsense, for a moment's blurry addlement?

Going where? he asked.

To the island of Run, I said. That place. Right over there. I might have added: to the world's most inconspicuous yet eloquent symbol of changing commodity values and myopic diplomacy. I had been reading about Run in a guidebook titled *Spice Islands: Exotic Eastern Indonesia,* by Kal Muller. According to Muller: "In the 1667 Treaty of Breda, the formerly British-held island of Run was ceded to the Dutch in exchange for a Dutch-held island on the other side of the globe—Manhattan." Run happened to be crucial to Holland's foreign policy, which entailed cornering the world nutmeg market, and that *other* island in the trade packet didn't seem nearly so promising or precious. New Amsterdam, as it then styled itself, was just a chilly slab of granite near the mouth of a turbid river, unlikely to yield even a good crop of potatoes.

No, said Piet. Why would we go to Run? It's just a tiny wooded island with a couple of fishing villages. There's no exceptional snorkeling, no carvings or trinkets to be bought, no quaint native rituals obligingly reenacted. Why would we go there?

For me it was obvious: to see the mercantile equivalent of the Borough of Manhattan as measured in nutmeg, of course. But I guess the idea didn't translate.

THE NUTMEG tree, *Myristica fragrans,* is endemic to the Moluccas, and until about two hundred years ago it was found nowhere else. It's a broadleaf evergreen that favors wet lowland areas in the tropics, thriving best on the rich volcanic soils of equatorial islands. It grows about forty feet tall and produces a pendulous fruit, roughly the shape of an avocado, with apricot-colored pulp. The pulp doesn't ripen palatably and it isn't harvested commercially, though it can be cooked into an interesting jelly, tasting faintly like A.1 steak sauce. At the core of the fruit is a brown pit the size of a quail's egg, around which is wrapped a sinuous scarlet aril, like an octopus hugging a football. The aril constitutes mace, one of the twofer set of spices that this tree produces. Within the pit's thin outer shell is a single seed: the nutmeg.

A whole nutmeg seems hard and woody, but anyone who has ever seasoned a cup of eggnog knows that it surrenders easily to a grater. In cross section it shows the network of dark veins, like worm tracks, holding the volatile oil that gives it aroma and flavor—and that in an earlier age gave it geopolitical importance. Among the factors that allowed nutmeg to achieve its global appeal, no doubt, was this accident of natural packaging. In the whole-seed form, it traveled well while remaining fresh. It came in its own convenient, preservative dispenser. In the days before canning, shrink-wrapping, and freezers, it could ride for hundreds of miles on the back of a camel and for thousands in the hull of a ship. It was almost as useful as money.

No wonder it had the power to cause trouble.

Today we think of nutmeg as a sweet, cloying, decidedly minor spice, seldom pulled off the shelf except for a Thanksgiving or Christmas dessert. In earlier times, its utility was more broad. At the end of the twelfth century, for instance, when Emperor Henry VI entered Rome before his coronation, the streets of the city were fumigated with nutmeg. Chaucer mentioned it in *The Canterbury Tales* as a seasoning for ale, and a fifteenth-century cookbook includes nutmeg (as well as saffron, cinnamon, pepper, and cloves, which were other precious imports from the Indies) in recipes for rabbit and chicken. The Middle Ages were a spice-hungry era, more given to excess than to subtlety, at least in the kitchens of the gentry and clergy. A social historian named Wolfgang Schivelbusch has written that banquet dishes "were virtually buried under spices; food was little more than a vehicle for condiments which were used in combinations we nowadays would consider quite bizarre." Furthermore, a spice platter was sometimes passed down the table like a relish tray. "Guests helped themselves, adding spices as desired to the already seasoned dish, or they used the tray as a cheese or dessert platter. They consumed pepper, cinnamon, and nutmeg as we nowadays might partake of a delicacy, a glass of sherry, or a cup of coffee." Schivelbusch was tiptoeing at the edge of a larger issue with his mention of sherry and coffee, because evidence also exists that nutmeg in such dosage serves as a drug.

The evidence was summarized in an article titled "Nutmeg as a Narcotic," by Andrew T. Weil, which appeared in the journal *Economic Botany* three decades ago. Besides describing its narcotic effects and uses, Weil offered a scholarly survey of nutmeg's repute as a folk remedy—in India, in the Arab world, and in Europe until the nineteenth century. He cited a sixty-page dissertation on nutmeg pharmacology that was published in 1681, and a nine-hundred-page treatise on nutmeg that tumbled off the presses a generation later. That tome prescribed nutmeg for treating no fewer than 138 diseases. One explanation for this former medicinal popularity is that, whether or not a large dose of nutmeg actually cured a particular condition—palsy or gas or eczema or worms or asthma or impotence or tuberculosis, as variously claimed—it probably did console the patient with a narcotic high. It achieved this, most likely, by way of an organic compound called *myrisiticin,* one of the active ingredients of nutmeg oil. After quoting a number of case reports, Weil concluded: "The seeds and arils of M. *fragrans*"—that is, both mace and nutmeg—"have powerful narcotic properties. In man, they have frequently caused serious but almost never fatal intoxications."

A less rigorously scientific source, published in 1969, expressed it differently: "In an attempt to escape from reality at 'nutmeg parties,' beatniks and hippies sometimes eat two or three tablespoonfuls of powdered nutmeg as a hallucinogenic drug for 'kicks.'" Just another of the elemental Sixties experiences that I seem to have missed while I was irremediably distracted by reality.

AMONG the great mercantile empires that emerged in the wake of Magellan, the one that most jealously fastened upon M. *fragrans* was the Dutch. It began in 1599, when Jacob van Neck's expedition reached the Bandas and took on a lucrative load of nutmegs. Van Neck probably called at the central island of the group, with its trading village, Bandaneira, and its good anchorage. The histories I've seen don't say whether he got to the island of Run.

Early spice cargoes were sold in Amsterdam at as much as 32,000 percent markup, and so the Dutch burghers who had financed those expeditions moved quickly to corner the trade. To eliminate competition among themselves, they united in 1602 as the Dutch East India Company. To eliminate international competition, they began nudging aside the Portuguese, who had reached the Moluccas first; the Spanish, who had gained a regional foothold in the Philippines; and the British, who had established an East India Company of their own. The Dutch focused on the Bandas, where the other colonial powers had no prior commanding presence, and in 1611 they built a fort on the slope above Bandaneira. Meanwhile the British had established a more modest trading post on Run, just a few miles eastward. The British, if Muller's book can be trusted, offered better prices for nutmeg than the Dutch. And the Dutch company made itself still more unpopular with the Bandanese people by demanding a monopoly concession. This led to rebellion, murder, reprisal, and war—between the Dutch and the Bandanese, between the Dutch and the British. At one early stage, the Dutch tortured and beheaded eighteen (or eight, depending on which source you believe) British subjects for conspiring to subvert Dutch colonial authority. That caused a stink back in England, but the Bandanese fared even worse.

The Dutch company officials were truculent, firm, and purblind, as imperialists of all flags usually are. Beginning in 1621, under a fierce governor-general named Jan Pieterszoon Coen, they began killing off the Bandanese population. Another measure was equally barbaric, though less bloody: They also killed nutmeg trees. They did their best to extirpate *M. fragrans* from most of its range—everywhere but on those few islands where the Dutch hegemony was absolute, namely Ambon and the larger Bandas. The smaller outliers of Banda, according to Muller, weren't secure enough to be spared: "Because the eastern islands of Run and Ai were less tightly controlled by the Dutch, they exterminated all nutmeg trees there." Within a few decades, three-fourths of the nutmeg trees in the Moluccas (and therefore in the world) had been destroyed, so as to preserve the monopoly and keep prices artificially high.

When most of the Bandanese population had been murdered or driven into exile, Jan Pieterszoon Coen set to remaking the system of nutmeg agriculture. He divided the good land into dozens of *perken,* three-acre parcels, and allotted them to licensed Dutch planters, who came to be known as *perkeniers.* All the perken together encompassed maybe a half-million trees. "Since there were no Bandanese to work them," Muller reports, "slaves were brought in." The company made huge profits, while the perkeniers were paid just a minuscule fraction of the sale value of nutmeg in Europe. But rural luxury came cheaply in the Moluccas, and the perkeniers presumably lived the same sort of comfortable, halcyon lives as did slave-owning colonial growers of other places and times—such as George Washington and Thomas Jefferson in Virginia. For almost two centuries, people everywhere bought nutmeg from the Dutch East India Company or not at all. And when the supply threatened to sate the demand, the company willfully destroyed tons of its own nutmeg in order to reinflate prices.

As a mercantile strategy it worked, but not forever. By the end of the eighteenth century, the monopoly had been broken and the Dutch East India Company was dead. What had killed it? One factor was smuggling. Adventuresome Frenchmen had managed to sneak nutmeg plants out of the Moluccas and establish thriving plantations on other tropical islands, in the Indian Ocean. A second factor was rising British sea power—a blockade of Dutch ports in the East Indies, followed by outright usurpation of Dutch colonies. The British were assembling an empire of their own. A third factor is mentioned in historical sources, with no evidence given, and some recent authors find this one implausible: that fruit pigeons had been swallowing nutmeg seeds and voiding them (either by regurgitation or defecation) onto other islands, where the seeds managed to germinate without Dutch permission.

Personally, I find the third factor both plausible and appealing. Its plausibility rests on *Ducula concinna,* a handsome pigeon that's native to Banda, known to eat nutmegs, and capable of crossing from one island to another. Its appeal rests on this: an empire thwarted by bird poop.

AT BANDANEIRA, when I went ashore with Piet and the others, the stigmata of history were still visible. Each lamppost on the main street rose from a base of sculpted concrete in the shape of a nutmeg fruit. I saw a young Bandanese boy wearing a T-shirt that read I ♥ NUTMEG MACE. Near the waterfront was a decrepit warehouse with a sign saying THE BANDA NUTMEG AGRICULTURE COMPANY in Indonesian. The Dutch fort on the slope above town had lately been restored for the edification of tourists, and even with ghosts for a garrison, it cast a stern presence. Then we visited a half-derelict nutmeg plantation at the edge of the forest, where an aging Dutch-Moluccan man told us feelingly in Dutch: "Nutmeg on Banda is a lousy business."

The man's name was Mr. van der Broeke. He had a few pounds of mace spread out to dry in flat baskets. He called himself "the last perkenier."

We also made an excursion to an old Dutch church, built about the same time as the fort. It was a stark little building with a rickety belfry, a hand-rung brass bell not much bigger than a dinner bell, and a few rows of roughly planed pews. The altar was bare. No crucifix, no statues, no candelabra; obviously not a Catholic mission. In the churchyard, overgrown by weedy vines, were gravestones. One of them marked the remains of a certain Heer van der Broeke, who until his death in 1754 had been—like his descendant two centuries later—a perkenier. Stepping among these graves, I talked with Annelies and Max, two of my fellow passengers, whom I'd discovered as blessedly good company for a slow-boat cruise to wherever.

Max is a distinguished Dutch novelist. Annelies is a tough-minded woman with a sparkle of mischievous humor. Quietly, as we hung at the fringe of the group, Annelies told me that she felt very uncomfortable doing the tourist waddle through this scene of her national guilt. She mentioned the thousands of dead Bandanese, slaughtered by Dutch imperialists to make the world safe for overpriced nutmeg. Max, hearing our murmurs, agreed. The Dutch had been horribly vicious during their imperial era out here, he said. More vicious than the Portuguese during theirs, or the Spanish during theirs? Yes indeed, more. Why? Because we didn't take priests with us, he said, so there was no mitigating influence by men who at least professed to value holiness and mercy. Holland was already Protestant, and colonialism was just a business enterprise, without pretense of missionary purpose. The Dutch were in it strictly for cash. Consequently our sins of empire, Max asserted, were worse.

I followed his logic, I respected his judgment and his contrition. But I wasn't convinced that the Dutch empire in its day had been utterly different from the Portuguese empire, or the Spanish, or the British—or for that matter from the Akkadian, the Egyptian, the Hittite, the Assyrian, the Persian, the Macedonian, the Parthian, the Roman, the Mogul, the Napoleonic, the Czarist, the Soviet, or the American.

NEXT DAY I split from the group and chartered my own boat for a trip back to the island of Run. I was still intrigued by the Bargain of Breda, and I wanted to see just what it was that the Dutch negotiators had valued more highly than Manhattan. My boat jockey, a young Moluccan employee of a Bandaneira hotel, put me ashore in a cove at the north of the island, fronting a village, and then roared away. He saw no reason to linger, but he promised to come back.

A handful of one-masted praus stood at anchor in the cove, but not a single boat with a motor. There was no dock and, beyond the beach, no road. There seemed to be no internal combustion engine of any sort on the island. A lane of hard clay, packed smooth by centuries of barefoot pedestrians, led through the village. Attended by a swarm of curious children, I followed that lane between tin-roofed houses of stucco and thatch, set neatly behind fences of split bamboo. The children dinned me cheerily with their two words of English—"Hallo meester!"—over and over, and I responded in my moronic, elementary Indonesian. My initial impression was that this place was cleaner and friendlier than Manhattan. No doubt safer too.

I nodded politely to the women in doorways, who stared back, some smiling and some blank-faced, all of them wondering who the devil I was and why I had come. *"Dimana?"* the children hollered—Where are you going?—to which I had no sensible answer. I couldn't put "I've simply come to wander and gawk" into their language. I passed a large half-built boat, propped in a dry-dock scaffold near the beach. The boat's planking was adze-cut from logs, but its overall lines were graceful. Walking along, I exchanged greetings with a man in a yard, and then stopped when I saw that the ground beside him was covered with small brown ovoids. I recognized those ovoids.

Flattered by my interest, the man invited me through the fence. Splayed fish lay drying on a rack. A photoelectric panel stood on sawhorses, and an extension cord led incongruously in through the window of his house. I was curious what the cord might be feeding. Electric lights? A refrigerator? A Macintosh? A dialysis machine? But I was more interested in the ovoids. The man cracked one obligingly with his teeth and showed me the seed. *"Pala,"* he said. "Nutmeg?" I translated, expecting him to confirm what I knew. No sign of recognition. He'd never heard the word. *"Pala,"* he repeated pedagogically.

"Ada banyak?" I asked. Is there much of it hereabouts?

"Ya. Banyak." He gestured up toward the forested hillside above the village. He was pleased to assure me: *"Ada banyak."*

Clearly this was a place of great riches. I wondered in passing whether it had been the Dutch who brought in those trees, reestablishing orchards of *M. fragrans* amid the palm forest after having solidified their claim at Breda. Or was it the enterprising Runians, the indigenous survivors (if there were any) who outlasted the Dutch? Maybe the ancestors of this very man? Or was it the pigeons, who care nothing for human borders, or treaties, or mercantile schemes, and who shit on the dreams of empire?

There may be no biological evidence, but history tells us, I think, to bet on the pigeons.

HARD PARTS

A Skeletal View of Trilobites and Other Objets d'Art

Let me pose an intrusive but well-meant question: When you pass from this life, what will you leave behind? And don't try to tell me you haven't thought about it.

Will you leave children, each of whom carries a random half-share of your genes and remembers you (if you've been loving and lucky) with a nonrandom, full share of devotion? Will you leave a house with two BMWs in the garage, all paid for, gas tanks full? Will you leave your name on a marble headstone and on a couple of bitter ex-wives? Each of us yearns to generate some sort of notable entity, an extension or token of our selfhood, that will hold its shape on the planet long after we've checked out. But differences of inclination and talent dictate a variety of forms. Will you leave your eyes to a blind person, your brain to science (assuming science wants it), the rest of your carcass to the local worm fauna, and your money to a church? Will you leave curiosity and zeal in the minds of a handful of students? Will you leave a three-foot shelf of ponderous books with your authorial name on the spines—or, better yet, one perfect poem? Will you leave a towering granite building that you've designed, an honest wooden boat that you've built with your hands, a single delicate watercolor that you've painted? Will you leave four minutes of happy saxophone solo on a cassette? Will you leave your baby shoes in bronze and your softball trophies in plastic? Whatever you leave, will it partake somehow of both beauty and permanence?

Then again, maybe we shouldn't dwell on this issue. The trilobites of the Cambrian period never did, and look how well things worked out for them. They left only themselves—transmogrified into configurations of stone and still beautiful after five hundred million years.

THE COMELINESS of the average trilobite, I admit, is an arcane felicity that most of us rarely see. You wouldn't notice it in the austere pen diagrams of a paleontology text, designed to show only the basics of trilobitic anatomy—the horseshoe head, the multi-segmented thorax, the tail, and the three longitudinal lobes (one axial, two pleural, like a caterpillar with fancy flanges) that give these extinct arthropods their name. But you can't miss the aesthetic dimension if you browse through a certain book, simply called *Trilobites,* by an unusual man named Riccardo Levi-Setti.

Levi-Setti is a distinguished physicist at the University of Chicago. Whereas his day job includes the directorship of the Enrico Fermi Institute, his after-hours energies are devoted in large part to the collection, study, and photographing of trilobite fossils. His *Trilobites* is a coffee-table volume for people with odd tastes in coffee. It includes a modest bit of scientific commentary and some taxonomic annotation, but mostly it's a gallery of photos—adoringly large black-and-white portraits of *Olenoides superbus, Elrathia kingii, Calymene celebra,* and other species. Here is *Paradoxides davidis,* from a middle Cambrian deposit in Newfoundland, a magnificent lanky thing with twenty thoracic segments, resembling the breastplate of a Mycenaean warrior-king. Here is *Isotelus maximus,* from the Ordovician period, smooth and symmetrical as a polished mahogany bowl. Here is *Phacops rana,* from the Devonian, with its rolled-up body and its gaping compound eyes. And here is *Dicranurus monstrosus,* also Devonian, a fierce-looking little beast consisting of long wiry spines, so spooky that you'll flinch when you turn the page. Although the shapes from the later periods are more elaborate (another wild one from the Devonian is *Psychopyge elegans,* like a thistle blossom modeled in cast iron), the oldest forms, from the Cambrian, have a special gravity. It's amazing to contemplate that, three hundred million years before the first dinosaur had evolved, the same *Olenoides superbus* portrayed on Levi-Setti's page was scuttering along the bottom of a sea in what is now Utah.

Notwithstanding my chatter about them, the bizarre variousness and the collective force of these photographs just can't be put into words. So I ask you to take it on hearsay that, if trilobites can have their own Richard Avedon, their own Annie Leibowitz, their own Diane Arbus, Riccardo Levi-Setti is the guy. He has seen them so lovingly and photographed them so knowingly as to turn arthropods into art.

Wait, though, that's not quite right. No, he hasn't turned them into art. He has simply seen and photographed, artfully, what was there—what the trilobites themselves left behind. Evolutionary and geological forces made these elegant shapes, not Levi-Setti. It's no diminishment of his work to recall that, after all the eons of struggle and adaptation that the trilobites underwent, and then all the further eons of their adamantine endurance as fossils, taking their portraits was the easy part.

TRILOBITES hold a special position in the history of life. They are the first great success story embodying (literally) an ingenious innovation in zoological anatomy, of which the importance can hardly be overstated: the skeleton.

Fifteen hundred genera of the class Trilobita, encompassing about ten thousand species, are represented in the fossil record. Their survival spanned 350 million years, from near the start of the Cambrian period (almost 600 million years ago) until the end of the Permian. By these standards, they did well—and at their peak, in the later Cambrian, they were a dominant ecological presence in shallow marine environments. Levi-Setti makes no claim in *Trilobites* to encyclopedic coverage of the subject. He has concerned himself more, he says, with the pure visual appeal of his selection.

"I like to dig for trilobites," he admits plainly. He began doing it as an escape from his addiction to physics. "I also like photography, and trilobites provide an endless source of form and composition." By now he has been a serious trilobite amateur for more than thirty years. To some small degree he has mixed his vocation and his avocation, applying a touch of the physicist's expertise as he coauthored such technical papers as "Trilobite Eyes and the Optics of Descartes and Huygens," published in *Nature*. But mostly his trilobite work has been a kind of "time travel," his phrase, to eras far earlier and stranger than the seventeenth century of Huygens and Descartes. One of his goals, he confides, has been to demonstrate that "dinosaurs were not the only prehistoric animals that inspire awe and fascination. Trilobites tell us of an earlier world, perhaps less threatening, when life on earth could still explode into a myriad of new, unseen, uncounted forms discovering their own way to survive."

That last sentence is loaded with scientific content. The world-changing blast of newness to which he's alluding was the so-called Cambrian explosion, and it didn't involve only trilobites. It was the greatest episode of large-scale biological diversification that ever occurred—or as Levi-Setti writes, "the most revolutionary and far reaching single event in the history of life." The new tools of survival included that ingenious anatomical innovation I've already mentioned—the skeleton—which allowed animals of many different kinds to increase their mobility, their efficiency, their strength, their security against predators, and in consequence their evolutionary success. Life on Earth was never the same again after the invention of shells and bones.

Before the Cambrian explosion, back in Precambrian time, all animals were soft and gooey, like jellyfish. None of them possessed skeletons—neither the intricate external sort (exoskeletons) as later evolved by arthropods, nor the simpler external sort (shells) as in snails and clams, nor the internal sort (endoskeletons) as in vertebrates like us and in a few anomalous invertebrates such as squid. Closely linked to the absence of skeletons (maybe as cause, maybe also as consequence) was the fact that animal evolution hadn't progressed far. There did exist, by about 630 million years ago, an interesting assemblage of soft-bodied animals, flat creatures showing quilted or leaflike anatomy, which are now known collectively as the Ediacarian fauna. This fauna took its name from the Ediacara Hills of South Australia, where its fossil remnants were first found in 1946. But the Ediacarian fauna, though intriguing, was nowhere near as diverse or successful as later phases of animal evolution, and it doesn't seem to have led to the major faunal lineages that have prevailed throughout the past half-billion years. One authority, Stephen Jay Gould, suspects that the Ediacarian animals "may represent a failed, independent experiment in multicellular life, not a set of simpler ancestors for later creatures with hard parts." We can't confidently attribute that failure to the absence of skeletons, but it's a plausible guess.

The age of hard parts began about 600 million years ago, and even the experts are still asking themselves why. Richard Fortey of the British Museum puts it this way: "The acquisition of shells and skeletons is one of the great milestones in the history of the biosphere, and the difficulty of finding a single neat explanation only adds to its fascination." George Gaylord Simpson, an eminent American paleontologist, has called it "a mystery to speculate about: Why and how did many animals begin to have hard parts—skeletons of sorts—with apparent suddenness around the beginning of the Cambrian?" The earliest skeleton-bearing animals seem to have been tiny things that lived unassumingly on the sea bottom, equipped with mineralized little widgets that functioned nobody-knows-how. Formally these creatures are assigned the label Tommotian; less formally they're called the small shelly fauna. Gould suggests that the Tommotian creatures might represent ancestors of more familiar animal lineages that "had not yet developed full skeletons, but only laid down bits of mineralized matter in small and separate places all over their bodies." On the other hand, he adds, they might be another failed experiment, ancestral to nothing we've ever seen.

Relatively soon after the Tommotian fauna, maybe 570 million years ago, the trilobites made their first appearance in the fossil record. By that time they had already carried the skeleton principle to a rather advanced stage—their carapaces were elaborately segmented, integrally articulated, and (except in a few species) hardened with calcium carbonate. With these advantages, the trilobites would achieve what the Ediacarian and the Tommotian faunas hadn't: vast success, as measured in their abundance, their diversity, their breadth of geographical distribution, their duration as a class, and (the measure of those other measures) their conspicuous representation as fossils in sedimentary rocks. Still another measure of their success, I suppose, is popular appeal. No one has published a handsome coffee-table book titled *The Tommotian Fauna as Revealed in Their Itty Bits of Shell*.

But trilobites weren't the only group to turn hard-bodied during the early Cambrian. Various lineages of mollusks, brachiopods, and coral-like animals were doing it too. Some of them seem to have favored calcium phosphate as the concrete for their skeletal engineering, while others (notably the trilobites) used calcium carbonate. The roughly simultaneous development of hard parts in those disparate lineages, and the rapid evolutionary diversification that hard parts made possible, figured importantly in the Cambrian explosion—which was really more of a building boom than a detonation. To return to the mystery mentioned by George Gaylord Simpson: Why *then?* What triggered this revolution in skeletal engineering at the start of the Cambrian?

Although a single neat explanation is impossible, as Richard Fortey warned, one school of thought points to environmental changes. Those changes include the episodes of glaciation and thaw that alternately lowered and raised sea levels, the transgressions and regressions of seawater across continental shelves that attended each glaciation and thaw, the losses and gains of shallow marine habitat that resulted from the transgressions and regressions, and—most suggestively—the increase in atmospheric oxygen, which may have been a biochemical prerequisite for building mineralized skeletons. There's some evidence, according to Fortey, that "it was not possible for calcium carbonate (or perhaps other skeletal minerals) to be deposited by living tissues until the pressure of oxygen in the atmosphere had reached a critical level." Increased availability of calcium carbonate was a boon to later paleontologists as well as to early sea creatures, because the stuff makes for nice fossils.

Whatever combination of factors did trigger the skeletal revolution, that revolution was immeasurably consequential. Without the appearance of hard parts in the early Cambrian, to be followed by vertebrate skeletons in the Ordovician, there would have been no fish, no amphibians, no reptiles, no birds, no mammals, no us, no paleontology, no art, no photography, no major-league baseball, no television, no rock-and-roll, and no cell phones. A world without television and cell phones might be nice, but otherwise, what a shame.

ABOUT EIGHT years ago I paid a visit to a small private museum in a village in southern Germany, not far from a series of quarries renowned for their high-quality Jurassic shales. The village was Holzmaden, in Württemberg, not far southeast of Stuttgart. The shales were famed in paleontological circles as *die Posidonienschiefer,* named for a little shell-bearing marine creature that constituted their predominant fossil, *Posidonia bronni,* which in turn had been named for the Greek sea god.

Those shales, formed of fine-grain sediments that had settled onto a sludgy sea bottom about 170 million years ago, were smooth slabs of darkish-gray rock. In addition to their larding of *Posidonia bronni,* they contained some spectacularly detailed fossils of other Jurassic sea creatures—ichthyosaurs and plesiosaurs (two groups of marine reptiles, both distinct from the dinosaurs), ammonites (spiral-shelled mollusks, like a chambered nautilus but now extinct), sea lilies (plantlike animals related to starfish), and much more. The little museum and its workshop, run by a family named Hauff, were devoted to the extraction and display of these fossils. The Hauffs were perfectionists, sensitive to the sheer visual beauty as well as the scientific significance of the fossils they processed. Because the rock was so fine, because the conditions of preservation on that sea bottom had been so ideally gentle, and because the fossil preparations done in the Hauff workshop were so painstaking, the results were extraordinary. Some of the ichthyosaurs contained what appeared to be embryos, delicate little skeletons within the skeleton of the mother's abdomen. Others showed not just the hard parts, the reptilian skeleton modified for swimming, but also the faint impression of soft tissue, resembling the silhouette of a dolphin. Besides adorning the walls of this little museum, Hauff preparations hang like Pre-Raphaelite paintings in some of the major public museums of the world.

I had been sent over by a little-known but very solvent magazine—it was a car magazine, actually, with a special reverence for German workmanship in any mode—to write an article about Museum Hauff. I spent one day there, gawking at the great dark slabs and visiting with a bright, likable man named Rolf Bernhard Hauff, third-generation purveyor of ichthyosaurs. He showed me the workshop. We shared lunch and some excellent pilsner. He talked about his great-grandfather, who had come to Holzmaden as an industrial chemist; about his grandfather, who began the fossil-processing enterprise; about his father, who ran the museum until recently; and he mentioned his own abandonment of a doctoral program in geology to come home to the family business. He also spoke with some passion about the extinction of species—not just of ichthyosaurs, not just of ammonites, but also the countless extinctions that humans have caused within recent centuries. He made a point with which I didn't disagree: Humanity is presently perpetrating a mass-extinction event surpassing any such catastrophe since the death of the last dinosaurs. But that's another story—not the one I was chasing for the car magazine and not precisely the one I'm telling now.

I flew home, taking two souvenirs from the museum's shop: a small slab of Jurassic shale and a book. The shale contained an ammonite fossil. The book, titled *Das Holzmadenbuch,* included many large black-and-white photographs of the Hauff ichthyosaurs, plesiosaurs, and sea lilies in exquisite detail.

Das Holzmadenbuch is in German. I can't read a sentence of it but that doesn't matter. It's one of the most beautiful things I own.

THE AMMONITE was a gift for the biologist whose husband I am. She keeps it now with her collection of other biological treasures. They all reside, carefully arranged upon a swatch of red velvet, inside a dry aquarium that fills one bookshelf in our dining room. There's the skull of a gray fox, the skull of a beaver, the shell of a nautilus, the lower jaw of a piranha from the Amazon headwaters, the skull of a coyote from suburban Los Angeles, a three-point antler, a flake of beige rock containing a fossil fish, a vertebra from an Asian buffalo, a sand dollar, a few cowries, a few cone shells, the breastbone of what seems to have been a Canada goose, and a number of other skulls, jawbones, vertebrae, shells, and fossils. All of the animals in question died natural deaths, so far as we know, except for the piranha, which I ate. The softest and most perishable item on display is the shed skin of a rattlesnake.

She has gathered and saved these things for two reasons: because she loves wild creatures and because she loves graceful shapes. Like Levi-Setti, she finds aesthetic delight in the forms by which evolution has met functional demands. Her collection consists almost entirely of hard parts, not just because an aquarium full of little carcasses in formaldehyde would stink up our dining room but, more essentially, because hard parts convey a structural certitude and a permanence that no flesh (not even beef jerky) can match.

This biologist whose husband I am happens also to be a graphic artist. At times she has worked as a scientific illustrator. During one of those times, she collaborated with the paleontologist Jack Horner on a monograph he was writing about hadrosaurs (duck-billed dinosaurs) from the late Cretaceous. Her role, among others, was to create dozens of precise, richly textured drawings of cranial fragments—drawings meant to serve other paleontologists in place of having the fossils themselves in their hands. The monograph was eventually published as *Cranial Morphology of Prosaurolophus (Ornithischia: Hadrosauridae), With Descriptions of Two New Hadrosaurid Species and an Evaluation of Hadrosaurid Phylogenetic Relationships,* a handsome volume not available at Barnes & Noble. Although the work had been exhausting and she was glad to finish, she remained mildly amazed that someone would pay her for drawing pictures of bones. On her own time, over a span of years, she had been doing the same thing for the sheer love of it.

She was invited to hang some of those prosaurolophid drawings as part of a fine-art show at a gallery in Butte, Montana. She put them up in a grid pattern, twenty-four organic shapes without explanation, and let people make of it all what they would.

LIKEWISE I invite you to make of these facts and anecdotes what you will.

My own inclination is to take them at face value. It's intriguing—and it really doesn't need to be *more* than intriguing—that, for the past 570 million years, animal evolution has been creating skeletal structures in which can be seen, at least by some human observers, the qualities for which we normally turn to art: grace, harmony, beauty, majesty, surprise, truth. The proof lies here on my desk: *Das Holzmadenbuch, Cranial Morphology of Prosaurolophus,* and *Trilobites.* To the same shelf of images I would add Ernst Haeckel's classic book of lithographs, *Art Forms in Nature,* and a stunning volume of scanning electron microscope photos published by Harvard University Press under the winsome title *Identification Guide to the Ant Genera of the World.* These are books to be seen, to be savored visually, not to be read. They express more about our planet's half-billion-year saga of zoological diversification than could be packed into a thousand pages of purple prose. And they do it largely by displaying the hard parts that various (I mean *really* various) creatures have left behind.

Look past their face value, though, and these images challenge us to address another question: What will *we* as a species leave behind?

Rolf Bernhard Hauff had an opinion. I recorded it in my notebook at the time, but found it unsuitable for my car-magazine story. For eight years I forgot about it, until I pulled out the notebook recently. Having voiced his concern about human-caused extinctions, Herr Hauff wondered aloud how the era of modern civilization—in his caustic phrase, "our Coca-Cola culture"—would appear to paleontological observers in the distant future. Inglorious, he thought. "They will know us by our Coca-Cola cans." His eyes showed a glint of irony, then, as he remembered my assigned task for the Mercedes Benz company. Accommodatingly, he added, "And perhaps a few automobiles."

Herr Hauff's comment carried an echo, probably unintentional, of that famous passage from T. S. Eliot's poem "The Rock," written sixty years ago with a certain late-modern gloom:

> And the wind shall say: "Here were decent godless people:
> Their only monument the asphalt road
> And a thousand lost golf balls."

Me, I'm slightly more of an optimist. I'm hoping we might also leave a few libraries, full of poetry and science and the great art forms, including life.

❊ II ❊

DUBIOUS CERTITUDES, DAUNTLESS THEORIES

CERTAINTY AND DOUBT IN BAJA

Scientific Confidence Goes South

Two men and thirty-two lizards are at work in a Mexican motel room. They are united in effort, but their motives are various. One of the men is a biologist. He seeks scientific insight of a seemingly paradoxical sort, the sort that can do justice to the diversity of living creatures yet reveal itself as a neat pattern of numbers. The other man is a journalist. He seeks drama, a simplified understanding of an impossibly complex subject, and of course cheap laughs. Precisely what drives the lizards is anyone's guess.

This motel room is a long day's trip down the Baja peninsula. It sits at the edge of a small village overlooking the Gulf of California, surrounded by raw rocky mountains and boojum trees. No telephone. No electric power between noon and sunset. The room is strewn with extension cords, duct tape, double-A batteries, jars of preserving alcohol, chocolate-chip cookies, dissecting instruments, day-old tortillas that seem to have been chewed upon overnight by some discreet rodent, and a burgeoning population of dust bunnies. A scorpion has been sighted in the bathroom. There's also a laptop computer.

It all looks godawful suspicious. A modest cocaine factory would probably look less suspicious. But the motel's maids have backed off, leaving fresh towels each morning on the veranda outside, and so far the *policia* haven't visited.

The computer is linked to an analog-digital converter, which is linked to a strange piece of paraphernalia roughly as long as a coffin. This piece of paraphernalia has been cobbled together from sheets of Plexiglas, metal brackets, tiny lightbulbs, photoactivated transistors, and a lot of gaily colored wire, all of which give it a garage-shop look of ingenious amateurism. It was brought to the motel room in pieces. Assembled, it amounts to a set of high walls confining a long rubber track, which is marked off with photoelectric gates. This piece of paraphernalia is a portable racetrack for lizards.

A state-of-the-art herpetological speedway. The amateurishness is cosmetic only. You can't buy a better one.

The journalist reaches into the incubator. Yes, excuse me for omitting that, there's also an incubator. The journalist reaches into the incubator and carefully lifts out a covered plastic cup, the kind intended for urine specimens. In the cup is a reptile, a handsome little member of the species *Uta stansburiana,* brownish gray with spots of orange and turquoise. More commonly known as the side-blotched lizard, *U. stansburiana* is common on mainland Baja as well as on many small islands of the Gulf, and this particular individual was captured yesterday on a desolate offshore nub called La Ventana. Today it has been resting in incubated comfort at exactly 36 degrees Celsius—which, to a lizard, should be the optimal body temperature for sprinting. Will a side-blotched lizard from La Ventana run as fast as a side-blotched lizard from the mainland? If not, what could that mean? Does the absence of predator species on La Ventana allow those side-blotched lizards the luxury of being slower? Or is evolution indifferent to the matter of how fast a lizard can sprint? Maybe endurance running is more important. Maybe wariness. These are questions of a type that biological fieldwork might be able to answer. The trick is in designing a way to ask them. Accepting the specimen cup, the biologist dumps the lizard onto the racetrack.

He chases it down the track with his right hand. Lights flash, phototransistors wink, the computer goes *tweet,* and the monitor shows that this lizard attained a top speed of 2.38 meters per second. For a *U. stansburiana,* that's pretty fast. Then the little bastard jumps out of the racetrack and dashes away into chaos under the bed. After fifteen minutes of belly-crawling and fervent profanity, filthy from chest to knees, the biologist and the journalist succeed in recapturing it. Perhaps we should let the maids in tomorrow, the journalist wonders silently.

Using a wooden pencil, the biologist records "2.38" in his field log. The field log isn't computerized. Don't ask the journalist why. He's been told but he missed that part.

The biologist's name is Jon Herron. He is a bright and candid young Ph.D. student from the University of Washington. "The only thing I can conceive of that's more boring than what I'm doing," he says to the journalist without provocation, "is what you're doing."

What the biologist is doing is called science. What the journalist is doing has no dignified name.

FIELDWORK in evolutionary biology is not all binoculars and gorillas, unfortunately. It's not all safari pants and hammocks and radio-collared jaguars and machete trails through the forest to a water hole where at dusk you can watch the rhinoceros drink. Add a few other factors— monsoon, mud, biting flies, sunburn, thorn scratches that may or may not heal, unwashed clothes, loneliness, fungus in your headlamp, ear-wigs in your chloroquine stash, crotch rot, toe rot, instant coffee, leeches that go for your armpits, fear of setting foot on a rattlesnake or a bush-master, fear that the local guerrillas will kill you for your propane, fear that the local villagers will cut down the trees or kill the animals you've been studying, leishmaniasis, diarrhea, hypothermia, shipwreck—add those and you still won't have it all. You've got to consider two other fac-tors. Fieldwork in evolutionary biology is also tedium and reductionism.

Without tedium and reductionism, it's not science. It's natural his-tory. Natural history is a noble enterprise, yes, but not the same noble enterprise as science. Natural history addresses the thing-in-itself. Sci-ence looks at, and then past, the thing-in-itself, seeking some pattern that might connect one thing-in-itself with others. Since nature is chaotic and almost infinitely various, the search for patterns must involve reduction: complex living creatures and systems reduced to a rough sketch of themselves. Most often, in recent decades, the rough sketch is drawn with mathematics. Observations must be made quanti-tative; life's variety must be translated into decimals. Even for a biologist with the soul of a mathematician—and there are enough of them nowa-days—that task of number-gathering can be tedious. (Pure mathematical fun resides not in gathering numbers but in manipulating them—though the journalist only knows this by hearsay.) For a biologist with the soul of a biologist, it can be deadly.

There's more. Besides tedium and reductionism, snakebite and dysentery, one other danger faces the biological fieldworker. This one is so large and scary, so terrifyingly amorphous, that it's best described in the negative: lack of validity. Are you really measuring what you *think* you're measuring? Are you really counting what you *think* you're counting? Are you really therefore proving what you claim to be proving? Or possibly not? Maybe you're rowing like hell but your oars aren't in the water.

Quantification must be meaningful as well as precise, and the assumptions by which numbers are linked to biological realities must be correct. If so, you have not only precision but validity. If not, you're wasting your time. Does the number of rings in a tree trunk really represent years of age? In most cases, yes. Does the number of wolf sightings in Glacier National Park really represent the current wolf population of that area? Possibly. Does the number of UFO stories in *The National Enquirer,* this year compared with last year, really represent the trend in visits by alien spacecraft? Uh, maybe not. Mathematized meaning, like any other kind, can be illusory.

There's always the chance that a nice set of numbers might describe nothing more than a carefully measured red herring. There's always the chance that 2.38 meters per second does not represent how fast a lizard can run when escaping from enemies on the desert landscape—that it represents only how fast a lizard might *choose* to run when chased by a human hand down a rubber runway in a motel room.

Jon Herron knows all this. He's familiar with most of those things that make biological fieldwork difficult—the perils of quantification, the perils of boredom, the others. Yesterday, while they collected lizards together on Isla La Ventana, he gave the journalist a sound explanation of why he came south to Baja with a portable racetrack. "After spending two years studying caiman at Manu," he said, referring to the big crocodilians of Peru's preeminent jungle park, "I decided it was time to work on something small enough that it couldn't rip my arm off when I screwed up."

◉   ◉   ◉

ONE BY ONE, the journalist hands Jon Herron all thirty-two plastic cups. One by one, each of the thirty-two side-blotched lizards takes a run down the racetrack. Flash, wink, *tweet,* and its top speed is penciled into the log. Then each lizard goes back to the incubator for a half-hour of rest. Six trials for every lizard in the course of a day. Repetition is essential to science. Repetition gives increased confidence of precision and, to a lesser degree, of validity. It also brings tedium. By noon, when the electric power shuts off and the computer falls dead, Jon and the journalist are both bored. Possibly the lizards are bored too, though this is harder to know.

The journalist fires up a gas-burning Coleman generator. Jon shifts his computer to this source of power, and the time trials continue. Running a laptop computer off a cheap, noisy generator seems to the journalist somewhat odd, like feeding a cockatoo on hog fodder. But if the computer doesn't balk, and Jon doesn't mind, and the lizards don't care, then so be it.

Sixteen of the lizards come from La Ventana. The other sixteen were collected on a different island. Eventually their speeds will be compared against each other, against speeds for at least one other island population, and against speeds for *U. stansburiana* from the mainland. Possibly it will all yield some small, significant insight about peak performance by reptiles in different ecological circumstances. That might in turn point a finger of light at how evolution can shape an animal's physiology, not just at moderate levels of activity but at the extremes. Possibly, on the other hand, it will all yield zilch.

One lizard hits 2.74 meters per second. Jon gives an appreciative mutter as he pencils that into the log. Another tops out at 1.54. Middling. A third does no better than 1.15. Slow. Some of the lizards achieve higher speeds on their later trials, some get worse. Some of the lizards from La Ventana are faster than some from the other island, and vice versa. Some of the males are faster than most of the females, but perhaps only because they are larger. If significant patterns exist, those will be sorted out later from the numbers.

One female from La Ventana, on her fourth or fifth trial, moves down the track sluggishly. Finally the biologist's hand prods her over the finish. Flash, *tweet,* and the computer screen shows a very low maximum speed figured to two decimal places. The racetrack knows precisely how slowly this lizard ran. The racetrack is smart but not sapient.

"She's getting tired," says the journalist.

"Yeah," says Jon Herron. "Or else she's getting wise to the game and isn't interested anymore."

CREDIT where credit is due: In 1981, the semi-obscure Swiss journal *Experientia* published a paper titled "A Field-Portable Racetrack and Timer for Measuring Acceleration and Speed of Small Cursorial Animals." It was written by Raymond B. Huey and three collaborators. Ray Huey is a biologist at the University of Washington with a particular interest in physiological ecology. He studies questions like, How does evolution affect an animal's peak performance? and, What role does temperature regulation play, among ectotherms, in maintaining that capacity? Ectotherms are those animals, including lizards, whose body temperatures are not internally stabilized. Since a cold lizard is a lizard incapable of vigorous activity, and since a lizard can only warm itself by seeking some external (usually solar) source of heat, temperature regulation is an important part of how lizards spend their time and effort. But how much time and effort can they afford to spend on maintaining just the right temperature for some sort of peak performance—say, a sprint—if that peak capacity is seldom useful or used? Back when the paper appeared in *Experientia,* no one knew. Huey, among others, had been wondering.

While it's easy enough to measure the *average* speed of a little running critter, the paper noted, measuring *peak* speed and acceleration is much more difficult. "The usual technique involves frame-by-frame analysis of films or videotapes. However, this method is relatively expensive, tedious, and inconvenient for field research. More importantly, data reduction is not immediate." So Huey and his coauthors offered design details for a better method, one that was inexpensive, somewhat less tedious, convenient to use in the field, and capable of squirting out data instantly. Only a physiological ecologist, perhaps, could appreciate what a sweet tool this racetrack might be.

Over the years since, Huey and other scientists have applied it to various questions—questions of foraging strategy among lizards of the Kalahari, questions of defensive response among lizards of the Negev, questions of how nocturnal lizards (such as geckos) might cope with their own special problem of maintaining performance capability without sunlight, and questions of sprint speed as a function of predation pressure upon lizard populations in the western United States. The last of these studies has involved both *U. stansburiana* and Jon Herron. Professor Huey is Jon's dissertation adviser, and the racetrack is one tool that Jon has been given to use. Finally, when another scientist invited Huey's racetrack along on an expedition to Baja, an expedition that would study island-dwelling reptiles of the Gulf of California, Jon Herron was the logical choice to go with it.

The racetrack has gotten around. In Israel, in the Kalahari, and elsewhere, it has answered just what was asked of it: How fast will a lizard run down a rubber track when chased by a human hand? It has answered to two decimal places of precision. It has answered quickly and conveniently. Validity, of course, is another matter.

Maybe the validity of the technique is unimpeachable. Maybe not. This isn't physics or pure math, and that particular question can't be answered to two decimal places of precision.

AFTER three days on a different island with the rest of the expedition, the journalist returns to the motel. The dust bunnies have multiplied. Some of the duct tape and all of the chocolate-chip cookies are gone. Except to collect lizards, Jon Herron has scarcely left the room. He is probably more pale-skinned than anyone south of Ensenada. "Been getting some good data?" asks the journalist.

Jon sighs. "Sometimes, as I'm racing the lizards, I think this is all bullshit. They behave so differently on the track from how they do in the field," he says. Ambivalence rides in his stomach, as heavy as tortillas and beans. "When you take the data away, though, and look at it in the lab, it begins to make some sense. Sometimes."

The journalist lays down his pack. When the next set of trials is ready to start, he hands Jon the first plastic cup. A lizard runs down the track. Flash, wink, *tweet*. So many meters, and hundredths of a meter, per second. Two decimal places of precision.

It goes into the log. Later, from the disorderly jumble of crisp little numbers, someone will deduce a meaning. The journalist has great respect for people like Jon Herron, people like Ray Huey, exploring this risky and paradoxical corner of science where precision intersects with the ineffable. He knows that their certainty, sometimes, may be illusory. He doubts that any of us do better.

Phobia and Philia

A Barefoot Psyche in the Forest of Spiders and Snakes

As a person who suffers from an inordinate fear of spiders, I'm continually amazed to discover how many otherwise sensible, doughty, well-adjusted people suffer from an inordinate fear of snakes. Seems like they ought to grow out of it. Seems like they ought to recognize that an emerald boa, for instance, is a gorgeous animal, comparable aesthetically to a leopard or a cockatoo; that a diamondback rattler is a handsome and honest-hearted predator that would never harm any person who didn't provoke it; that a twenty-foot anaconda is a beast of magisterial dignity. But they don't, those snake-fearing folk. Instead of showing proper appreciation, they shudder and cringe with irrational anxiety. And another thing that amazes me about these very people is that many of them are completely unaffected by the gut-curdling repugnance of spiders. They don't shudder and cringe when they *should*.

The point I take from this pair of amazements is that animal phobias are among the most mystifying and intricately illogical forms of human behavior. They're even less fathomable than romantic love, anorexia, and golf.

Phobia itself is a technical term that psychologists use carefully—to denote a fear that's exaggerated, inexplicable, uncontrollable, and debilitating—but we nonpsychologists can be forgiven for using it more loosely, in reference to the inexplicable but controllable loathings we cope with discreetly. A reasonable synonym might be "the willies." Some people get the willies at the sight of a cockroach or a horse. Others get the willies on the observation deck of a skyscraper. For spider-specific willies, as you know, the applicable term is *arachnophobia*. For snakes it's the slightly less familiar *ophidiophobia,* derived from the Greek word for serpent. Part of what makes these two phobias intriguing is that they seem so similar, yet they occur independently.

What makes them seem similar? Well, they focus on two of the world's least popular groups of animals. Spiders and snakes, as commonly thought of, are the leading exemplars of a single subjective category that cuts across all their objective differences: spooky vermin. Scorpions and centipedes and leeches, though not quite so infamous, fall into the same category. Is it simply a matter of leg count? Is it that spiders (and centipedes and scorpions) have too many walking limbs, and that snakes (and leeches) have too few? Each group does lie outside the numerical range of legginess that's standard for most of the animal kingdom—namely, four legs give or take two. But if that were the whole secret of arachnophobia and ophidiophobia, more people would be terrified of oysters (zero legs), snails (one smeary leg), and lobsters (ten legs, plus a half dozen supplemental appendages waving every which way), and seafood restaurants would be unthinkable.

Of course, oysters and lobsters don't sting or bite. Then again, mosquitoes bite vastly more humans than spiders do, and their bites cause vastly more misery and death. Bees and wasps take a higher fatality toll, in some countries, than snakes do. Even chiggers feed heavily on humans, and in Asia they carry a nasty disease known as scrub typhus; if you look at a chigger through a microscope, furthermore, it's god-awful ugly. But you don't hear of many people who suffer from raving chiggaphobia.

For reasons ineffable, chiggers and bees and mosquitoes just don't command the same psychological mojo as spiders and snakes. Neither do centipedes, scorpions, or leeches. The phobic dimension of snakes and spiders is a phenomenon that eludes easy explanation.

OPHIDIOPHOBIA is even more puzzling than arachnophobia, in that it shows up not just as personal fear among some individuals but also as a deeply ambivalent, obsessive fascination that has permeated folklore, religion, and iconography all over the world. From the ancient Egyptians to the Hopi of New Mexico, from the Shang Dynasty in China to the Kgatla tribes in southeastern Botswana, cultures throughout time and space have incorporated serpent spirits into their metaphysics and serpent images into their art. The Aztecs had Xiuhcoatl, the fire serpent; the Ainu of Japan have a snake god named Kinashut kamui; the Australian Aborigines have their Rainbow Serpent, sometimes wrathful, sometimes beneficent, always gigantic. The ancient Egyptians had Netjer-ankh, a deity embodied as a cobra, and the Kgatla have Kgwanyape, a snake spirit crucial to rainmaking rituals. In northwestern Canada, where snakebite is no issue, the folklore of the Kwakiutl nevertheless includes a menacing beast known as the *sisiutl*, portrayed in serpentine form with a snake's head at each end. The list could be extended to dozens of other cultures, time periods, and places—as it has been, by a biologist and polymathic scholar named Balaji Mundkur.

In his book *The Cult of the Serpent,* Mundkur presents a huge dossier of evidence about ophidiophobia and its perverse complement, ophidiolatry. He's the encyclopedist of humanity's long loathing-and-awe relationship with snakes. "In the ontogeny of specific fears, exceedingly few animals fall into the same category as the serpent or cause the intense emotion known as dysthymic neurosis," Mundkur writes. His "dysthymic neurosis" is another synonym for the willies. He adds: "'Dangerous' carnivores like the tiger, bear, or wolf, though 'fearsome,' do not repel man as serpents do." Everywhere on the planet, it seems, people fear and detest snakes but can't stop thinking about them.

Sigmund Freud had a facile explanation for ophidiophobia— roughly the same facile explanation he had for virtually everything. "There is a valid sexual meaning," Freud argued, in *The Interpretation of Dreams,* "behind the enormous exaggeration in neurotics of the natural human dread of snakes." Without explaining why *any* dread of snakes should be considered natural in civilized humans, he went on to say that many of the animals "used as genital symbols in mythology and folklore play the same part in dreams," and he listed specifically fishes, snails, cats, mice, plus "above all those most important symbols of the male organ—snakes." Symbolism was the language of the psyche, Freud believed, and the topic of its discourse was invariably sexual.

In his zeal to decode and interpret that discourse, he ignored the possibility that some dreamt-of snakes might represent not penile anxiety, not the sinuous gropings of the id, but actual legless reptiles of the suborder Serpentes. Then again, what did Freud know about herpetology? He lived his life in downtown Vienna, where an esteemed neurologist might easily forget that sometimes a snake is just a snake.

Another shortcoming of Freud's approach was that it said little or nothing about arachnophobia. Some later psychoanalytic theorists, such as K. A. Adams, have filled that gap. Almost two decades ago, Adams proposed in the *Journal of Psychoanalytic Anthropology* that an adult's fear of spiders can be traced to a childhood struggle to escape maternal entanglement. The child's sense of self, according to this view, represents an insect caught in the web of Mom's all-enwrapping femininity and affection. Adams seems to have found the syndrome more prevalent in our culture than elsewhere, and titled his paper "Arachnophobia: Love American Style." If there was any response to that notion by Adams's own mother (I like to imagine she pounced on K.A. with a smothering but affectionate refutation), the *Journal of Psychoanalytic Anthropology* doesn't seem to have carried it.

The biologist Edward O. Wilson has offered several insights of his own, grounded more in reality than in symbolism. In his 1984 book *Biophilia,* an autobiographical essay on the affective bond between humans and other species, he devoted a full chapter to the subject of how primates (monkeys, chimpanzees, and lemurs, as well as humans) react to snakes. It's interesting that African monkeys and chimps tend to show vehement alarm in the presence of a snake, whereas lemurs—indigenous to the island of Madagascar, where there are no dangerous snakes—seem indifferent. Wilson raised the possibility that snake aversion might be an inherent trait, inculcated by natural selection during the evolutionary process and only secondarily activated by an individual's learning experiences. "There is a principle of many ramifications to consider here," he wrote, "which extends well beyond the ordinary concerns of psychoanalytic reasoning about sexual symbols." The principle is that we humans, like other primates whose evolutionary adolescence was spent in the snake-infested habitats of tropical Africa, might carry a predisposition toward ophidiophobia in our genes. The many ramifications include this: If ophidiophobia has been built into the human genetic heritage, certain other phobias and philias might be genetically influenced as well.

Wilson himself had spent an ophidiophilic childhood in the snaky forests and swamps of Alabama and Florida. As a boy naturalist he was enthralled by snakes, collecting them, absorbing the folklore and teaching himself a bit of the science, gathering his own little herpetological zoo, until the bite of a pygmy rattlesnake helped to shift him toward other specialties. As an underweight end on his high-school football team, he still carried the nickname Snake. Years later, he was doing field-work in New Guinea when some of the native people raised a great nervous hubbub around a small brown snake; Wilson calmly collected the snake and got it preserved in alcohol for the Harvard museum, an act of bravado that earned him notoriety in the village. Next day, one of the children who followed him as he collected insects brought Wilson "an immense orb-weaving spider gripped in his fingers, its hairy legs waving and the evil-looking black fangs working up and down. I felt panicky and sick. It so happens that I suffer from mild arachnophobia. To each his own."

Wilson acknowledged the question—why one sort of phobia, and not the other?—but left it unanswered. Still, his admission of panic is a cheery message to arachnophobic ophidiophiles like myself. It tells us that we do our shuddering and cringing in good company.

IN AUGUST 1992 a small group of scholars and scientists met quietly at the Woods Hole Oceanographic Institute, on Cape Cod, to discuss the central idea of Wilson's autobiographical book: biophilia. It's important to remember that what Wilson had proposed was more than a vague, dreamy notion about love for nature; his biophilia entailed the controversial hypothesis that an emotional affinity for nature's diversity might be programmed genetically into the human species. More precisely, he had suggested that humans might be genetically equipped not necessarily with biophilia itself, but with a predisposition to learn biophilic attitudes and behaviors through individual or collective experiences. Implicit within this formulation (and later to be invoked explicitly) was the concept of biologically prepared learning, which had already been delineated in the literature of experimental psychology. With the pre-

pared-learning concept built into it, biophilia takes account of the combined effects of both genes and experience.

The group at Woods Hole pondered Wilson's idea from fifteen different angles. Eventually their presentations and discussions yielded a
book, edited by Wilson himself and the sociologist Stephen R. Kellert,
and published as *The Biophilia Hypothesis*. One provocative chapter is
by a psychologist named Roger S. Ulrich, long a student of how humans
feel about landscape.

Ulrich approaches biophilia in a roundabout way, through the cluster of attitudes and behaviors that he calls biophobia. The linchpin of
Ulrich's logic is that evidence of bio*phobia* does not, as it might seem,
undermine the bio*philia* hypothesis. He argues the contrary: If specific
types of biophobia are genetically based, that fact only adds plausibility
to the hypothesis that generalized biophilia might be genetically based
too. If genes can prepare us to loathe snakes, genes can also prepare us
to prefer forests over pavement. If evolution can predispose us to fear
spiders, evolution can also predispose us to feel that a diverse ecosystem
is the appropriate and necessary context for human life. It's a cleverly
counterintuitive argument. Any evidence for genetically based animal
phobias, according to Ulrich, tends to bolster the broader hypothesis of
biophilia.

Of exactly such evidence, he has collected a heap. "The most common phobic fears in Western societies may be fears of snakes and spiders," Ulrich notes. For that reason, a number of experimental
psychologists have used snake and spider images as "fear-relevant stimuli," matched against "neutral stimuli" such as geometric figures, in conditioning experiments designed to induce a defensive reaction at the mere
sight of one image or another. The conditioning phase of these experiments typically involves showing the volunteer subject a spider or snake
image (or, alternatively, a geometric figure) while giving the poor soul an
electric shock. After a sequence of repetitions, the volunteer has been
conditioned to feel the willies at sight of either the snake-and-spider
images or the geometric figures. During a second phase, the images are
shown without accompanying shocks, while the monitoring for defensive reactions continues. Results indicate that spider-and-snake willies
linger more persistently after conditioning than geometric-figure willies.

Similar experiments have added the insight that even images of handguns and frayed electrical wiring, which are certainly fear-relevant to modern humans, don't hold their conditioned emotional power as long as spider and snake images do. The photo of a pistol simply isn't as memorably scary, to most people, as the photo of a snake.

Another type of evidence comes from subliminal presentations of stimuli—that is, images flashed on a screen for milliseconds and gone again too quickly to allow conscious recognition. Results from these experiments suggest that arachnophobia and ophidiophobia are lightning-fast instincts, not dependent on conscious thought but operative at the subliminal pace. Still another type of evidence derives from studies of human twins: Specific animal phobias tend to be shared, even between twins who have had separate educational experiences. The implication, again, is that genes might play an important part in separating arachnophobes from ophidiophobes, and in separating both from the aphobic.

Basing his conclusions on a survey of such evidence, Ulrich writes: "The findings suggesting a robust genetic role in biophobia imply tenability and even optimism for the biophilia hypothesis." At first it sounds paradoxical, but on reflection it's compelling. Our cringe reflexes at the sight of a snake or a spider hint that we humans, deep in our souls, deep in our DNA, remain connected to the natural landscape.

SCIENTIFIC scrutiny of the biophilia idea has barely begun. Even *The Biophilia Hypothesis*, a hefty and authoritative volume, leaves most of the issues unresolved. Among them is the question I keep raising: Why is a given person susceptible to one sort of phobia but not another? What manner of quirky difference—in genetic endowment or formative experience or both—makes me an arachnophobe, makes you an ophidiophobe, and allows still other (smug, impassive, maybe downright deceitful) people to claim that they suffer no inordinate zoological fears whatsoever?

I've wondered about that for decades. I had occasion to wonder with particular urgency, several years ago, while dodging my way through a piece of tropical landscape that resides vividly in my memory as the Forest of Spiders and Snakes.

This forest is on the island of Guam. It's a woodland of monsoon vegetation—pandanus and breadfruit trees, cycads and palms, hibiscus and figs, knitted together with vines and shrubbery and ferns—on a plateau of uplifted limestone. The limestone consists of coral skeletons that have been compacted into rock, ragged and sharp. It has a texture like petrified sea froth, and it's pocked with old foxholes and ammunition-storage trenches left behind by the Japanese army. In river sandals with stiff soles, I walked through it carefully. I was wary of slicing a toe—especially wary because foot injuries, in the tropics, heal slowly.

I wouldn't have ventured into this iffy terrain without a purpose, but I was helping a herpetologist from the U.S. Fish and Wildlife Service make his daily rounds of a trapline. Our chore was to check eighty snake traps, set out in a broad grid and baited with geckos, for specimens of a mildly poisonous tree snake called *Boiga irregularis*. The snake is an exotic species that invaded Guam about fifty years ago and has multiplied catastrophically in the time since, making itself an ecological terror. Among other offenses, it has caused a series of electrical outages (by climbing power poles and shorting out the lines), attacked sleeping infants as though they were edible prey, and gobbled up virtually all of Guam's native forest birds. My herpetologist pal was an experienced field man in charge of orchestrating the effort to control it, and the trapline was one step toward learning how that might be done. In this particular forest, the snake density had gone extraordinarily high, though more recently it seemed to have declined. I was optimistic that we'd catch at least a few. Better still if we caught lots.

Noticing the old, rusty muzzle of what looked like a mortar sticking out of the ground, I asked the herpetologist about unexploded ordnance. Yes, there's some risk, he told me, and mentioned the two native Guamanians who had been killed within recent memory, when they tried to crack open a three-hundred-pound bomb. I made a note about the mortar and the bomb, then forgot them. Notwithstanding the snakes in the trees and the war debris underfoot, what caused me greater discomfort that morning were the spiders.

The forest was full of them. They were big. They were silent. They were black, yellow, orange, shaped variously, some gaudy, some subtle, oy, don't ask. By a cautious estimate, there were zillions. Many were specimens of *Cyrtophora moluccensis*, an orb-weaving species that tends to affiliate in labyrinthine communal webs. They were enjoying a population explosion of their own—possibly because the newcomer snakes had eaten their natural enemies, the birds. The *C. moluccensis* and the others had assembled in gangs, filling gaps in the understory with huge three-dimensional webs, thick as lace, large as dome tents, threatening to block my escape. These spiders were harmless to humans, I knew, but it didn't matter. Yeah, sometimes they are a nuisance, the herpetologist allowed—so he would carry a stout stick and carve the webs out of his way, like hacking through bamboo with a machete. OK for him, he was clearly a nonarachnophobic ophidiophile; but I made a point of leaving the webs undisturbed. I circled around them on long detours, or gathered my nerve and ducked underneath. Each web held dozens of major spiders, and I shied at the idea of having that many mad at me.

Eventually I made a misstep. My attention strayed at the wrong moment and I marched forward recklessly, pushing my face into one of those webs. At the first touch of silk on my eyelids, air-raid alarms went off in my brain and the floor of my stomach dropped away like a falling elevator. No doubt my galvanic skin response, whatever that is, spiked up to a personal lifetime high. But I tried to stay calm. I backed slowly out. As I did, I saw a single black spider, very large, at roughly eye level just in front of me.

She made no move to attack. She didn't even growl and wiggle her fangs. She simply waited, forbearingly, for me to get my mug out of her web.

THERE'S A poem by Jim Harrison that bears on all this, titled "Cobra" but applicable to scary critters of all breed. "What are these nightmares, / so wildly colored?" it begins. After a few lines on the nature of every person's most personal fears, it continues:

> Long ago
> in Kenya where I examined the
> grass closely before I sat down
> to a poisonous lunch, I worried
> about cobras. When going insane I worried
> about cobra venom in Major Grey's Chutney.
> Simple as that. Then in overnight sleep I became
> a lordly cobra, feeling the pasture grass
> at high noon glide beneath my
> stomach.

As a cobra, with his head arched above the weeds, he surveyed the land-scape. Then he slept in the cool dirt under a granary. He had entered upon a fresh perspective.

I aspire to the same kind of karmic freshening. My own goal for the next life is to come back as an orb-weaving spider. I want to be big as a prune and black, with yellow markings. When I retreat to a corner of my web, I'll leave a silken inscription in the middle, as a gesture of homage to a certain children's book from the era of my childhood—*Charlotte's Web,* the greatest arachnophilic document of our time. Instead of weaving the words SOME PIG! or TERRIFIC, like E. B. White's heroic spider, I'll weave BIOPHILIA, or maybe just DAVE'S NOT HERE. I can only hope that the food will be good, that I'll see some new angles, and that people will find it in themselves to be nice to me.

WHO SWIMS
WITH THE TUNA

Confronting the Intricate Moral Ambivalence
of Canned Fish

The yellowfin tuna is not celebrated for its intelligence. It's celebrated for its flavor. The spotted dolphin, on the other hand, is famously brainy and no one will tell us how it tastes. The killing of dolphins is a national outrage; the killing of tuna is a given. I keep asking myself why. There are some good reasons and some bad reasons, I think, which haven't been closely examined, or even sorted apart.

One of these animals breathes air. The other doesn't. One is a mammal, one isn't. And so on: Among the possible ways of describing dolphins and tuna, though not the only way, is to recite a litany of such invidious comparisons. One is homoiothermic and one isn't. One seems to have an elaborate system of social behavior and one doesn't. One has performed altruistic and astonishing rescues of human swimmers; the other is prized for sushi. One shrieks with terror and squeals with pain. The other maintains a stoic piscine silence. Furthermore, on our grocery shelves nowadays we find cans of a product called dolphin-safe tuna. But no tuna-safe dolphin.

There are other differences. Entangled in a net, unable to swim backward, panicked, hampered from raising its blowhole clear of the water, a dolphin will drown. The sight is pathetic and gruesome—as I can attest, having once watched a certain videotape of dolphin misfortunes at the hands of tuna fishermen during a purse-seining operation.

To be more precise, I did not watch this videotape *once*—I watched it over and over in the course of a week, immersing myself in ugly visions of drowning dolphins, crushed dolphins, bleeding dolphins. I froze frames, rewound, and jabbed the play button again to see large dolphin bodies, mashed and twisted beyond hope of recovery, being tossed back into the ocean like so much offal. It's an important document, this particular tape, potently distressing yet eloquent on the subject of humankind's wasteful, abusive treatment of other creatures. It was shot by a young man named Sam LaBudde, at serious personal risk, while he worked for some months on a tuna boat in the Eastern Tropical Pacific, that zone of ocean encompassing the warm waters along the west coast of Latin America.

During the past thirty years, dolphins of several different species have died in great number because commercial tuna fishermen found it convenient and cost-effective, at least in the Eastern Tropical Pacific, to catch one kind of animal by setting their nets around another. By a conservative estimate, purse-seining for tuna has caused more than six million dolphin deaths. Although U.S. tuna fishermen claim that they are more careful than their foreign competitors, that they safely release almost all the dolphins they net, those same U.S. fishermen have fought stubbornly for a legal provision that lets them continue killing up to 20,050 dolphins each year.

The dolphins are netted because they serve as a marker: encircle them and chances are good that you've also got tuna. Despite all their differences, the fish and the mammal tend to associate closely. Maybe that connection is symbiotic, or maybe it's just coincidence. We humans don't know. We aren't privy. Trapped in a huge corral of floating net, along with their tuna associates, the dolphins can in some cases be released unharmed. In other cases they turn hysterical, or the boat captain simply ignores them; the net is hauled, the dolphins tangle themselves and flail desperately, like antelope caught in the web of a gigantic spider; a few are lifted high, to be crushed in the power block (the huge spool) that gobbles up the net; more than a few, still trapped in the water beneath doubled-over netting, drown. Drowning is ugly; drowning makes four minutes seem like eternity. A tuna will not drown, though it will suffocate inconspicuously while it flops around on a deck.

For all the value of the LaBudde tape, something is missing. At least it's missing from the edited version, supplied to me by Earth Island Institute, the organization with which LaBudde is affiliated. There's no footage, not so much as a glimpse, of dead or dying tuna.

Tuna are not the point, I know. Canned tunafish is the given; dolphin-safe or dolphin-unsafe is the point. But it still seems to me odd that tuna, as living and dying creatures, have so completely disappeared. Not just from the videotape. From our minds.

Are we concerned with humanity's relationship with nature, or are we merely concerned about Man's Special Friend at Sea, the dolphin? These are two different things.

A FEW years ago, Kenneth Brower published in *The Atlantic* a long, excellent article about the destruction of dolphins by tuna fishermen in the Eastern Tropical Pacific, and about the daring gambit of Sam LaBudde. The article is full of facts, full of fair-minded argument, but its most subtle effect is achieved by another method—point of view. It begins:

> Of the thirty-odd species of oceanic dolphins, none makes a more striking entrance than *Stenella attenuata,* the spotted dolphin. Under water spotted dolphins first appear as white dots against the blue. The beaks of the adults are white-tipped, and that distinctive blaze, viewed head-on, makes a perfect circle. When the vanguard of the school is "echolocating" on you— examining you sonically—the beaks all swing your way, and each circular blaze reflects light before any of the rest of the animal does.

Brower describes the habitat of these dolphins—clear, deep, tropical ocean—and the sensation of floating within it. A blue void, he calls it, seemingly sterile as a desert. Then:

> Five or six quick strokes of the flukes and they are upon you, sleek, fast, graceful legions. They come a little larger than life, for water magnifies. They animate the void. With barrages of clicks and choruses of high-pitched whistling, with speed and hydrodynamic perfection, with curiosity, mission, agenda, and something like humor, they fill up the empty blue.

You are surrounded by dolphins, caressed by their clicking voices. And then: "The last dolphin of the last wave pumps by, glances at you in passing, hurries to catch up." Kenneth Brower has been in the water with these animals, obviously, and before even mentioning tuna boats or purse seines, he deftly pulls the reader in there with him. He offers a vicarious opportunity to look dolphins in the face and share the sensation of being explored, known, by their sonar and their big liquidy eyes. Why? Because he wants us—you and me and whoever else might pick up *The Atlantic*—to feel especially bonded with dolphins, and he evidently believes that direct physical acquaintance (or even a literary rendition of it) is the best way to generate such a bond.

Later in the article, he makes that premise explicit. Alluding to the doom awaiting a certain newborn dolphin calf that LaBudde saw pitched back into the water, where without its mother it faced starvation and sharks, Brower declares: "Anyone who has swum with wild dolphins can imagine how it went."

Ani H. Moss, a former fashion model living in Los Angeles and latterly a conservation activist, broke into public view about the same time as Brower's article, representing a physical embodiment of the anyone-who-has-swum-with-them premise. Like Brower, she harbors a warm and specific affinity for dolphins. One newspaper photograph shows her, afloat, in a life jacket, kissing a pleased-looking dolphin on the side of its beak. According to the *San Francisco Chronicle,* Ani Moss has swum with dolphins in Bermuda, Florida, and Hawaii. This fact merits newsprint because she is one of the cluster of people—including Sam LaBudde, David Phillips of Earth Island Institute, Anthony J. F. O'Reilly of the H. J. Heinz Company, and Ani's husband, a music-industry executive named Jerry Moss—most responsible for a great triumph won in the crusade to protect dolphins. On April 12, 1990, Heinz announced that its StarKist subsidiary, the world's largest tuna-canning business, would no longer purchase any tuna caught by methods that were harmful to dolphins.

Behind that decision lay a domino chain of persuasion that went roughly like this: Ani Moss saw LaBudde's videotape and talked with her husband; Mr. and Mrs. Moss talked with Phillips about dolphin conservation and Earth Island's consumer boycott against Heinz; Jerry Moss then talked honcho-to-honcho with Anthony J. F. O'Reilly; the

Heinz people eventually talked with Phillips and even, it seems, with Sam LaBudde. Behind the boardroom doors at H. J. Heinz, there was "an epic debate, almost theological in tone," as O'Reilly himself later told the *New York Times*. At last, with a suddenness that startled everyone on the outside and probably more than a few people on the inside, Heinz decided to leap acrobatically from one side of the issue to the other. Seldom in the history of conservation politics has jawboning proven so concretely effective.

The announcement caused an abrupt revolution in the international tuna trade. That same afternoon, StarKist's two main competitors, Chicken of the Sea and Bumble Bee, vowed that they also would cease their complicity in the death of dolphins; StarKist had seized what appeared to be the moral high ground, and in this case the moral high ground was so good for public relations, perhaps also for business, that Chicken of the Sea and Bumble Bee were compelled to scramble up-slope in the same direction. Before long, tuna canners in Thailand, France, and Italy made similar announcements. Some of the U.S. tuna boats in the Eastern Tropical Pacific immediately applied for clearance to move westward, into waters where tuna and dolphins don't associate. Heinz began printing "dolphin-safe" labels, while Earth Island Institute declared victory and offered peace with honor.

Anthony J. F. O'Reilly, the man who effected (or at least accepted) this sea change, is a hardheaded Irish millionaire and a fancier of race-horses. If he has ever jumped into a tank or an ocean and swum with dolphins, the newspaper accounts don't mention it. But the calculus of the businessman has its own heartfelt power.

Back when the Earth Island boycott was in force, before the Heinz capitulation, Sam LaBudde said: "The reason this issue remains an issue, and the reason that it's not going to go away, is that human beings have a very special kinship with dolphins." It's an honest and accurate statement, so far as it goes, and one with which Anthony J. F. O'Reilly came to agree.

THE LABUDDE videotape does not diminish in grisliness with repeated viewing. While the information content becomes familiar, while the words and the numbers blur away, the moving images come forward more vividly. Like the photographer played by David Hemmings in the movie *Blowup,* you start noticing nasty details that you had missed. You see the flying bits of flesh from some anatomical breakage—a fin ripped away, maybe, or a beak—when a tangled dolphin suddenly falls from the hoisted net. You see an animal pass through the power block, like wet laundry through a wringer, and you recognize that its thrashing has turned into twitching. On the fourth replay, as you stare at the sleek dark shapes in a pocket of tightened seine, big animals bunched like spawning salmon, you realize that they are all floating limp with their blowholes submerged. Watching the crewmen work, you begin to distinguish between when they're releasing live dolphins and when they're disposing of carcasses. Mostly it's the latter. Then there's the scene with the knife.

The captain of LaBudde's ship, a burly man wearing only a pair of soaked shorts, is stooping over the body of a dolphin, filleting it deftly. With quick slashes, he strips off a long panel of muscle. He glances up into the camera—once, then back to his work, then up again. The tape ends.

This scene with the knife is hard to watch and tricky to contemplate. It's a crux at which the emotional import of the LaBudde videotape diverges (for some of us, anyway) from the philosophical import. The captain's knife cuts through more than flesh; it also divides attitudes. It divided my own, clarifyingly, into two successive but contradictory reactions. First reaction: My God, he's slicing that dolphin into meat. My God, they're going to *eat* it. Witnessing the butchery, you feel a surge of horrified outrage to which you may not be entitled. I know I felt one to which I'm probably not entitled. Butchery, not as a metaphor but the literal fact, is just what brings animal parts—including, occasionally, a bit of mammal—to my kitchen counter. Sam LaBudde, when he made the tape, was a vegetarian; so arguably he was entitled. Maybe he also felt some outrage at the notion of eating tuna. Or maybe not. Second reaction: Who am I, a confirmed carnivore, to say that they *shouldn't* eat dolphin flesh? If the creature is dead, better to eat it than to discard it. Both these reactions have merit, I think, and the dichotomy between them helps untangle that confusion of good logic and bad logic, earned emotion and specious emotion, surrounding the subject of dolphin-unsafe tuna.

A person might object to the killing on grounds that dolphins are big-brained mammals. If that were my position, I'd want also to know more than I know about the size of the brain of a Hereford, and I'd be uncomfortable with reports of high intelligence among octopuses and pigs. A person might object on grounds that dolphins are charming and communicative creatures capable of forming exceptional bonds with our species. That position is admirably loyal. But if it were mine I'd feel forced to admit that my view of nature was rigidly anthropocentric, and that I was therefore prevented from arguing that a hectare of beetle-infested rainforest might be more valuable than a hectare of slash-and-burn rice. A person might object on grounds that the death of six million dolphins in thirty years—as a by-product of purse-seining, merely to bring us cheap tuna, with most of those six million carcasses dumped back into the ocean—has been unconscionably wasteful; and that just such contemptuous, self-indulgent wastefulness is the greatest sin that our species commits against nature. This *is* my position. But probably it's no more consistent than the others.

Or a person might object, as some have, that the drownings of dolphins are slow and cruel, much worse than the quick death of a cow or a chicken in a slaughterhouse. If that were my position, I'd deserve to be haunted by a nightmare of suffocating tuna, big fish flopping paroxysmally on a deck, their sticky-dry gills unable to extract oxygen from the air. And I'd need to swear off live-boiled lobster.

Mix all these positions together and what you don't get is a single, unassailable ethical stance. What you do get is a successful consumer boycott against one kind of canned fish. The fight to protect dolphins from tuna fishermen brought a great victory for mammalian empathy, but not for clear thinking about humanity's responsibility within the wider diversity of life.

There's no question that *Stenella attenuata* and the other dolphins have an unmatched appeal to us humans. From our point of view, as Sam LaBudde said, it's a special kinship. They are bright, sophisticated, cheery, generous, perceptive, affectionate, and yet mysterious—all the things that we value in our friends. They seem to possess important secrets. They seem to reciprocate our infatuation. Plus they consent to let us swim with them.

On the other hand, who swims with the yellowfin tuna? The answer is that dolphins do.

TROPICAL PASSENGERS

How to Stay Healthy in Maluku Utara

It says here in this gruesome book, *How to Stay Healthy Abroad,* compiled by Dr. Richard Dawood and a roster of other experts in order to educate and terrify travelers, that a person could get schistosomiasis from windsurfing on Lake Volta. Waterskiing the river Euphrates could likewise be risky. The parasite *Schistosoma haematobium* might splash aboard, burrow in through your skin, and establish a franchise in your bladder.

It says here that the pork tapeworm *Taenia solium* can cause epilepsy, cerebral degeneration, and death. It says here, in the same fearful volume, that the fatal ingredient of fugu (puffer fish, to those of us who aren't Japanese epicures) when it has been incorrectly prepared is something called tetrodotoxin, and that a fugu-poisoned victim's last mortal sensation will be a delicate tingling on the lips. It says here that the fruit of the *Blighia sapida* tree, served in Jamaica under the name akee, can bring on convulsions if eaten unripe. And it says here that two-thirds of the chefs in Taiwan restaurants, during an exhaustive 1988 survey, had athlete's foot. From where I presently sit, holed up in a rat-haunted hotel on a small island in the outback of equatorial Asia, these are four of the book's more cheerful points, because akee and fugu and Lake Volta water sports—let alone the temptation to loan my shower clogs to a Taiwanese chef—can all be so easily avoided. The rev-

73

elations in *How to Stay Healthy Abroad* that I find rather more scary are the ones implicating certain ineluctable basics: potable water, simple food, and the necessity of occasionally coming in contact with a bath-room, a doorknob, a mattress, an insect, a gasp of unfriendly air, or the unwashed hand of another human. I should have known better than to bring Dr. Dawood's macabre treatise as light reading on a trip to Maluku Utara.

Maluku Utara is a region of mountainous, jungle-wrapped islands in eastern Indonesia. It might be slightly more familiar (though not much more, I suppose) as the northern Moluccas. My particular loca-tion is a tiny volcanic nub called Ternate, just off the west coast of Halmahera, which is a day's boat journey east of Sulawesi, which is north of Flores, which is three island hops east of Bali, if that's any help. Borneo and New Guinea flank these out-of-the-way little places like cinder-block bookends. Ternate itself is an island too minuscule to appear in any but the heftiest atlas. It's an ancient trading port dating back to the heyday of the Dutch East India Company, when it held high strategic significance as the world's leading export center for nutmeg (see "The Narcotic of Empire," page 25) and cloves. But the endemic spices have long since been transplanted elsewhere, and the world's taste in strategic resources has changed, and so the Ternate of today is noth-ing more than a pony-cart town trading in fish and bananas and copra, well off the lanes of international commerce and at peace with its shrunken destiny as the provincial capital of Maluku Utara. Tourists don't come here. You can't buy a picture postcard.

But allow me to say a thing or three on behalf of Maluku Utara. Its people are handsome and friendly. Its atolls are lambent turquoise. Its endemic mammals are gentle beasts such as the cuscus, a tree-climbing marsupial with a pussycat disposition. Its forests are graced also with cockatoos, lorikeets, racquet-tailed kingfishers, big-footed ground birds known as megapodes that incubate their eggs in huge mounds of com-post, surrealistic beetles, gigantic spiders, and a bounteous variety of wild tropical fruits, including the legendary durian. Its largest settle-ments are small coastal towns, its villages are mere flecks, and there aren't many roads in between. Its innocence is nearly intact. Its food is exotic, savory, and almost embarrassingly cheap. All of which is to say: Maluku Utara ranks high among the planet's most wonderful places.

But if I had read *How to Stay Healthy Abroad* before leaving America, and taken its warnings to heart, I probably wouldn't have come.

CONSIDER just the perils of food. "If not eaten straight away," Dr. Dawood's book warns, "cooked food should be protected from possible sources of contamination, and refrigerated immediately." Right. And monkeys should fly out of Dr. Dawood's ass. From my current vantage point, that kind of talk about instant and scrupulous refrigeration reads like a sadistic taunt.

Cooked food in Maluku Utara is displayed proudly on shelves in the sun-warmed front windows of restaurants: bowls of roasted fish and stewed jackfruit and fried squid and coconut-curry chicken set out in full sight as enticement to passersby. This is generally true throughout Indonesia, at least within the modest food stalls known as *warungs* and in the restaurants that feature a spicy buffet-style cuisine called *padang*. Window-shopping, at such establishments, takes the place of a menu. But up here in Maluku Utara the practice is still more pervasive—or anyway it seems so to me, partly because there aren't many local alternatives to warungs and houses-of-padang, and partly no doubt because Dr. Dawood has made me excruciatingly aware of the microbial implications. People browse by, flies come and go, the heat of the day rises to its peak, and there the food sits. A given morsel of meat might be delivered to one table at lunchtime, sniffed at, breathed upon, rejected, and replaced on its shelf to await a second chance with someone else around dinner. Refrigerators—what few exist in Maluku Utara—are reserved for the undeniably crucial purpose of chilling beer.

Dawood would not approve. "Small numbers of surviving bacteria may grow at phenomenal rates if left in a slowly cooling medium (i.e., recently cooked food)," says the good doctor's doom-mongering book. What constitutes a phenomenal rate? "Bacteria of the type relevant to this discussion may divide once every twenty minutes: a single bacterial cell weighing one millionth of a gram could (under optimum conditions) divide enough times in twenty-four hours for its offspring to weigh around four million kilograms—or about the weight of a small ship." So if the bacteria grown on one dish of leftover mackerel don't happen to kill you by poisoning, they might crush you to death as they fall off the shelf.

Suddenly it occurs to me: Maybe I should play safe and eat nothing but rice. Rice, of course, is the staff of life in this part of the world. Boiled rice for breakfast, cold rice for lunch, and as a hedge against waste the remnants turn up as *nasi goreng* (fried rice) for dinner. Something called black-rice pudding for dessert. OK, the book allows grudgingly, fresh-cooked rice is likely to be safe. But then I come to the part about *Bacillus cereus,* a rice-contaminating bacterium that's clever enough to produce heat-resistant spores. "Left to their own devices in the interval between meals, these spores germinate and the subsequent bacterial growth converts the surrounding rice into a deadly emetic cocktail, lying in wait for the unwary consumer." So there's no reassurance from rice. Those consumers who aren't unwary, left to *their* own devices in the interval between meals, might catch the next plane out.

But fresh vegetables, at least, ought to be wholesome, yes? Within the fool's paradise of my ignorance I embrace that notion, momentarily, until Dawood's book reminds me about night soil. "The use of human faeces as fertilizer (nightsoil)—a practice widespread in the tropics—makes salads and uncooked fresh vegetables risky unless they have been carefully washed with clean water." In the real world, or in this tiny corner of it anyway, that "unless" represents a deal-breaker. Where's the nearest clean water? Tap water of doubtful purity doesn't satisfy Dawood's standard. Unimpeachably clean water is only available, in Maluku Utara, from rainspouts and boiling kettles and expensive plastic bottles labeled AQUA, none of which sources is likely to be used in a street-corner restaurant for the rinsing of spinach. Therefore a wholesome-looking side dish of night-soiled greens could carry giardia, shigella, *Entamoeba histolytica,* typhoid, cholera, or hepatitis.

There's still fruit. Fruit, unlike vegetables, is mostly arborescent—growing high up in trees, that is, beyond range of ambient night soil except in the most peculiar circumstances. The market stalls of Maluku Utara happen to be rich with superb local fruit: durians, mangosteens, langsats, papayas, litchi-like rambutans, pineapples, salaks. The problem with fruit is that, to eat it, you gotta touch it. Touch is contamination. Germs are everywhere, Dr. Dawood assures me, but especially on hands. So the healthy precaution is to wash your hands before peeling that salak or wolfing that glob of durian. Wash your hands early and often; wash them, in fact, on general principles whenever confronted with a sink. But don't lay your fingers back on the faucet handles to turn off the water, huh-uh; and don't use a public towel, huh-uh; and don't handle a newspaper or a piece of money or anything else that's been handled by God knows how many unsanitary strangers. And therefore don't touch the outside of a mangosteen that you've just bought at the market—or, if you do, don't touch the pearly and succulent little sections on the inside. All right now, Houdini, with those stipulations: Enjoy your fruit.

Eventually it can make a person crazy. The logical end point of fastidious hygiene, after all, was Howard Hughes in a darkened hotel suite with an empty Kleenex box over each hand. (Or was it white gloves on his hands and the boxes on his feet?) I feel a new twinge of empathy for the demented Mr. Hughes when I realize, thanks to Dawood, that I can't possibly eat a durian or a salak without sullying the edible part with my own filthy fingers.

This, as the book explains smugly, is why God gave us bananas.

Maluku Utara does offer bananas. It offers bananas like the sky offers stars. Banana trees grow here in every backyard and empty lot. They grow along the highway, and at the airport, and in the foothills above the villages, and outside the sultan's mosque. The local bananas are thick-skinned and cheap, not as sweet and delicate as some Indonesian bananas, but infinitely available. So that's one way to go, I suppose. Call it The Cautious Traveler's Maluku Utara Diet: bananas, bottled water, and beer.

An equally appealing option might be to stay home and forget the whole thing.

BUT PANIC IS tiring. So after the first wave of Dawood-induced panic has passed through me like a malarial shiver, I take a different tack. I embark on a two-pronged program. Prong one is that, while continuing to read Dr. Dawood's book, I avoid any passage that has immediate relevance and confine my attention instead to all the sad, unfortunate, morbidly fascinating forms of bad health that might befall other folk in other parts of the world but are not likely to get me in Maluku Utara.

African eye worm, for instance. This is a variety of filariasis—an infestation of long, threadlike, parasitic worms spread from one human to another by insects. African eye worm (also known, more clinically, as loiasis) occurs in the rainforests of West and Central Africa. It's carried by large biting flies of the genus *Chrysops,* which breed in exactly those shady forest pools where a jungle-weary trekker would take respite. The eye-worm infection usually shows itself as recurrent, itchy swellings just under the skin. Each attack lasts only a few days, but the swellings might come and go for fifteen years. And sometimes, says the book, this particular filarial worm can be seen crawling across the surface of the victim's eye.

Tropical warble fly is another tribulation passed between humans and insects. This one, like so many others, travels by mosquito. The life history of the tropical warble fly is "complex"—as Dawood's book notes tantalizingly, without offering ecological detail except to say that the female lays her eggs on a mosquito's thorax and that those eggs hatch to maggots while the mosquito is biting a human. The maggots leap off (evolution having granted them good timing) and burrow into the person's skin. Evidently there's no pharmaceutical cure. So warble-fly attack is something to keep in mind if you're planning a vacation on the east slope of the tropical Andes, which I'm happy to say I am not.

Tumbu fly, native to East Africa, also punishes humans with its maggots. The tumbu-fly female lays her eggs on clothing, with a marked predilection for clothes that bear traces of urine or sweat; imperfectly clean laundry, hung outside to dry, makes an especially inviting target. By way of safeguard against tumbu-fly maggots, accordingly, the book decrees: "All clothes dried outdoors should be pressed with a good, hot iron to destroy any eggs that may be present." A hot iron, did the man say? We've got access to a hot iron in the tropical outback? He might as well tell us to have our expedition shirts frequently Martinized. Along the margin of my Dawood, beside the hot-iron passage, I've penned a small piece of reciprocal advice: "Get real."

On the opposite page appears a line illustration of the tumbu-fly maggot itself, which seems to resemble an Austrian coffee cake, though presumably not quite so large.

These lurid maladies are all serious human problems, of course. What makes them most serious is not that they hit an occasional traveler, but that they can make life hard, painful, in some cases short, for millions of rural people who permanently inhabit the tropics. Malaria still afflicts more than 200 million humans each year, for instance, and kills a million children in Africa alone, while we affluent visitors breeze through the danger zones with our chloroquine and our mefloquine and our deet. Cholera and yellow fever and typhoid still kill people too, owing mainly to a lack of good health care, whereas an American tourist carries that magical yellow card inside his or her passport, attesting to immunization. Notwithstanding the seriousness, though, Dr. Dawood's book reads like a catalog of bizarre pathogenic interactions, some dire, some only inconvenient, even the names of which ring with their own ghoulish music: Lassa fever, Ebola, and green monkey disease; Chagas' disease, carried by cone-nosed bugs and suspected of having caused lifelong torment to Charles Darwin; river blindness, Kyasanur Forest disease, Crimean haemorrhagic fever, o'nyong nyong; louping ill, a rare occupational hazard to British shepherds; rabies and scabies and scrub typhus; larva migrans, larva currens, creeping eruption; yeccch.

Yeccch is a comment, not an arcane tropical parasite.

Taken in this spirit, *How to Stay Healthy Abroad* makes vivid reading—vivid enough to keep a traveler up late in a rat-haunted hotel. It reminds me of the hours I once spent, mesmerized, in the middle of a New Guinea forest, with my rear parked on a soggy log until I turned the last page of *The Silence of the Lambs*.

PRONG TWO of my personal health program is to proceed blithely as though I'd never read Dr. Dawood. For the duration in Maluku Utara, then, I simply go where I need to go, do what I need to do, letting the insects and microbes and poisonous snakes and filarial worms and rabid cuscuses, if any, do what *they* need to do. I pretend that the Ternate volcano won't erupt, not this week at least, though the plume of smoke at its summit serves as reminder that it certainly could. I pretend that the boat from Ternate to Halmahera won't sink, ramshackle as it is, and ignore the Dawoodian advice that I acquaint myself with the muster stations for lifeboats, of which there seem to be none anyway. I maintain a stout optimism, use my hands as though they are sterile utensils just freshly emerged from Kleenex boxes, and eat everything that looks or smells appetizing, no matter how long it's been functioning as a petri dish.

Even Dr. Dawood himself sanctions this approach, sort of. "A positive attitude to health," he says (though I'm quoting selectively from an unrepresentative passage in his generally downbeat book), is a powerful weapon for the traveler.

I sample the boiled coconut crab—*kepiting rebus,* on local menus—for which Maluku Utara is justly famed. I eat cherrylike jambulangs, knocked ripe from their tree, which have rolled only briefly on the ground. I share durian in the forest (see "The Great Stinking Clue," page 93) with a disreputable pack of small boys. I gobble nameless pastries and custardy substances wrapped in banana leaf. I consume enough tepid rice to grow a battleship's weight of *Bacillus cereus.* I test my luck with spinach. Now admittedly, eating isn't the purpose of my visit to Maluku Utara. (History is what brought me, and a heroic man named Alfred Russel Wallace, who while based here conceived a great scientific idea, despite being—come to think of it—deathly sick.) But the joys and risks of eating can stand as token for the various modest challenges entailed in pursuing that purpose. That is, if the food doesn't get me, the cabdrivers or the malaria or the local Liberation Army might. Travel isn't really travel without some measure of uncertainty, and uncertainty in turn implies jeopardy. For the illusion of travel without the jeopardy, God gave us Imax as well as bananas.

I embark on my little "leap now/worry later" program knowing that one of two things will happen. Maybe I'll get miserably ill. Maybe some nasty creature will make itself a passenger in my bowels, or in my eye, or in my liver. Maybe I'll lose ten pounds of fluid and have to consult the local shaman. Maybe I'll carry home some new skin inflammation to amuse Brian, my ever-appreciative dermatologist. Maybe I'll blunder into a harrowing medical misadventure of one sort or another, which might provide a splashy denouement to this discussion of the perils of tropical travel. It's a prospect not to be wished for. But the alternative is also troubling.

Despite all my heedlessness, I might return safe and healthy to the international nexus at Bali, and then board my flight for America feeling just fine. In that case, God forbid, I could offer no firsthand testimony about the symptomatic expressions of shigella, coconut-crab ptomaine, Malayan tongue-worm, or mangosteen toxosis. I'd have lost the little bet that I made with myself when I started writing, while still in the field, about how to get sick in Maluku Utara. If I had learned anything, I'd have learned only that positive thinking might be a good travel strategy, but not necessarily a good literary one. I'd be deprived of a splashy denouement. This essay would simply stop.

SPATULA THEORY

The Continuation of Courtship by Other Means

No doubt you've often asked yourself, over the years, why it is that owls don't have penises.

And no doubt you've noticed, if so, that this is one of those hauntingly stupid questions that allows of no smart, easy answer. Half of the reason is circumstantially moot; half of all owls are female. It's the other half, regarding the other sex, that's the hard part: If male owls don't have penises, how come? Be assured that you're not alone in your wondering. Biologists, serious-minded scientific people with no tincture of prurient curiosity—or not much tincture, anyway—have wondered too. An eagle has no penis either. A crow has no penis. These facts are somewhat peculiar.

The peculiarity lies in those birds being excluded from an otherwise very inclusive category. To be equipped with a penis (actually, that word by its strict definition is specific to mammals) or penislike organ represents no elite evolutionary attainment. A male crocodile has one. A male ladybug has one. So do a wombat and a whale and a slug and a butterfly and a turtle. This is one of the few anatomical features that a man shares (pride yourselves, guys) with a nematode or a mite. These protrusive male thingamajigs turn up among a wide range of animal groups, in a heady variety of shapes, under a handful of names. For insects, the technical term is *aedeagus*. For millipedes, it's *gonopodia*, translating roughly as "legs modified into genitalia." Spiders do their mating with *pedipalps,* another form of modified leg, to which sperm is applied from a separate male orifice, like guacamole on a chip, before insertion. The male of the black widow spider bears on its pedipalp a fine, pointy structure called an *embolus,* the tip of which breaks off inside the female (bad enough in itself, but portending an even worse fate in store for the poor little dude). Most fish have no use for any such appendage, since their eggs are fertilized externally, out in the hospitable liquid medium that surrounds them. Still, even the fish world does include some exceptions. Male guppies have gonopodia, not be to confused with the milli-pedes' gonopodia, since the guppy version is anal fins, not legs, that have been modified for internal fertilization. In sharks, the equivalent is called claspers. Biological jargon offers one generalized term for the lot: *intromittent organs.* What they commonly intromit is sperm, from the male's body into the female's (or from one hermaphrodite's into another's), so that the jissom doesn't get dried out or spilled or other-wise squandered in transit.

Internal fertilization has evolved independently a number of times in the animal world, and in almost all cases it's the male sex-cell contri-bution that's transferred from one body to another, by way of some sort of extensible dingus, while the female sex cell stays put. One remarkable reversal of this pattern shows up in the sea horses, those giraffe-faced and prehensile-tailed fish of the family Syngnathidae. Among at least some of the syngnathids (including pipefish as well as sea horses), both fertilization and incubation occur inside the male's body, and it's the female who delivers her contribution through an intromittent organ. What's the fancy terminology for hers? you might reasonably ask. Unfortunately, my sources don't say. Maybe none has been coined. If not, somebody should sponsor a contest: Invent a name for the female penis, win a free trip to Delaware! And does the female sea horse take foolish pride in the size of her thing? This is a question that science hasn't yet answered.

In certain species of barnacles, the intromittent organ is forty times as long as the rest of the animal's body, which evidently makes up for the fact that barnacles are glued to their substrate and can't go galloping after one another in quest of sex. A snail also uses a sinuous, groping tube, not quite so long as the barnacle's but still remarkable in that it's extruded at will, like a randy idea, from an aperture on the snail's head. A male gorilla has its dainty little penis, a billy goat has its big one, males of some opossum species have forked penises, and a male snake has two penises, which the experts call *hemipenes,* one for left-sided mating and one for right. In mammals, of course, the penis serves as a conduit of urine as well as semen, but some mammals are more highly evolved than others and *Homo sapiens* is still the sole species, according to current observational data, among whom a male is capable of writing his name in the snow. Even the male platypus has a penis, but that's just another tip-off that a platypus, notwithstanding its duckish bill and its egg-laying mode of procreation, is no bird.

Birds are another story. In most bird species, not just owls and eagles and crows, the male lacks an intromittent organ. Instead, those birds do their mating cloaca-to-cloaca, a crude but workable arrangement that roughly resembles two vacuum-cleaner hoses spliced together with duct tape. Ironic as it may seem, even a woodpecker has nothing you might call a pecker except its beak. And a cockatoo has no intromittent organ either.

This anatomical omission among avian species is a mystery that helps put in relief another mystery: What drives the evolution of bizarre forms of penis among the many animals that *do* have them? In recent years, a biologist named William G. Eberhard has offered a cheerfully perverse hypothesis. Male genitalia, Eberhard argues, are shaped by the excesses of female whim.

IT'S AN area of evolutionary theory that traces straight back to Charles Darwin. In 1871, Darwin published a hefty tome titled *The Descent of Man and Selection in Relation to Sex,* which was really more like two books bound as one. In the second half, he propounded the concept of sexual selection to explain all those gaudy male decorations (tail feathers on a peacock, nasal protuberances on a chameleon, long spiral horns on a South African kudu) that are useless, or worse, in the struggle for survival. The struggle for survival, Darwin realized, is not the real test of evolutionary failure or success. The real test is this: Notwithstanding whether a creature dies young or dies old, how many offspring does it leave? In some cases, reproductive success is directly related to traits that do also help a particular animal to survive—and those cases exemplify

Darwin's more famous concept, natural selection, in its familiar form. In other cases, the traits that contribute toward reproductive success are irrelevant to survival, or even downright costly—and it's these reckless, impractical traits that embody sexual selection. The four-foot-long tail feathers on a male ribbon-tailed bird of paradise will never help one of those animals live to be old. On the contrary, they may shorten his life. But they will help him proliferate his genes in the limited time he has. How? By making him madly attractive to the females of his species.

Darwin described two alternate modes of sexual selection: 1) combat between members of the same sex for the prize of mating with relatively passive partners, and 2) direct choice of mates by individuals of the sought-after sex who are anything but passive on such a crucial matter. What that dichotomy boils down to, generally, is 1) male combat or 2) female choice. Females seldom fight over stud services, within any province of the animal kingdom, and males are seldom choosy. Why? Because horny males are excessively abundant, whereas receptive females exist in preciously short supply. And why is the receptive-female supply short? Because females are obliged (except maybe among sea horses) to make a larger investment of resources in each of their offspring than males do. Eggs are expensive, pregnancy is expensive, pregnancy takes time and time is expensive; sperm is cheap. (More about this in "The Dope on Eggs," page 103.) Females, therefore, stand to suffer greater loss from the ill-advised choice of a genetically inferior mate. So sexual selection is most often directed at males. Call it Aphrodite's Revenge. Never mind that the tail of a peacock, or the horns of a kudu, or the outlandish protrusion on the snout of a chameleon might make day-to-day survival just a bit harder. If those features are somehow useful in competitive mating, then the damn troublesome things will be favored by evolution.

This is the background to William Eberhard's work. He presented his hypothesis some years ago in a book titled *Sexual Selection and Animal Genitalia,* an entertaining but serious volume published by Harvard University Press, and he has continued to develop it since. The purpose of that hypothesis is to account for a bewildering pattern apparent throughout the natural world: extravagant male genitalia among species who fertilize internally.

In a great number of animal groups, according to Eberhard, male genitalia have evolved more rapidly and divergently than any other aspect of anatomy. By divergently he means that they have transmogrified into a wide range of different shapes, and by rapidly he means that such differences have arisen even between closely related, recently separated species. One testimony to the trend is that taxonomists use male genitalia as key characters—that is, traits for distinguishing between species so closely related that with pants on they would seem virtually identical. When there's no other visible difference between two similar species of beetle, a taxonomist looks at their aedeagi; when there's no other anatomical grounds for sorting a jumble of spiders into separate species, a wise eye peers at their pedipalps. The groups that lend themselves to such male-organ taxonomy include primates, rodents, bats, armadillos, sharks, rays, snakes, lizards, mollusks, crustaceans, flatworms, and opilionids (whatever the devil they are), as well as insects and spiders.

Why all this rapid and divergent evolution of male genitalia? Eberhard's answer: It's because females are choosy.

Other explanations have been offered. The lock-and-key hypothesis is the oldest, dating back to a treatise on beetle classification from 1844. The idea here is that the male and female genitalia of a particular species are matched to each other like a key to a lock. Failing an appropriate matchup, the lock's tumblers won't tumble; mating and fertilization won't happen. By this view, the intricately complementary genitalia represent a form of defense against hybridism between species, which wastes the precious female resources by producing (at best) sterile offspring. It sounds good, and a glance at some lock-and-key pairings seems to suggest that it should work. But the lock-and-key hypothesis fell into disrepute, Eberhard writes, "when it was established that locks are too easily picked." The more intricate female genitalia don't seem to exclude wrong-species males after all, and in many other cases the female genitalia are not nearly so intricate as the male. It's more like putting a key into a coat pocket than into a lock.

Another hypothesis invokes pleiotropy, the phenomenon of multiple effects from a single genetic change. Although pleiotropy is a familiar concept within evolutionary theory, whether it explains the pattern of divergence among male genitalia is questionable. But exactly that suggestion was made, thirty years ago, by the evolutionary biologist and science historian Ernst Mayr. Mayr's notion was that bizarre genital modifications might have no adaptive significance in themselves, either for survival or for reproduction; they might simply be pleiotropic effects, reflecting genetic changes that affect other anatomical zones, where those changes do have adaptive significance. In other words: Maybe an armadillo has a filigreed penis for no purpose at all, but merely as the side effect of a gene that helps dictate, say, the shape of its feet.

Eberhard dislikes the pleiotropy hypothesis for several reasons. First, it fails to explain why the side effects of adaptive changes should so often involve the male genitalia, rather than some other aspect of anatomy. Second, it fails to explain why similar effects are generally absent in animals practicing external fertilization, like all those aquatic species that spawn out their eggs and sperm into a randomly mixing cloud. Pleiotropy also offers no logical link between primary genital modifications (as in mammals and insects), and secondary conversion of nongenital appendages to genital uses (as in spiders and millipedes and guppies). If pleiotropy is the sole mechanism, functioning by sheer chance, why does it chase the genital function from one part of the body to another?

Eberhard sets up a few other hypotheses and knocks them right down: the genitalic-recognition hypothesis, the mechanical-conflict-of-interest hypothesis, Arnold's variant of Mayr's pleiotropy hypothesis— don't worry, I'm not going to explain them. I thought I'd skip the logical edifice and get straight to the dirty part. If pleiotropy and locksmith taxonomy and the rest of that mumbo seem aridly theoretical, you can take heart. You have now reached the portion of this essay that can't help but be lewd and unseemly.

Parental discretion is advised.

From here on, in fact, I'd better not even use the word *penis*. It might get a little too vivid. I'd better not chatter about *genitalia*. Even *pedipalp* and *aedeagus* and *gonopodia* could prove to be overly blunt. So here's what let's do: Let's me substitute a more respectable word, and each time I use it, let's you bear in mind that what we're engaged upon jointly is a dignified, cerebral consideration of the evolutionary significance of the morphological eccentricities of the male organ. OK?

In place of those words, I'll use *spatula*. It sounds kind of scientific, but it's clean.

* * *

HAVING dismissed all the other hypotheses, Eberhard offers what he considers a better one: female choice. The essence of his argument is that "females discriminate among males of their own species on the basis of the [spatula], and that males with favored [spatula] morphologies sire more offspring than others."

The trickiest part of this phenomenon is its starting point. At first, the females might show only a mild preference for one sort of spatula versus another. Why would they show any preference at all? Well, maybe one sort is just slightly more effective at stimulating certain hormone releases—essential to the female's reproductive physiology—than another sort. Once initiated, the mild preference can become self-reinforcing. It can turn into what Eberhard calls "runaway sexual selection by female choice," in the course of which "males develop increasingly elaborate [spatulas] and females become increasingly discriminating." Such runaway selection is a theoretical postulate, not an experimentally documented process, but it does seem like a plausible explanation for the panoply of ridiculous spatulas.

This hypothesis is more complicated than it sounds. Behind it lies the biological fact that insemination isn't synonymous with fertilization. Most female animals mate with more than one male, and many actually exercise some physiological control over which dose of sperm reaches their eggs. Does the female accept a given male's sperm into her sperm-storage organ, or does she dump it? Does she allow it to move from her sperm-storage organ to the site where her eggs are to be fertilized? Does she give precedence to the sperm of one male over the sperm of another? Eberhard's research suggests that each of these forms of discretion is exercised by at least some female animals, and possibly by many. So even *after* she starts to mate with a given male, the female may still be deciding about whether to let him father her young. "In short, I am suggesting that [spatulas] function as 'internal courtship' devices and that their use is properly considered as an extension of the male's courtship of the female." It's the continuation of wooing by other means.

The notion of runaway selection by females is another venerable bit of evolutionary theory, dating back to a classic work by R. A. Fisher, *The Genetical Theory of Natural Selection,* published in 1930. It explains certain collective genetic changes—lurches of evolution within a group—that would otherwise seem inexplicable. What causes this process to surge beyond normal bounds is a positive feedback relationship between arbitrary sensory signals, on the one hand, and on the other hand a presumption of evolutionary value. It starts when the females of a species begin relying on some form of sensory signal (a slightly enlarged set of tail feathers, say, or a modest nasal knob) to tell which males might carry superior genes for either survival or reproduction. Before long, the signal itself takes on inherent value, not for survival but solely for reproduction. Females begin to appreciate it more highly, and even to demand it; males compete with one another to produce it more strongly; the presumption of value escalates and, zingo, there's runaway selection. Suddenly the knob or the tail feathers become codified as a standard of sexiness.

Sexiness is far from irrelevant to ultimate evolutionary success. Female animals experience a powerful compulsion to get their eggs fertilized by the sexiest males available, because females (like males) want to maximize their own total number of offspring, and one way of doing that is by producing sexy sons. Sexy sons are a route to evolutionary success? Yes, because sexy sons win more mating opportunities than nerdy sons or loutish sons, and therefore they ultimately yield more grandchildren. (Among most species they do, anyway; contraception blurs that correlation among humans.) Grandchildren are how evolution keeps score. Fisher's sixty-year-old idea, now known as the sexy-son hypothesis, forms the crucial underpinning to William Eberhard's explanation of the mystery of exaggerated spatulas.

Runaway selection doesn't operate in all cases where females exercise controlling discretion, but it seems to be fairly common. Once it gets started, the results are conspicuous. Females choose—and thereby exaggerate—and choose still more avidly—and exaggerate further—whatever is currently fashionable among male sexual signals. Some signals are visual, like the tail of a peacock. Some are tactile, like a fine fancy spatula. Eberhard's point is that female choosiness continues into the mating act itself—will she let this male's sperm reach her eggs, or will she not?—and that the pressure of such sedulous scrutiny directed at male equipment has resulted in a worldwide trend of rapid and divergent evolution. It's the only hypothesis, Eberhard claims, that accounts for the whole range of evidence, including the very strange illustrations in his book, most of which couldn't be printed in a family newspaper. Maybe he's right.

What it fails to account for is why owls have no spatulas whatsoever.

Eberhard doesn't address that one. Neither does Ernst Mayr, nor R. A. Fisher, nor even Charles Darwin himself—at least not explicitly, as far as I've managed to ascertain. Probably I've missed something. No doubt the experts have a hypothesis.

If so, they can keep it. The male owl seems more compelling to me as he is: a creature that stands boldly apart from prevailing convention and reminds us that spatulas, though amusing, are ultimately unnecessary.

THE GREAT
STINKING CLUE

In Search of a Fruit Called Durian

Fruit is the means that trees have invented for traveling from one place to another. But not every fruit travels as well, or as far, as others. Some kinds are adventurous. Some are more laggard. Some hit the ground unswallowed and don't even roll. So to get to the core of the matter, you'll need to do a little traveling yourself. My advice is: Start with a flight to the island of Bali. Then follow your nose upwind toward a species of tree called *Durio zibethinus*.

The fruit of that tree is a yellow-green ovoid, big as a rugby ball, heavy as fate, upholstered all over with thorns. It goes by the name durian, from the Malaysian word *duri,* for thorn. It's a hard capsule that hangs from a stout stem and God help you if you're beneath when it falls. It looks about as succulent as a stuffed porcupine, but it splits open along suture lines to reveal its amazing innards. Each inner chamber contains several large gobbets of ivory-white pulp. That's the edible stuff. Inside each gobbet, a seed. The seed itself is as big as a chestnut. Durian is renowned throughout Asia for its luxuriant flavor, its peculiar anatomy, and its indecent stench.

Besides being a delicious fruit, and one of the world's largest, scientifically it's among the most interesting. You could think of it—as one botanist has done—as the great stinking clue to the evolution of tropical forests.

But by now, let's say, you've arrived in Bali, touching down at Denpasar Airport along the southern coast. Bali, your gateway to Indonesia, is an anciently civilized island just south of the vast equatorial forests of Borneo. Some scientists believe that those forests, or others nearby, are where the phenomenon of fruition first arose. The markets of Bali are bounteous with tropical fruits—salaks and mangoes and mangosteens, langsats and rambutans, mandarin oranges, papayas, litchis on the branch, tiny bananas as sweet as candy—but in your quest for fresh durian you'll do best to ignore that temptation and keep traveling. From Denpasar, catch a small plane eastward to Ambon, capital of Maluku Province, more familiarly known as the Moluccas. Here, if you've come at the right season, you'll notice fruit vendors seated patiently along roadsides, their precious few durians stacked beside them like cannonballs. For a dollar's worth of rupiahs, big money on an Ambonese roadside, you can buy one. Your fruit vendor will open it with a machete. Maybe you're curious now, notwithstanding the smell, but then again maybe you aren't—which is fine, since Ambon isn't the ideal place for your first taste of durian anyway. You board another small plane, this one headed north, on a low-altitude flight across the coralline shallows and then the deep Seram Sea and up the west coast of Halmahera, to a tiny volcanic cone of an island called Ternate.

You check into a little hotel (beware of rats and certain other hazards, as described in "Tropical Passengers," above) near the town market and, dropping your bags, notice a sign on the inside of your door: IT IS FORBIDDEN TO EAT DURIAN IN THE ROOM. An edict mostly honored in the breach. One stroll down the corridor has told your olfactory radar that, this time of year, everyone's doing it.

You charter a taxi—and not for a ride to the market. You would find durian at the market, sure, but that would be too easy. You tell your driver instead to head inland, up the volcano's slope, toward a village called Marikurubu at the end of the pavement, where the coconut and papaya trees of suburban Ternate give way to the true mountain forest. Here you start walking. You'll want a canteen. Your shirt will be sweat-drenched in minutes. Enjoy the giant butterflies and try not to anger the giant spiders. Follow the trail until the trail disappears. Then hike on through the understory, groping upward along the volcano's slope, and stay ever alert for falling ovoids. Pretty soon you'll be lost. At about that point, if you're as lucky as I was, you'll meet a gang of disreputable kids.

They will be as friendly and roguish as any pack of boys, and not quite utterly mercenary. Their names will be Junai, Sunardi, Saiful, Wan, or similar variants. This forest is their playground and their turf. They will offer, in clamorous Indonesian which you can only imperfectly decode, all manner of invaluable services. They will happily guide you, for instance, to wherever the hell it is you think that you're going. They could take you to the world's oldest clove tree? They could take you to the summit? Forget about destination and just walk with them. In passing they'll want to know whether you, an American, might be personally acquainted with their heroes: Chuck Norris, Rambo, Batman, and Mike Tyson. Offhandedly, they'll invite you to share a snack.

It's a durian, tree-ripened and freshly dropped.

When a fruit falls in the forest, these are the kids who hear it. Few of the world's most sybaritic gourmets will ever eat tree-ripened durian. But here you are.

You accept a handful of pulp. It's creamy and slightly fibrous, like a raw oyster that's been force-fed vanilla ice cream. There's also a hint of almond. It tastes strange, rich, wonderful. It smells like a jockstrap. It doesn't remotely resemble any substance that you've ever touched, let alone eaten.

Inside your gobbet is the chestnut-size seed. Sucking that clean, you toss it away through the forest. Your offhand act represents a crucial step in a long chain of many: The *Durio zibethinus* tree, with your help, has sent its genes on a journey. You are a seed-disperser. The fruit has fulfilled its destiny.

BOTANISTS use the word *fruit* in two senses. In the more technical sense, it applies to any seed-bearing structure formed from an ovary of a flowering plant and shaped so as to facilitate the seed's dispersal. Whether the seed-bearing structure travels by wind-power, or by floating on water, or by catching a ride aboard an animal, is immaterial. According to this strict definition, the downy white parachute of a dandelion seed constitutes fruit. The whirlybird wing that carries a maple seed is a fruit. A leathery acacia pod is a fruit, and so is an acorn, and so is a burr. Botanic professionals, with their uncommon love for jargon, have coined abstruse bits of terminology to distinguish the various modes of travel and give the illusion that plant evolution has been programmatic and orderly: *anemochory* for dispersal by wind, *hydrochory* for dispersal by water, *zoochory* for dispersal by animal. *Endozoochory* means dispersal via the interior of an animal—as distinct from *epizoochory,* riding along outside, the cheap trick of a burr. Endozoochory, then, is the method practiced by what you and I and a greengrocer would commonly call fruit.

This is the word's more familiar sense: a flavorful and nutritious packet of vegetable pulp that seems made to be eaten. In fact, it *is* made to be eaten. It's a bribe of concentrated carbohydrates and water and in some cases fats, offered to animals in exchange for seed transport. The seeds are hidden within the pulp and protected one way or another (either inside a hard sheath or a stony pit, or by their small size and numerousness) from being destroyed in the course of the animal's chewing and digestion. The indigestible seeds are offloaded from one end or the other—by regurgitation (as common among frugivorous tropical birds) or by defecation, the latter of which enhances a seed's growth prospects with a godparent's gift of manure. Evolution has taught flowering plants that this is an effective way to launch and position their offspring. True, the production of fruit entails some high metabolic costs, but the costs are justified by the rewards. Seed dispersal is that crucial. A plant species doesn't flourish if it doesn't travel.

So when a thirsty South African aardvark eats a water-rich melon and then buries its own dung in a hole, the benefits to plant and animal have been mutual. When a Galápagos tortoise eats a wild Galápagos tomato and then craps out the seeds a week later on a piece of terrain hitherto uncolonized by tomatoes, it's a classic instance of endosaurochory (dispersal via the gut of a reptile) and everyone is happy. Not least happy are the botanical jargoneers, who invent that sort of terminology, I suspect, while they're out on a field site waiting for plants to grow.

Why is dispersal so crucial? Because it allows a plant to enlarge the number and range of its own offspring. Why is *that* crucial? Because it's the standard on which evolution mediates survival, extinction, and change. A tree that has no means of dispersal, dropping all of its seeds in its own shade, will be especially vulnerable to seed predators adapted for taking advantage of its helplessness. A plague of seed predators, descending on such an improvident tree, can destroy every single seed.

And if the predators carelessly let a few seedlings spring up, those young plants will tend to be stunted by competition with the overshadowing parent. The seedlings will also compete with one another, so most of the seed crop will be wasted. And if the local climate goes bad, turning permanently intolerable, the tree and its few clustered seedlings will die without leaving offspring. Dispersal of seeds to distant new patches of habitat obviates all of those problems.

It's an ingenious biological strategy, this matter of travel by fruit. But how did it originate? To that difficult question, an eminent British botanist named E. J. H. Corner offered what he called The Durian Theory of plant evolution.

In 1949, Corner published a journal paper titled "The Durian Theory or the Origin of the Modern Tree." He refined it in later publications, including a bold essay that appeared in 1954, "The Evolution of Tropical Forest." His notion was that endozoochory (again, the enticement of animals to transport seeds in their bellies) arose before all other methods of dispersal, and that primitive ancestors of *Durio zibethinus* were the earliest practitioners of that strategy. His supporting argument was complicated, involving big seeds versus small seeds, many seeds versus few seeds, dehiscence (splitting neatly open, as a pea pod does) versus indehiscence (the flesh of a mango may rot away, but it isn't designed to split), and a type of fruit known as *arillate* versus all others. I'll skip over the complications and move straight to the aril.

Arillate fruits are rare. In the tropics, arillate-fruiting trees account for about one species in a hundred. Most fleshy fruits are considered drupes (such as a peach, with its single hard pit) or pomes (such as a pear, with its accessory flesh surrounding a seedy core) or berries (which category, God knows why, includes tomatoes, potatoes, and asparagus). In an arillate fruit, the aril itself is a fleshy outgrowth of the seed's own integument, which wraps down around the seed like melted caramel on a Halloween apple. In many cases, the aril is both nutritious and brightly colored. Red is common. When such an arillate fruit falls to the ground and splits open, the wink of the aril beckons animals to a rewarding meal. Nutmeg is an arillate fruit on exactly this pattern: The aril is a gaudy little scarlet octopus embracing a dull brown seed. Nutmeg arils are avidly eaten by pigeons, if the tree is growing wild in a forest; if the tree isn't so wild, the arils are avidly harvested by spice farmers (see "The Narcotic of Empire," page 25), who sell them for processing as mace. The durian, according to E. J. H. Corner, is also an arillate fruit. That creamy white pulp is nothing other than aril run spectacularly amok. In lieu of a flashy color, it advertises itself with a garish smell.

It's clear from his writings that Corner loved durian trees with a passion that paralleled his botanical judgment. The durian, in his view, provided an important clue to the evolution of tropical plants. Furthermore, one of the lessons of what he wryly called durianology was that plants of the temperate zones too should be understood in the light of this tropical model. Evolutionary botany in the tropics has remained especially obscure because the primeval species have left almost no fossil record, but in *D. zibethinus* and its closest relatives Corner found what he took to be living fossils. The durian illuminates tree evolution, he believed, in something the same way that the coelacanth illuminates the evolution of land-walking vertebrates.

At the heart of Corner's argument is that delectably gooey durian aril. Because the arillate condition is so rare, yet so broadly scattered among many different tree families, and so similar anatomically wherever it occurs, it's most likely a vestige of the primitive form shared by all early fruits, rather than a recently evolved derivation. The bright red coloration seems to be primitive too. Although the pulp of *D. zibethinus* is white, Corner noted, at least one other species of *Durio* produces a red fruit with red pulp. Based on these facts and others, he wrote: "The first, and overwhelming, postulate of the durian theory, therefore, is that a red durian-fruit exemplifies the primitive fruit of flowering plants." He envisioned *Iguanodon* and other herbivorous dinosaurs gobbling those red globs of pulp and performing the service of dispersal—which is good news for any of us who have been waiting for a chance to use *endosaurochory* in a casual sentence.

Big seeds dispersed by big animals gave the proto-durians an evolutionary advantage that revolutionized plant ecology, according to Corner. A big seed provides the young seedling with a nutritional head start, and therefore a competitive edge, as it begins life as a pioneer in some new patch of habitat. But big seeds embedded in generous bribes of aril require big fruit capsules to contain them, and big fruit capsules impose their own structural requirements on the trees in which they hang. Thus the second postulate of Corner's theory: Although the earliest flowering plants were probably shaped like a tree fern—with a thick columnar trunk that rose to a single point, not much firm wood, and virtually no limb structure—the necessity of supporting a sizable crop of heavy fruit capsules drove plant evolution toward the development of stronger trunks and stout, woody branches. Trees became bigger and sturdier. They spread their limbs. The tropical canopy blossomed. Insects and birds and arboreal reptiles and mammals evolved to inhabit it, feeding on nectar and leaves and more advanced sorts of fruits and one another.

Meanwhile the proto-durian paradigm, at the level of fruit anatomy, also gave way to great diversity. As Corner hypothesized: "From such arillate fruits all other kinds have been derived by loss of the aril, by drying up into the rattling pod or capsule with its dry seeds, by indehiscence leading to the general succulence of berries, by increasing lignification leading to stone fruits and nuts, and by decreasing size leading to small editions of all these kinds."

This evolutionary upheaval began, if we can trust Corner's guess, in the vicinity of what is now mainland Malaysia. From there, the new plant and animal forms and relationships spread to other regions, including Borneo, southwestern Asia, and tropical Africa. During subsequent episodes of climate change, the forests in some of those regions receded for lack of moisture, zones of savanna opened, and big herds of grazing mammals began to appear. Recapitulating that much, Corner added: "The durian theory can contemplate the hairless arboreal mammal that lurched from the forest in its increasing austerity, to slaughter the wild herds, to harvest the wild grain, and to hack down the testimony of his origin." He meant us.

So there's not much that his durian theory *can't* contemplate. The evidence may be tenuous, the logic may be disputed by some other botanists, but no one can complain that E. J. H. Corner's thinking lacked scope.

IF YOU'RE A lucky traveler, as I was, you'll arrive at the height of what Corner called durian-time. "Usually the fruits detach when ripe and crash to the ground, where the pulp turns rancid in a day or two. In Malaya the smell of fruiting trees in the forest attracts elephants, which congregate for first choice; then come tiger, pigs, deer, tapir, rhinoceros, and jungle men. Gibbons, monkeys, bears, and squirrels may eat the fruit in the trees; the orang-outan may dominate the repast in Sumatra and Borneo; ants and beetles scour the remains on the ground." The scene on Ternate, a small island set far apart from those raucous forests, is more sedate: no rhinos, no bears, no tapirs, no tigers, no elephants or orangutans competing for durian. Besides ants and beetles, and maybe a few species of birds, here it's entrepreneurial fruit-gatherers and small boys and American visitors who police up what hits the ground.

If luck serves you as it served me, you'll be slave to no hasty schedule. You'll linger in Ternate while the daily flights come and go. You'll hike through the forest in late afternoon and visit the market at dawn. From the market, you'll carry away fruit. You'll live contentedly on a diet of fruit, coffee, fresh fish, fruit, rice, Bintang beer, and fruit. You'll learn the best way to peel langsats out of their chamois-soft skins and you'll grow fond of their mild grapefruity flavor. You'll binge on rambutans. Papaya and good little bananas will be your staples for breakfast. You'll make a thorough study of mangosteens (which are far more spectacular than, and not to be confused with, mangoes), slurping immoderate quantities of those little cream-and-lemonade-flavored sections out of their leathery red husks, and you'll reach the conclusion that Queen Victoria was right: This is indeed the world's most delicious fruit. But unlike Victoria, who reportedly offered a prize to whoever could deliver a fresh mangosteen to her in England, you'll buy yours locally, cheap as turnips. That's another piece of good luck, since mangosteens don't travel. And of course you'll flout the hotel rule shamelessly, eating durians in your room.

You'll learn what you can about this primitive dehiscent arillate odoriferous packet of sublimely tasty glop. If the writings of E. J. H. Corner aren't available, and sadly they won't be, you might read an account by the naturalist Alfred Russel Wallace, who spent some months right here on Ternate back in 1858: "A rich butter-like custard highly flavoured with almonds gives the best general idea of it, but intermingled with it come wafts of flavour that call to mind cream-cheese, onion-sauce, brown sherry, and other incongruities. Then there is a rich glutinous smoothness in the pulp which nothing else possesses, but which adds to its delicacy." Wallace advised that the ideal durian is a tree-ripened one, freshly fallen, because "the smell is then less overpowering." The pulp isn't juicy, or acidic, or even exactly sweet, he wrote, but entirely unique. "It produces no nausea or other bad effect, and the more you eat of it the less you feel inclined to stop. In fact to eat Durians is a new sensation, worth a voyage to the East to experience." He was right.

But after some period of days, or maybe weeks, you'll have eaten your fill: *enough* of the buttery custard with onion-sauce intimations, *enough* of the ice-creamy oysters with jockstrap bouquet. You'll feel indifferent to the prospect of haggling amiably with still another fruit vendor. You'll have no great desire to watch still another machete splitting open still another big thorny capsule. You'll be happy to pass, thanks, on still another blast of that perversely promising smell. I'm not saying you'll be disgusted with durian. You'll merely be sated.

This brings us to my own durian theory, far more modest in scope than E. J. H. Corner's. When you're tired of durian, says my theory, you're tired of the tropics. That's your clue that it's time to go home to a land of raisins and prunes.

The Dope on Eggs

Anisogamy, Science Journalism, and
Other Food for Thought

Monday afternoon of a fresh new week and here's a grown man, damn near forty years old, college graduate, stalking the upper floors of a university library with a notebook in one hand, a sheaf of photocopied pages in the other, and the pinched worried ruthless countenance of a starving coyote. The clock is running. He is a magazine columnist working on deadline, poor fool. His monthly mandate is to demonstrate that evolutionary biology, theoretical ecology, and the incisive contemplation of nature can provide piquant entertainment for people in dental waiting rooms. As usual, he's three weeks behind. The subject this month is eggs. Eggs, yes, as in chickens and zygotes and nature's ultimate self-contained package for a developing embryo. His notebook is full of scribbled citations and call numbers; his brain is full of eggs. He scowls at the nattering undergraduates in designer denim and moves briskly among the stacks. He knows a few facts about eggs. He knows that the ostrich lays an egg weighing more than three pounds, with a shell strong enough to support the weight of two men. He knows that a starfish can produce forty million eggs in a year. He knows that a marsupial frog carries her eggs until hatching in a pouch on her back. What he doesn't know is how these amusing and utterly disconnected facts can be garbage-compacted into a single essay. Sometimes, and this is exactly such a time, he feels that he has the most ridiculous job in America.

The sheaf of pages is a monograph from the *Journal of Theoretical Biology* entitled "Why Are There So Many Tiny Sperm?" It's exactly the sort of scientific question that commands his attention. The week is young and he is still hoping to follow a logical trail on a gentle meander through meadows of biological fact to a neat little conclusion. At this point he is scouting for spoor. Where there are sperm there must also be eggs, correct? After an hour of dashing around the library, though, he can't remember just how this article got into his hand. Nor why. Something he does know is that the wandering albatross lays only a single egg every two years. He knows about egg-care behavior in the maternal octopus. He knows a thing or two about yolk.

And he has begun gathering a mental list of other eggy questions. Mere facts are no good to him unless they answer (or can be made to seem to answer, or can be twisted and wrenched and piled into odd shapes until they hint at being somehow perhaps on the verge of answering) a question that someone might conceivably want asked. What are the major unanswered egg questions? he has been wondering.

Of course there's the obvious one: Which came first, the chicken or . . . ? But that's not really unanswered, since anyone except a creationist knows that the first egg preceded the first chicken, in the evolution of life, by dozens of millions of years. A better question is, Why does a duck-billed platypus lay eggs, whereas a hammerhead shark or a rattlesnake gives birth to live young? And another, closely related: If some species of reptile lay eggs and some species don't, if some fish do and some don't, if some mammals do and some don't, why is it that every *bird* species on the planet lays eggs? Now we're cooking, he thinks. There are more. Why do some eggs hatch before being laid? How does a vulture, on a low-calcium diet, come up with enough calcium for its eggshells? Does an egg need to breathe? Does an egg need to drink? How does an egg know when to hatch? Then suddenly he is visited by a question possessing such promising scientific depth and such a stupid surface that he wishes immediately he hadn't thought of it: *If we eat chicken eggs for breakfast, why don't we eat chicken sperm?*

He doesn't know the answer. Maybe it's a matter of theoretical biology, maybe just good taste. Maybe the difference is packaging. With any sort of luck, this week, he will be able to leave that one unasked.

◉   ◉   ◉

DOWN A corridor between the stacks he happens upon his chum the dinosaur paleontologist, seated cross-legged on the carpet like an angry janitor drinking wine, after hours, from a paper bag. On the paleontologist's lap is a heavy green volume. This paleontologist holds an international reputation for his discoveries and analyses of nests full of dinosaur eggs, and today he is browsing for ideas among the books on bird biology. "What are *you* up to?" the paleontologist asks our man.

"Eggs."

"What about 'em?"

"Anything. I'm open to suggestions."

The paleontologist rolls his eyes pityingly. Then he points to a sentence on the open page of his fat green book. It says that the newly hatched young of the echidna (an egg-laying Australian mammal, related to the platypus) possesses an egg tooth. An egg tooth is a temporary structure that shows up on the beaks of some hatchling reptiles and some hatchling birds, used by the weak little animal to bust its way out of the shell. The occurrence of an egg tooth in this weird mammal represents an interesting primitive trait, says the paleontologist.

"Gimme," says our fellow, and snatches the green volume to scamper off for a photocopy.

He knows that a tapeworm can release two billion eggs in its lifetime. He knows that a parasitic insect called the sheep ked, on the other hand, can expect a lifetime fecundity of only twelve eggs. He knows that the yolk of a hen's egg is rich with two kinds of protein (ovovitellin, ovolivetin) that will serve as construction material for an embryo chick, and with fats that will gather like creosote in the arteries of a human. He knows that an alligator incubates her eggs in a cozy pile of rotting compost. And now he knows that baby echidnas have egg teeth. He is frantic.

He feeds the word *eggs* into the computerized periodical index and the computer chortles at him condescendingly, as though to say, Can't help you if you're so vague, you dumb-ass. He photocopies a few scattered pages from back issues of a few scattered journals—*Science, Science News, Natural History, Business Week*—and grabs an armload of books. By this time he knows why NASA planned to send thirty-two eggs into space (evidently on board the *Challenger,* alas) and what the distinguished food writer M. F. K. Fisher thinks of scrambled ostrich. He knows about the optimal-egg-size theory, never mind what that is, and that a recent study of freshwater turtles tends to refute it. He knows that the male of the emperor penguin stands around for nine weeks on the Antarctic ice holding an egg on the tops of its feet.

He has also found a good concise definition, praise God, for the entity at issue: "Fundamentally, the egg is comprised of a minute center of life, about which are accumulated relatively enormous amounts of inanimate food substances, the whole enclosed in protective structures. Given the proper combination of circumstances, the living fraction of the egg is activated and transforms the nonliving mass into an organism capable of independent existence." This comes from a book called *The Avian Egg*, but he knows that it applies just as well to the eggs of grasshoppers, snails, giant squid, corals, crocodiles, fish lice, dogwhelks, echidnas, water fleas, trout, and some species of algae. He leaves the library, well informed and utterly hopeless.

It isn't too late to veer off toward a different subject. No one will ever know that he wasted a day on eggs.

BY TUESDAY afternoon it is too late. He has devoted another half-day to filling his brain with intriguing kibble. He knows that cliff-nesting birds called guillemots lay eggs that are tapered sharply, like chicken cro-quettes, so that they roll in tight circles and are less likely therefore to go wheeling off a narrow ledge. He knows that maternal earwigs spend great effort keeping their eggs licked clean of fungi. He knows that the eggs of the crested cuckoo have an extraordinarily thick shell, evidently an adaptation to the fact that the cuckoo drops her eggs rather rudely, for foster rearing, into the nests of other species. He knows that corals of the Great Barrier Reef indulge in mass orgies of synchronized spawn-ing. Much of this kibble comes out of a book titled *Eggs: Nature's Per-fect Package,* from a publishing house that calls itself Facts On File. He is grateful to the author, Robert Burton, and would also very much like to strangle him, since the book is full of information but offers virtually no footnotes or bibliography. Nothing can be traced to its scientific source. The FCC or someone should require that this publisher rename itself Facts Adrift. He knows from Mr. Burton's book that certain scien-tists have discovered prehatching communication among eggs of the bobwhite quail (mutually audible tapping, like in *Darkness at Noon*), but he doesn't know which scientists announced such a discovery, or when, or where.

On Wednesday morning his editor calls from Chicago, sounding cheerful. "How's the column coming?" His editor is a young man of saintly equanimity who has consented over the years to publish all manner of creep-show biological comedies and whose sole demands seem to be decent grammar and promptness.

"Fine," our man lies. "Pretty good. I think you'll have it by Friday. Is Friday OK?"

"Uh. All right, sure. Friday's OK."

"In that case, how's Monday?"

He knows of a certain Black Orpington hen that once turned heads by laying 361 eggs in less than a year. He knows that the common mussel can deliver itself of twelve million eggs in fifteen minutes. He knows that these two beasts belong side by side in the *Guinness Book of World Records* but not in any coherent science essay that he can so far imagine himself writing. He knows the difference between *isogamy* (sexual reproduction in which all the sex cells, or gametes, are of similar size) and *anisogamy* (sexual reproduction in which some members of the species produce big passive gametes containing nutritional supplies, while other members of the species produce tiny fast-moving gametes containing only genetic information), and he knows that those two types of anisogamous gametes go by the names egg and sperm. He senses now that in the mystery of anisogamy lies the answer to at least one of the great eggish questions. He is not sure he knows which one.

He has been back to the library three times, he has photocopied from the *Journal of Theoretical Biology* a half-dozen more monographs on the subject of anisogamy, and as a hedge against desperation, he has phoned the manager of a local chicken ranch. Yes, the manager will give him a tour tomorrow.

Now it's late Wednesday night, and our egg guy has begun decoding the anisogamy monographs. Some of them say things like:

$$\frac{\hat{x}_1}{\hat{x}_2} = \frac{1-(1+\theta)^{-k}\{\theta 2^k+[2p/(1-p)](\theta-\theta^k)\}}{1-(1+\theta)^{-k}\{\theta^{k-1}2^k+[2p/(1-p)](\theta^{k-1}-1)\}}.$$

See what I go through for you people, he murmurs silently. Another begins with a sentence so wonderfully scientific that it almost brings tears to his eyes: "Sex has always been an embarrassment to population biologists." These articles originally appeared over a span of ten years, but they seem to be interconnected; the authors are talking to each other, homing in toward the truth about anisogamy. The first article in the series, and the one that seems to have sparked all the rest, was published in 1972 by Parker and Baker and Smith, which sounds more like a double-play combination than a group of scientists. Its title is "The Origin and Evolution of Gamete Dimorphism and the Male-Female Phenomenon," no less. Clearly it's a seminal piece of work.

The gist of this whole packet of monographs seems to be: 1) that the world knows two (and only two) different genders within the realm of sexually reproductive species, which two genders produce two (not one and not three, not four, not twenty) different relative sizes of gamete, a large slow size containing a nutritional legacy for the future youngster and a tiny quick one containing genetic instructions only; and 2) that the world knows these unremittingly binary circumstances for a small number of reasons comprehensible in the terms of theoretical biology, among which reasons are the factor of competition among galloping herds of sperm, the improbability of two overstuffed eggs being able to locate each other for sapphistic union in an ocean of loneliness, and the fateful fact that $f_{31}\hat{x}_1 + f_{32}\hat{x}_2$ is less than or equal to $\hat{W}$. Our man on the egg beat now recognizes the whole thing for a fascinating scientific question that might lend itself rather well to vulgarization and mockery, but unfortunately by this time his column is nearly written and there's no space left for doing justice to anisogamy and it's time he departed for his tour of the chicken ranch.

Cherry Lane Farms consists of six huge metal sheds and a processing building on the outskirts of Three Forks, Montana. It is the workplace of 150,000 assiduous leghorn hens and the amiable man charged with their supervision, Don Zeiger. Mr. Zeiger has been in the business nine years. Mr. Zeiger likes eggs. "Well, yeah, let's see. I had four for breakfast this morning in Helena. Had four yesterday morning. And I'll probably have six for supper." Each week Mr. Zeiger ships about 900,000 eggs and eats about three dozen.

No, says Mr. Zeiger, there isn't a rooster on the place. He doesn't breed his own stock. He buys young hens from breeder farms in Iowa and Minnesota, keeps them for an egg-laying career of roughly two years, then ships them back to a slaughterhouse that is also in Minnesota. Throughout their time in Montana, the hens lay hard, live a claustrophobic but otherwise decent existence, and get one ten-week vacation. During the vacation they molt. Unlike some chickens raised purely for meat, they are allowed to keep their beaks and their feet and their combs. The combs on these hens are long and red and floppy. Cutting the combs, says Mr. Zeiger, is bad for morale.

A young hen with good morale lays about six eggs per week. As she gets older, her eggs tend to be fewer and bigger.

Inside one of the henhouses, the egg journalist looks upon rows of cages stretching away to the vanishing point. He breathes an atmosphere thick and sour with he prefers not to imagine what. He peers down one narrow corridor between those rows of cages, and hundreds of white heads with floppy red combs lean out to peer back at him. A single egg drops to the floor of one cage, rolls forward gently through a low slit, and comes to rest in a trough. All right, who *was* that?

"Mr. Zeiger, I want to ask you a question. I'm coming at all this from a scientific angle, remember. I hope you won't take me wrong."

"OK," says Don Zeiger.

"Have you ever wondered why we eat chicken eggs, but not chicken sperm?"

Of course it's because of anisogamy. It's because one contains food, the other contains only information. The question is not really trivial, or disgusting, or ridiculous.

"No," says Don Zeiger. His fleshy ranch-manager face softens with the faintest twitch of a smile. "No sir, I never have."

The man with the notebook nods. He changes the subject. What he would like to be able to say is "Neither have I."

✿ III ✿

FLESH OR FOWL
OR WHAT?

THE CATS THAT FLY
BY THEMSELVES

Felis catus at Terminal Velocity

Back when the tame animals were wild, according to Rudyard Kipling, the wildest of them all was the cat. The dog was a wild creature then, the cow was still wild, the horse was wild, the pig and the sheep were wild—but the cat belonged in a whole different category. He walked by himself, according to Kipling, and all places to him were alike. One day he walked up to the cave where humans were living and hornswoggled them into accepting him as a boarder. He made himself popular, marginally, by amusing the baby and killing mice. But he remained uncontrollable, even unknowable, in a way that those other animals, as they succumbed to domestication, didn't. At night, when the moon was up, he strayed back out to the wet wild woods and wandered there, unfettered by leash or loyalty. Nobody could say where he went, on his ramblings, and nobody could say why.

This allegorical portrait comes from a children's story titled "The Cat That Walked by Himself," which Kipling published in 1902. It may seem like a simpleminded tale, but the best efforts of modern science—in the forms of archaeology, evolutionary biology, ethology, and population genetics—haven't gone far to improve on it. Nowadays, true enough, we know quite a bit about cats. They've been dissected in uncountable numbers. Their anatomy, their physiology, and their behavior have been minutely studied. Symposia have been held, thick books and abstruse journal papers have been written. A grad student at Harvard has submitted a dissertation discussing "the catnip response." We now have scientific support for the pre-scientific intuition that cats are different from other domesticated animals. But there's much that we still don't know. Among all the other intractable issues, one in particular interests me: What's the terminal velocity of a plummeting cat?

Although the question sounds stupid and barbaric, it might actually be a matter of some gravity.

EVERYTHING that falls must previously have risen, and cats came to their zenith in the reign of Sheshonq I, a pharaoh who ruled Egypt during the Twenty-second Dynasty.

That was roughly a millennium before Christ—early in the history of culture, early in the history of spoiled pets, though thousands of years after the domestication of animals had begun. Cats were latecomers to the entourage of humanity. Evidence from a bog site in Germany shows that dogs, for instance, have been domesticated since about 9,000 B.C. Excavations from the ancient city of Jericho suggest that some residents, as early as 7,000 B.C., were keeping goats. The herding and breeding of sheep can be traced back to 6,000 B.C. in northern Persia, and domesticated pigs were a valued commodity among the Sumerians around 2,800 B.C. The domestication of cattle, from a wild ancestor known as *Bos primigenius,* had begun before 3,000 B.C., so that by 2,500 B.C. there were already several recognizably distinct breeds. Some of the early cattle-breeding occurred in Egypt. About the same time, by contrast, the ancestors of the domestic cat were still at large in the forests and savannas that bordered the Nile.

Those ancestors belonged to a subspecies of felid now known as *Felis sylvestris libyca,* the African wildcat. The animal-fancying Egyptians of the Middle Kingdom were probably the first humans to domesticate cats, but they don't seem to have done it until late.

The first convincing evidence comes from the Twelfth Dynasty, around 1,900 B.C. Seventeen pet cats were entombed, along with small pots for their afterworld milk. Their entombment with provisions implies that cats of the Twelfth Dynasty already enjoyed a special symbolic prestige. Eventually they became associated with certain deities—including Ra (the sun god), Sekhmet (a warrior goddess), and particularly Bastet (a cat-headed goddess of a more benign disposition). Bastet was the presiding local deity of a city called Bubastis, east of the Nile Delta. She was just one figure within a crowded Egyptian pantheon until about 950 B.C., when Sheshonq I took power.

For reasons unknown, this man Sheshonq was nutzo about the cat-headed goddess. He moved his capital to Bubastis and made Bastet the preeminent deity of the kingdom. A cult of cat-worshiping followed, with Bastet's temple as its ceremonial center. As many as 700,000 pilgrims attended the annual festival. The temple itself was graced with a huge statue of the goddess and filled with thousands of live cats, who were pampered as sacerdotal mascots. (Kitty litter wasn't invented until some centuries later, but menial labor in pharaonic Egypt was cheap.) Pet cats were also kept, and cherished fanatically, in secular Egyptian households. If a cat died, the family went into mourning, shaving their eyebrows in bereavement. If a cat was killed, even accidentally, the responsible person had hell to pay. The cult of Bastet spread throughout Egypt and lasted for centuries, so that around 50 B.C. a Roman soldier could still get himself lynched for the offense of having killed an Egyptian cat. From this high point, the prestige of *Felis catus* fell like a diving duck.

The goddess Bastet became anathema at the end of the fourth century A.D., when the emperor Theodosius I banned paganism. That was just the start of the bad times. Domesticated felines remained an elegant novelty for a few centuries longer—at least among the cultures of northern and western Europe, to which they had been imported by the occupiers from imperial Rome. They performed the important service of rodent control, plus they were decorative, graceful, and (when it suited them) friendly. In Saxony, as late as the twelfth century, a good adult mouser was worth sixty bushels of corn. Meanwhile, cats maintained their propensity for walking alone. Often they went feral; sometimes they interbred with the European wildcat, *Felis sylvestris sylvestris*, dragging new genes into the domesticated lineage. They hung at the margins of civilization—the back alley, the outskirts of town, the thicket that bordered the farm—where human influence blended away into the wild and unknown. Their stubborn marginality soon brought them to grief, because one way of construing it was: These critters aren't to be trusted.

They weren't loyal toward humans or reliant upon them, as dogs and horses were. They were smarter and snottier, not to mention infinitely more nimble, than sheep. They weren't God-fearing, bootlicking minions that came when called or followed instructions for a morning's work. They vanished when they chose to, for days at a time, on unauthorized and unexplained vacations. They weren't scrutable. They didn't permit themselves to be thought of as possessions or servants or livestock. They were something else, and nobody exactly knew what. Around the thirteenth century, as medieval Christian society became more violently defensive against the various external and internal factors that threatened it, the domestic cat got tagged with a heinous reputation.

Black cats in particular—but all cats, more generally—came to be seen as embodiments of evil. Febrile religious mythologizers, and the good gullible folk who followed their prompting, began to view cats as demonic. Now suddenly they weren't graceful and elegant, these animals; now they were spooky and unnatural. They moved fluidly, their footsteps were soundless, they skulked the night. When they shrieked, it was a weird yowly sound. They consorted with witches. People came to believe that they changed shape. They might represent Satan himself, prowling on Earth in the form of a yellow-eyed beast. Furthermore, and maybe most importantly, they had a preternatural resistance to death—or so it seemed, anyway.

From some sort of misapprehended evidence, during this era, there arose the canard that a cat has nine lives.

So people began persecuting them, as proxies for whatever was scary and loathsome about medieval life. The persecution was widespread and took various forms. "On feast days all over Europe," according to a modern expert named James A. Serpell, "as a symbolic means of driving out the Devil, they were captured and tortured, tossed onto bonfires, set alight and chased through the streets, impaled on spits and roasted alive, burned at the stake, plunged into boiling water, whipped to death, and *hurled from the tops of tall buildings,* all in an atmosphere of extreme festive merriment." The italics are added by me, to highlight one aspect of cat abuse that may have had special implications: the high-altitude heave. Likewise in the testimony of another authority, Muriel Beadle, who has written that "a town could celebrate a holy day, symbolically ridding itself of evil, by *tossing cats from a church belfry* or putting them into casks which horsemen would run through with swords." More than a few cats were flung down from heights, and the practice seems to have continued for centuries. It may even have energized itself into a cycle of cruelty, fear, and more fear-driven cruelty. What I mean by that is: If a cat somehow survived being tossed from a belfry, its very survival would have reinforced the presumption that it had extraordinary, demonic powers. As late as 1750, the English artist William Hogarth produced a set of engravings titled *The Four Stages of Cruelty,* one stage of which shows a cat being thrown from a third-story window. Hogarth's cat is a small figure in the background of a busy scene, but a curious detail shows clearly. The animal is wearing a pair of wings.

Were the wings in the picture literal or symbolic? Were they mockingly ineffectual contrivances, strapped onto the cat by that cat-tosser as a way of adding insult to injury? Or was Hogarth suggesting that a defenestrated cat would somehow, on its own, escape the death sentence of gravity?

Another bit of data appeared much earlier in the cat-tossing era. It's a passage, describing cats, from a thirteenth-century Latin treatise on natural history, translated into Middle English in 1397. A scholarly feliphile named Juliet Clutton-Brock has retrieved it from obscurity in her useful new book, *Cats: Ancient and Modern.* It has a Chaucerian sort of robustness, until the cool, perplexed comment at the end: "He is a full lecherous beast in youth, swift, pliant and merry . . . and is a right heavy beast in age and full sleepy, and lyeth slyly in wait for mice. . . . In time of love is hard fighting for wives. . . . And he maketh a rueful noise and ghastful . . . and *unneth is hurt when he is thrown off an high place.*" Is your Middle English as rusty as mine? Clutton-Brock offers no gloss but, according to the *Oxford English Dictionary,* the word *unneth* in those years meant "scarcely."

So the cat "scarcely is hurt when he is thrown off a high place." No wonder those anxious medieval believers found him loathsome and scary.

DURING our own century, the conventional notion about plummeting cats has been that they've got one crucial, lifesaving trick: They can land on their feet. The only real question seemed to be, How? How could a free-falling body acquire angular momentum—that is, start itself rotating toward a new position—without exerting leverage against another solid object?

Some scientists doubted that it was possible. Most scientists doubted that it was important. But a physiologist named Donald McDonald, about three decades ago, made an elaborate study. McDonald dropped cats from various (modest) heights, recorded their movements with a high-speed film camera, and published his diagrams and analysis in *New Scientist*. It's true, he concluded. Cats have perfected a little maneuver whereby they can right themselves, during free fall, within a blink. They do it by arching the back, twisting the torso independently of the hindquarters, and then finally bringing the hindquarters around too. McDonald's work focused mainly on the conventional notion: how cats cope with dangerous falls by landing feet-first.

But he touched on something more. "A further physical problem is raised by the fact that a cat can fall from far greater heights than a man." What he actually meant to say, of course, was not just that a cat can fall farther but that it can do so and *survive*. This led him to the subject of terminal velocity.

Terminal velocity is the speed at which a body falling through air stops accelerating. The force of gravity (which corresponds to body weight) reaches equilibrium with the force of air resistance (which corresponds to the size, shape, and posture of the falling body), and at that point of equilibrium the speed of descent remains constant. A small body will fall more slowly than a larger body, other factors being equal, because the surface-to-weight ratio of the small body (and therefore its air resistance) will be higher. A plummeting human will reach terminal velocity at about 120 miles per hour. For a plummeting cat, by McDonald's estimate, the figure is just forty miles per hour. On the basis of crude tests done with a feloid dummy, he guessed that a cat will achieve that velocity after falling about sixty feet. "Therefore," McDonald concluded, "if it can survive a fall of this height it should be able to manage any height."

Many cats wouldn't make it. Please don't test your own. But some cats, as McDonald knew, would.

What were the mortal limits of *Felis catus* in free fall? To explore that question experimentally would be moronic as well as heartless—and scientists hate to seem moronic. But then, in the early 1980s, two veterinarians found themselves gathering relevant data in the course of their everyday practice. They worked at an animal clinic on Sixty-second Street in New York City, where skydiving cats are just another hazard of life.

THE VETS were Wayne O. Whitney and Cheryl J. Mehlhaff. They published their findings in a major veterinary journal under the title "High-Rise Syndrome in Cats." Whitney and Mehlhaff had "diagnosed" this syndrome in 132 cats within just a five-month period. The surprising aspect of their data was not that so many cats were falling (or jumping, or being pushed) from the city's windows and roofs. The surprise was that 90 percent had survived. Some of these cats had fallen a hell of a distance. The average was 5.5 stories. Of the twenty-two individuals that fell from eight stories or higher, only a single cat was fatally injured; and one of those survivors had fallen thirty-two stories. This sounds like a piece of urban folklore, but Whitney and Mehlhaff recorded it as clinical fact. "The cat that free-fell 32 stories onto concrete was released after 48 hours of observation, having suffered mild pneumothorax and a chipped tooth."

The overall survival rate among their sample is still more impressive, given Whitney and Mehlhaff's figure for terminal velocity. According to them, McDonald's forty miles per hour was considerably too low. They estimated instead that, after accelerating earthward for several seconds, a cat settles into vertical cruise at a steady sixty miles per hour.

One aspect of their data is especially puzzling. In the lower range of elevations, there was a positive correlation between the distance fallen and the number of injuries per cat—fine, OK, that much seems logical. The positive correlation came to its peak, however, at the seven-story level. In the range beyond seven stories, the correlation reversed. The number of injuries per cat actually *decreased* among cats that had fallen eight stories or more. There were fewer total injuries to long-distance fallers than to cats that had fallen just five or six stories. There were fewer bone fractures. From the pattern in the data, it appears that a cat falling seventeen stories is less likely to be hurt than a cat falling seven.

The explanation for this anomaly, by the best guess of Whitney and

Mehlhaff, relates to terminal velocity and the way a cat reacts after attaining it. When the speed of descent reaches maximum, and the sensation of acceleration disappears, "the cat might relax and orient its limbs more horizontally, much like a flying squirrel. This horizontal position allows the impact to be more evenly distributed throughout the body." Cats survive their ten-story and twenty-story and thirty-two-story falls, in other words, by doing great soaring belly flops onto the streets of Manhattan.

Or at least: The luckier and more coolheaded survive. I described the Whitney-and-Mehlhaff hypothesis to a friend, who announced immediately that his aunt's cat once fell from a high-rise window. I was eager to hear the mystifying details of what happened. "What *happened?*" he said. "It *splatted.*"

The only moral I see here is an obvious one: *Felis catus* has ascended to great heights in the modern world, but its attainments have proved distinctly ambivalent. I suppose it shares that with us. Back when the tame animals were wild, and the wildest of them all was the cat, humans were still a little wild themselves. As caricatured by Kipling, they lived in a cave. Inside the cave burned a cozy fire. There was also a milk pot and a supply of mice. There were no religions, no pharaohs, no scientists, no witches, no belfries, no elevators, no windows. The cat walked by himself and, although he was smart, he was also curious. Then things got complicated.

LOCAL BIRD
MAKES GOOD

The Posthumous Journeys of *Tyrannosaurus rex*

Like the grizzly bear and the pronghorn antelope and the yellow-billed magpie, *Tyrannosaurus rex* is a beast unique to western North America. The breadth of its fame has obscured the narrowness of its geographical distribution—or at least its apparent distribution, with the uncertainties of the fossil record taken into account—and not many people are aware that all specimens of the world's largest flesh-eating dinosaur come from a small number of closely clustered sites. Some of the best *T. rex* material has been excavated in South Dakota. Alberta has yielded two important finds, and another was made recently in southwestern Saskatchewan. Partial skeletons or fragments have also turned up in North Dakota, Wyoming, and Colorado. Plot them all on a map, and the dots define a speckly pattern along the east side of the northern end of the Rockies, where exposures of late Cretaceous rock are as common as snow-covered sage and humanity is not quite so numerous as Angus cows. In the middle of that pattern, geographically central and historically preeminent, lies the tiny town of Jordan, Montana.

Four of the world's dozen major specimens have been found near Jordan, which could justly tout itself as World Headquarters for the Discovery and Export of *Tyrannosaurus rex*. But it's an unassuming community and, for one reason or another, it doesn't. If a boosterish brochure from a local real estate office can be trusted, it's equally proud of its rodeo. (Jordan's more recent claim to international notoriety, the standoff between so-called Freemen and FBI agents in spring of 1996, represents an aberrant event not nearly so anchored in the local terrain as *T. rex* fossils—and one which, for all its noisiness, doesn't carry quite the same depth of abiding importance.) This is a cattle and grain town, population five hundred, seat of Garfield County, graced with two bars and a hardware store and an Assembly of God and a VFW hall and a copse of senescent cottonwoods along the bottomland of Big Dry Creek, which happens to be small and wet. There's no stoplight, just a flashing yellow. The Garfield County Courthouse is a humble clapboard building with a few weedy sumacs in front and an annex for the sheriff out back. A shop called Country Crafts occupies the premium corner storefront, sharing space with The Athletic Supporter, a secondhand store. But the busy display windows of those two establishments betray not a single allusion to the town's one celebrated product—not even a needlepoint tyrannosaurid on a sofa pillow. Only two dinosaurian images show themselves on Jordan's main street. One is a triceratops (another Cretaceous animal that lived hereabouts and got itself impressively fossilized in the local sediments) painted on a wooden sign outside the Garfield County Museum. The other is the silhouette of a sauropod on the Sinclair sign at the Pioneer Garage. This cartoonish sauropod, by the way, is no more indigenous than a Texaco tiger.

So Jordan is modest about its role in scientific history. Whatever visible tokens may commemorate that role seem to be stored away in the county museum, a windowless tin-roofed building at the north end of town. Above the museum's door, a permanent notice says OPEN 1–5, without specifying what days, what months, what years. It suggests a timeless time-consciousness nicely appropriate to paleontology. When I arrive, the place is deserted.

I'VE COME on a balmy Saturday in October, late enough into Indian summer that the blackbirds have gone restless and the cottonwood foliage is flaming in shades of yellow and olivaceous orange. I've driven three hundred miles, drawn to Jordan by curiosity and a sense of civic mission, about which I'll say more in a moment. Taped to the museum door I find a disappointing message: CLOSED FOR THE SEASON.

The Pioneer Garage, on the other hand, is doing a brisk business.

Antelope season opens tomorrow morning, and Jordan is abuzz with hunters gassing up their rigs. In addition there's a card party scheduled for this afternoon at the senior center, I learn, and a football game at the high school. People are friendly but preoccupied. Under the press of other activities, they appear indisposed to concern themselves with my civic mission, which in any case might sound mildly ridiculous if detached from the relevant scientific context. It's not easy—not even in Jordan, Montana, I discover—to strike up a probing conversation about *T. rex* with a bartender or a Chevy mechanic.

The relevant scientific context involves a mass of new data and new thinking about the phylogeny of the dinosaurs and their nearest living relatives. It includes evidence of warm-bloodedness, high agility, parental care, anatomical affinities with the class Aves, and other non-reptilian characteristics now discernible from the fossils of certain dinosaur species. It encompasses a notable article published in *Scientific American* back in 1975 by an unconventional paleontologist named Robert Bakker. Bakker argued that recent research by himself and others revealed dinosaurs to be "more interesting creatures, better adapted to a wide range of environments and immensely more sophisticated in their bioenergetic machinery than had been thought." Bakker's own cheerful conclusion from the new data was that "the dinosaurs never died out completely. One group still lives. We call them birds."

The civic mission I mentioned, which took shape in my head some years ago, not long after I first read Bakker's article, is to get *Tyrannosaurus rex* designated the official Montana state bird.

It's much more suitable than the incumbent in that role—the western meadowlark, *Sturnella neglecta,* an undistinguished little yellow-breasted passerine found virtually everywhere west of the Mississippi. *T. rex* better matches the state's ethos, I submit, and the distributional fit is also more snug. So far I've been lobbying quietly. The head of the state tourism bureau has ignored me; the governor and the legislature are still oblivious; but Montana-based paleontologists to whom I've mentioned it (including Jack Horner, original model for the *Jurassic Park* character and coauthor himself of a book titled *The Complete T. rex*) see the logic and like the idea fine. Now I've come out to Jordan for a glimpse of the big bird in its habitat.

◉   ◉   ◉

THE HISTORY of Montana since its seizure by white people has been heavily marked with the theme of extraction: Gold, silver, copper, coal, timber, and big-game animals have been snatched from the landscape and sent elsewhere to be processed, profited from, or simply enjoyed. Even grass has been exported, in the form of beef and mutton. Dinosaur paleontology, especially regarding *T. rex*, has been another extractive enterprise in that tradition.

The type specimen of *T. rex*—that is, the prototypic set of fossils from which the species took its scientific identity—was discovered in 1902 by a professional collector named Barnum Brown. Although he had been born in Kansas, Brown was what's known hereabouts as an Eastern feller. He shipped the booty back to his sponsoring institution, the American Museum of Natural History in New York, where an eminent paleontologist named Henry Fairfield Osborn did the formal description. "I propose to make this animal the type of the new genus *Tyrannosaurus*," Osborn wrote, "in reference to its size, which greatly exceeds that of any carnivorous land animal hitherto described." The specimen, designated AMNH 973, had come out of the Hell Creek Formation, a body of fossil-rich Cretaceous deposits that lay partially exposed among the badlands just north of Jordan. Brown himself, in a popular article, depicted it as "a powerful creature, active and swift of movement when occasion arose. Its anatomical characters show distant relationship with lizards, crocodiles and birds." He elaborated: "Like those of birds, the bones are hollow and the hind limbs in contour and construction closely resemble those of birds." He was intimating the same theme that Bakker would eventually develop.

Specimen AMNH 973 was just the beginning. Another excellent *T. rex* turned up in the Jordan vicinity a few years later. It was extracted in 1908—both from the ground and from the region—and mounted for display back at the American Museum, where in subsequent decades it became maybe the most frequently gawked-at dinosaur relic on Earth. In 1966 a California-based fossil prospector named Harley Garbani found still another, weathering out of a hillside on the land of a Jordan-area rancher named Lester Engdahl. That specimen included only 30 percent of the full skeleton but about three-quarters of its skull. The Garbani-Engdahl skull, which was well preserved and large, went on display at the Los Angeles County Museum. Garbani also found two other partial skeletons from the Hell Creek Formation on behalf of the University of California. The fourth major specimen was spotted in 1988 by an alert local woman named Kathy Wankel and excavated by a crew from the Museum of the Rockies, down in Bozeman. The dig was supervised by an experienced field man named Pat Leiggi, in the Barnum Brown tradition but a Montana feller. Leiggi's Bozeman crew traversed the same three-hundred-mile route that I later did, coming out of the steep and forested Yellowstone ecosystem onto the high plains, the favored terrain of antelope and prairie dogs and anyone with an interest in *T. rex*. Again the fossils passed out of Jordan's ambit on the road to a wider world, though in this case they didn't leave the state. That fourth Jordan specimen, almost 90 percent complete, is one of the most telling batches of *T. rex* material ever found. It includes the first full set of bones representing those mysteriously tiny and seemingly useless front limbs. When I visited the Museum of the Rockies for a viewing, it was spread across a series of large shelves in the basement, protected behind multiple locked doors, while scientists there and elsewhere performed elaborate analyses on bits of its petrified tissue.

"Pretty darn amazing animal," Pat Leiggi said, having ushered me into its presence. "Looks a lot smaller when you put it on shelves, doesn't it?" Yes, he agreed, it would be excellent as the Montana state bird.

One piece of intriguing analysis derived from this specimen was described last summer in the journal *Science*. From their study of oxygen isotopes in the bone phosphate of the Bozeman *T. rex,* which suggested an absence of temperature variation between different parts of its body, two scientists from North Carolina deduced that "it was a nonmigratory endotherm"—that is, an animal not directly dependent on sunshine or seasonal warmth for its thermal balance. If so, it wasn't a reptile as that word is commonly understood. The North Carolina team added that the creature's body temperatures "were largely maintained by a controlled metabolic rate, unlike the metabolism of modern ectotherms." On these grounds among others, then, the living *T. rex* seems to have been less similar to a crocodile than to an ostrich.

MANY fundamental questions about *T. rex* remain unanswered. Was it warm-blooded or wasn't it? Was it birdlike or wasn't it? Was it the most ferocious predator that ever walked on land or wasn't it? (Jack Horner dissents from the predator notion; with an ecologist's sensitivity as to what constitutes pragmatic behavior, he imagines *T. rex* as a scavenger, feeding on carcasses left behind by great triceratops herds, and perhaps killing an occasional animal that was sick or lame.) Did it suffer extinction because of a gigantic asteroid impact, or from a less dramatic combination of causes? Why were its arms so ludicrously tiny? And what the hell was it doing in *Jurassic Park,* since it didn't even exist during the Jurassic period?

But the unanswered question most interesting to me is one that seldom gets asked: What accounts for the biogeography of *T. rex*? In other words, why did it live where it lived and not elsewhere?

Closely related species of carnosaur have been excavated in other parts of the world—for example *Tarbosaurus bataar* in Mongolia, so similar that one expert suggests it should be reclassified as *Tyrannosaurus bataar.* But *T. rex* itself has never been found in the eastern United States, or the Southwest, let alone overseas. Why is it geographically confined to the northeastern front of the Rockies? And why, therefore, is it so apropos as Montana state bird, so irrelevant to the civic imagery of Delaware or California or Latvia?

"*T. rex* may just have been limited to one kind of environment," Phil Currie told me by phone from his office in Drumheller, Alberta. Currie is another distinguished dinosaur scientist, based at the Tyrrell Museum of Paleontology, which houses two major specimens of *T. rex,* both collected nearby. "It may have evolved in this neighborhood." On the other hand, he explained, the relationship between where a species actually lived and where it has appeared in the fossil record isn't simple. For specimens of any ancient species to turn up in any given place, a sequence of conditions is necessary. First and most obviously, the species must have inhabited that place; second, sedimentary deposits incorporating animal carcasses must have been laid down in that place while the species lived there, and those deposits must have been buried by later deposits and eventually hardened into rock; third, the fossil-bearing sedimentary strata must have recently been exposed again by erosion. "All these factors came together in western North America," Currie said. There was a depositional zone just east of the Rockies during the time of *T. rex,* the last few million years of the Cretaceous, and many sections of that rock now stand exposed among the buttes, coulees, and labyrinthine bad-lands of the region. "So we have a *very* good late Cretaceous record. It really isn't matched anywhere else in the world." Furthermore, just to the east was a great tongue of water, sometimes called the Western Inte-rior Cretaceous Seaway, that covered most of the plains states and provinces but left the western Dakotas, eastern Montana, and much of Saskatchewan and Alberta with hospitable coastal habitats along its western shore. If the range of *T. rex* extended farther south along the seaway coast—into New Mexico, Texas, western Kansas, and Okla-homa—we'll never see evidence of that fact unless the other two condi-tions (rock deposited, rock exposed) are met.

In the meantime, those states will just have to be satisfied with their own mincing little state birds.

THE BIG new specimen at the Museum of the Rockies is designated MOR 555. Refer to it carelessly as "the Bozeman *T. rex*" in conversation on a street corner in Jordan, and you're liable to raise some hackles. Jack Horner and his coauthor Don Lessem were keen to that sense of per-sonal and community proprietorship when they studiedly called it "Kathy Wankel's *T. rex*" in their book.

I encounter a touch of the same sensitivity at the Hell Creek Marina, a backwater establishment (literally) on an arm of Fort Peck Lake, twenty-six miles north of Jordan. I've driven out through the bad-lands in search of the spot where Barnum Brown found the type speci-men in 1902. The landscape is lovely—brown hills grazed by antelope on their last day of peace and safety, coulees and miniature canyons gouged down through the gray Cretaceous sandstone, golden cottonwoods along the bottoms—but the exact location of Brown's dig is indeter-minable. I've stopped at the marina for a desultory chat with a woman named Shelly, who's minding the store. Yeah, the old fossil site is around here somewhere, she tells me, but there's no marker. Been some talk about putting one up. Just talk, no action. Down in Jordan, now, they don't make much fuss over it there either. The fossils are out, Shelly says—and I hear a regretful but philosophic finality in that flat state-ment, as though she were saying, The barn door is closed, sure, but the horse is done gone. The fossils are out.

Even at the Jordan museum, Shelly adds, they don't have any *real* fossils. Just some models of what's been taken away. I prompt her: Taken to Bozeman and New York? Yeah, well, and one of 'em's gone *across,* she says. Across? To France, she explains. Or maybe it's Germany. I buy a Dr Pepper and linger, hoping to hear more of Garfield County attitudes regarding the fossil drain. But a man wanders in after his morning's fishing, she greets him by name, and the talk turns to perch and antelope, species of greater immediate concern.

Back in Jordan, I stop again at the museum, frustrated at the prospect of leaving town without having seen what's inside this building. Although the CLOSED FOR THE SEASON notice is legible from a distance, I stroll up to the door. And then, with no expectations, no conscious criminal intent, I grab the knob and give it a twisting shove. To my surprise, the door opens.

I close it again at once. I glance furtively over my shoulder. I'm only a block from the sheriff's office and there are cars going by. Standing innocently with my face to the door, using the glass as a mirror, I wait till the coast is clear; then I dodge inside, close the door behind me, and flick on the light. It's not breaking and entering, I tell myself breathlessly, if I haven't broken anything. Is it?

What else could they charge me with? Maybe *unauthorized entry of a museum for the purpose of getting Tyrannosaurus rex declared the Montana state bird*? The worst that could bring me, I figure, would be a few months in a mental hospital.

I don't make a thorough inspection of the museum holdings, because I'm in rather a hurry. Also, the light is dim and I'm wearing my sunglasses, dammit, with my regular glasses left stupidly in the car. I can see well enough to make out a few antique cash registers and an old baseball uniform. There's a triceratops. At the far end of the room I find what I'm looking for: a great toothy skull of the largest flesh-eating animal that ever walked the landscape of Garfield County or anywhere else. Of course, it isn't really a skull, as Shelly at the marina has warned me. It's merely a cast of a skull, no doubt shipped back to Jordan as a token of gratitude from one of those museums that got the real thing.

It's roughly as hefty and valuable as a pulled Chevy engine down at the Pioneer Garage. But to me it's vastly more impressive. The teeth are as big as hunting knives. The fenestrae gape like eyes. It's grinning. From the tip of its chin to the occipital condyle, the whole thing is about five feet long. I feel suddenly gladdened, knowing that the town of Jordan owns at least some representation of its most renowned species of fauna.

Or does it? On the display stand beside the skull is a small card. I pull it up near my nose and peek beneath my sunglasses to read: "Property of Lester Engdahl." So there are ever-smaller concentric circles of jealous claimant: As far as Lester Engdahl is concerned, *he* owns the dang thing, not Jordan or Garfield County or Montana. But who's Lester Engdahl? Offhand I can't place the name, though it sounds familiar. As I make my getaway from Jordan, with the museum door closed behind me, the local constabulary none the wiser, I'm still wondering.

Having a better memory than mine, you'll recognize that Lester Engdahl was the rancher on whose land the tyranno-prospector Harley Garbani made his 1966 find. Mr. Engdahl's contribution to paleontological history consisted in letting Garbani dig into a stony hillside on his Hell Creek holdings and take a specimen away to Los Angeles, where it could be studied by experts and marveled at by an appreciative public. For that he deserves some sort of grateful acknowledgment. Still, the bald assertion of Lester Engdahl's property rights (recorded on that card by him or, on his behalf, by someone else) strikes me as poignant, misguided, and pointless. What exactly does ownership signify as applied to an effigial skull of an extinct species in a public museum of which the door doesn't even lock properly?

Later, safely back in Bozeman, I realize that my own civic mission is precisely as pointless as Mr. Engdahl's proprietary card. All right, so maybe it's not such a brilliant idea for us Montanans to appropriate *T. rex* as our avian icon. Local pride has its claims, yes. Science too has its claims. And important fossils are sold nowadays to rich collectors, at least in some unfortunate cases, like diamonds or rubies or upscale sculptures. Possession may be nine points of the law. But wildness is wildness, even after sixty-five million years in the ground. No one can own the king of beasts.

ONE MAN'S MEAT

The Dilemma of Fruit Bat Cuisine
on the Island of Guam

Sometimes the story is simple. Bad greedy men with chainsaws or guns. Poisoning and pillaging are always more cost-effective than forbearance. Craven bureaucrats, sleaze-hearted businessmen in Armani suits, mindlessly eager civil engineers, sellouts, buyouts, lunkhead development bankers who seek to transmogrify Borneo in the image of South Carolina. The so-called inevitable march of so-called progress. Poor folk in the low latitudes continue to make babies, uncountable babies, and then insist on trying to feed them; the rest of us insist on automobiles, air conditioning, and our two acres with an A-frame in the mountains; everyone shares guilt for the inexorable destruction of wild places and their diverse living creatures. These are stark, tedious, familiarly insoluble problems. Then again, sometimes the story is not simple.

The story of *Pteropus mariannus mariannus* on the island of Guam, for instance, is not simple.

Pteropus mariannus mariannus is a subspecies of bat. Large-bodied, frugivorous, it's one of those big tropical fruit-eaters known as the flying foxes. Although some species of *Pteropus* are broadly distributed, *Pteropus mariannus* is unique to the Marianas, a chain of volcanic islands in the western Pacific, of which Guam is the southernmost and largest. Within that range, the subspecies *P. mariannus mariannus* is still more restricted, occurring only on Saipan, Tinian, Aguijan, Rota, and Guam itself, where it happens to be a highly esteemed object of traditional Chamorro cuisine. The Chamorros are the native people of Guam. They have been on the island for millennia. They came by canoe from the Philippines, or maybe Southeast Asia, or possibly some part of Indonesia. They have been subjugated and abused by the Spanish, then by the Americans, then by the Japanese, then to a lesser degree by us again. They are possessed of a strong desire—and arguably, an inalienable moral right—to eat bats. Here's where the complications begin.

To explore the dilemma of *P. m. mariannus*, with its welter of improbable details, small ironies, kitchen recipes, import statistics, and unsolved ecological mysteries, one needs a guide. If one is lucky, the guide's name will be Gary Wiles.

Wiles is a bearded, reticent, solitude-loving biologist who works for the Guam Division of Aquatic and Wildlife Resources. He studies *P. m. mariannus*. On a Saturday morning not long ago, he led me to a secret spot, his favorite place on all of Guam. This was partly an act of press relations and partly an act of trust; over the years since he'd been coming to the site, he told me, he had taken about a dozen other people with him. It wasn't a spot I could have stumbled to on my own. We passed through the gate of an Air Force base, showed IDs at a security office, drove down the edge of a runway between bomb-storage bunkers and a row of B-52s, huge gray eight-engine planes parked in the sun like a dream of doom. The bunkers had once contained hydrogen bombs, but no longer. The B-52s, during Vietnam, had come off this runway like rolling thunder. We left the car, crossed through a fence, and began climbing down a heavily forested cliff. Great three-dimensional spider-webs, big as weather balloons, thick as cotton candy, blocked the trail. We lowered ourselves down small drops by the tautly strung air-roots of strangler figs. We went on all fours. The footing was good, but the hand-holds were rough, since the cliff itself was a wall of uplifted coral. Five hundred feet below, we could see a flat coastal terrace of vegetation uncut by roads or runways, then the Pacific Ocean. We were facing north, roughly toward Iwo Jima. Halfway down the cliff we stopped on a ledge.

Good, we were downwind from the colony, Gary noted. That was important. Instead of echolocation capabilities, like many bats, these creatures have keen eyesight and very sensitive noses, he told me. The stench of humanity, in particular, distresses them. They may not be highly intelligent, but they have learned over the centuries to associate human odor with persecution and death.

We steadied our tripods on the ragged coral rock and aimed our spotting scopes where Gary pointed—toward a cluster of trees in the middle distance eastward along the cliff line. A naked eye could barely detect that the upper branches were festooned with pendulous, dark shapes. Maybe three or four hundred bodies, each one like an eggplant hung up in a black mesh stocking.

Through the scopes, we could see better: bats. Big, graceful, languid, day-resting bats. "That's eighty percent of Guam's population right there," Gary said.

Once there had been thousands. No one knows just how many. Today they face a whole complex of new and old problems, but a single particular problem is paramount. Tradition-observing Chamorros have eaten them to the brink of extinction.

A few points of menu and etiquette.

When does one serve fruit bat? If you are a Chamorro, abiding by ancient cultural practices that have become entangled with Spanish imperial Catholicism, you might serve fruit bat on special occasions—baptisms, weddings, village fiestas, and perhaps Easter.

To whom does one serve fruit bat? To your good friends and family and honored guests.

How does one serve fruit bat? Poaching in coconut milk is a popular method. Another recipe advises: Boil the animal for forty-five minutes in plain water, then add salt and shredded coconut meat. Some cooks favor a sort of corn-and-bat chowder. Simplicity seems to govern.

How does one clean a fruit bat? One doesn't. *But certainly you gut it?* No. *Discard the wings and the head?* No. *Do you at least skin it, please?* No. You leave the pelt and the guts in place. You cook the animal whole or not at all. Queasy-making as this may sound, it can't on objective grounds be set apart from certain reckless gambits in the cuisines of other cultures, now can it? It's no more perverse than raw oysters or rat cheese or sea-urchin-egg sushi or plain yogurt. Lutefisk. A fruit bat is like a bristling sardine: Any part you can chew, you can swallow.

And the flavor? Reliable testimony from a non-Chamorro source (namely Gary Wiles, who despite his protectionist sentiments was once obliged at a formal occasion to partake) says that the flavor is good. That the flesh tastes, not surprisingly, fruity. That the contents of the gut resemble a stuffing of fruit compote. But that there is one drawback. When you have chewed for a long time, and the flesh is gone, you find yourself left with a mouthful of fur. Etiquette decrees that this too be swallowed.

Do all Chamorros eat bats? No, many do not. Especially among the younger generation, this tradition seems to be dying—but it's not dying so quickly as the bats.

What species of fruit bat is best? Among discerning Chamorros, *P. mariannus* is preferred, and the local population of *P. m. mariannus* (that is, Guam's own endangered subspecies) is reportedly valued above all others for its taste and smell. The familiar Chamorro name for this bat is *fanihi*. Some other species are too small and bony. Some other populations of *P. mariannus* have an unappealing bouquet. The Guam bat is big and tender and nicely aromatic. But precisely that population has been protected by Guamanian law since 1973 and by the U.S. Endangered Species Act since 1984. Here, again, come the complications.

Are Guam's bats killed illegally? Yes. Poaching is done not just with coconut milk but also, sometimes, with shotguns. Shotguns and population trends, in fact, have combined to produce the situation under which Guam's native bat requires legal protection from Guam's native people. Back at the turn of this century, when the island's Chamorro population was small (partly because so many had died from European diseases brought by the Spanish) and their bat-hunting weapons were unfancy, the bat population could endure the slow, steady level of harvest. No longer. Now the island holds more than 55,000 Chamorros and probably fewer than six hundred bats, of which one man with a bird gun can kill fifty in five minutes. Bag limits were lowered during the 1960s, yet the bat population continued to fall. Finally, in 1973, Guam outlawed any bat hunting whatsoever. Enforcement has not been draconian. *Is there a black market in dead bats?* Hearsay says yes.

But certain fruit bats can still be legally purchased on Guam? Yes. *Where do these come from?* They are imported from other parts of the western Pacific—especially from Palau, Samoa, and the tiny islands of Truk and Pohnpei. According to numbers gathered by Gary Wiles,

Guam during the last fiscal year received 13,587 imported bats. Because Guam's standard of living (judged on the basis of average cash income, anyway) is higher than in those other Pacific nations, the Guamanian Chamorros can afford to buy away other people's bats. *Why does Guam enjoy such a rich cash economy?* In large part, because it's an important outpost for the U.S. military. *Yet who is the foremost protector of bat habitat on the island?* Again, the U.S. military. Credit and blame overlap confusingly.

How do imported bats arrive? In the cargo bays of international airlines, frozen.

Where does one find them? In the freezer bin of your local Chamorro grocery.

So on Saturday afternoon, after my bat-watching experience with Gary Wiles, I went to a local Chamorro grocery. In the freezer bin, sure enough, surrounded by frozen pork snout and frozen pork blood and frozen pork ears, I found a single woebegone little bat. Taped above the bin was a hand-lettered sign: FRESH FANIHI. But despite that claim of freshness, the bat too was frozen. Wings drawn up around it, as though dead of hypothermia, on a Styrofoam tray and wrapped in cellophane, it looked like a barbecued chicken breast left too long on the grill. The tag said $13.95.

"When I get a good price on bats, I'll take all I can get," the store's owner told me. "When there are fiestas, I go through hundreds. I could sell thousands a year. But we don't have a steady supply. This is our last bat, and I don't know where the next one's coming from."

The owner's name was Joe Benavente. He was young and bright and half Chamorro himself. He wore a polo shirt and carried a clipboard. He had approached me warily as I stood over his pork-and-bat section. He was concerned at first that I might be (as he said) a spy for the competition (or possibly, as he didn't say, a government inspector), but I explained that I was just a journalist curious about fanihi and, trusting soul, he relaxed. He told me that outsiders sometimes set up a bat stand just down the road from his place, beside the fish stands. Couple of sawhorses and a big umbrella, they were in business. I refrained from asking him, Sort of a fly-by-night operation? "They can always undersell me," Joe Benavente said. "Because they got no overhead, right?"

With a fervor that caused me to believe him, he also said, "I don't buy from poachers. It's an endangered species on Guam. That's heavy stuff. You could get in trouble."

Joe catered to a trade of old-fashioned Chamorro customers who could tell, by smell, one kind of bat from another—even when the bat they were sniffing was frozen and cellophane-wrapped. One lady could tell a male from a female that way. She preferred the males. A heartier, muskier aroma. I asked Joe if he himself ate fanihi.

"I tried it once. My in-laws made it. In corn soup."

"Did you like it?"

"It was OK. The corn soup was OK."

"But the bat. Did you eat it?" He winced, he smiled, he shook his head.

Fourteen dollars seems like a lot to pay for eight ounces of frozen bat, I said. Joe didn't disagree. The prices used to be much lower. Supply was way down now, but not demand. Fanihi had gotten to be expensive at the wholesale level, therefore also expensive here in his freezer bin. "Some of the poor customers can't afford it. We've caught people shoplifting bats. Older ladies, even." One woman ripped a bat out of the cellophane and tried to hide it in her purse, according to Joe. She was caught. This absurdist tableau stored itself indelibly in my memory, representing the pathetic nadir for all concerned.

Various gloomy signals could be read from Joe's informal market-report data: supply down but demand still up, high incentive for poaching, as well as a downward trend in the average size of non-Guam bats supplied by the importers. "Sometimes they bring in real dinky ones," he noted. "I say, 'Hey, you guys, don't kill those small ones like that.' " The animals coming out of Samoa were bigger than most others, and Joe's customers liked them. Not so bony, those Samoan bats.

He also recalled being offered a shipment of bats from the Philippines. The Philippine bats were guaranteed to be large and meaty, more than a pound each. But there were some risks. The importer demanded a minimum order of five thousand dollars and a letter of credit. Joe asked for a sample bat, but the sample never came. Furthermore, he had to consider the fact that many Chamorros (as Joe explained to me delicately) bear a racial or cultural prejudice against anything Philippine. Could he conceal the provenance of these big bats? No, that's a bad way to do business. Was there danger that his clientele might approve the taste, maybe, but dislike the idea of this merchandise? Definitely. "You know, my customers might be suspicious of these Philippine bats. They could be flying dogs or something. Who knows what they might have been eating over there?"

Joe Benavente had taken a pass on the Philippine supply. It was understandable. No grocer wants to get stuck with five thousand dollars' worth of unpopular frozen bats.

GARY WILES and I sat on the ledge for an hour, watching bats dangle, watching them mate, watching them suckle their young, watching them cool themselves with a palpating motion of the wings. Occasionally one would become restless and take to the air, circle the roosting trees lazily or ride a thermal along the cliff line and sweep past within yards of where we sat. "I've done all my observations from up here," Gary said, meaning the forested escarpment that overlooks the north coast. He has gathered population data on Guam's fanihi—always from a discreet distance, watching and counting, noting the trends, denied their biological secrets but sensing the tenuousness of their survival—since 1981. "I've never had my hands on these bats. It'd be really interesting to tag some, and find out exactly what they're doing."

Among the many ecological mysteries that Gary would like to solve is the crucial question of whether this colony of *P. m. mariannus* is regenerating itself with births and maturation of its own offspring. He fears not. Somewhere between infancy and adulthood, the large juveniles are disappearing. Gary hasn't seen any of that age group in four or five years. These medium-size youngsters—just old enough to leave the mother's chest and be left alone while she goes to forage—may be falling prey to the same pestiferous exotic tree snake, *Boiga irregularis,* that has eaten up nearly all of Guam's native forest birds. But that's just a hypothesis, backed by precious little proof. Still, something is cutting away those young bats; and it's possible that the colony has only been able to sustain itself, even at its current marginal level, thanks to immigrant bats flying in from the nearby islands. If so, what happens when those outlier populations have themselves been destroyed by poachers? Answer unknown. And just how badly is *P. mariannus* endangered throughout its whole range? Unknown. And what is its breeding biology? How fast could the population rebound if protected from humans and snakes? Unknown. How vulnerable might this colony be to starvation, in the aftermath of one of Guam's characteristically violent typhoons? Unknown.

Will *P. m. mariannus* survive on the island of Guam? A small but difficult question.

At the moment, they looked safe and tranquil. Through the spotting scope, I could see one female who held a youngster on her breast, wrapped inside the protection of those big dark wings. She bent her head up and began grooming the little thing with her tongue. Suddenly a deep low rumbling noise gathered power in the air all around, then drew itself into a focused roar, and a B-52 came off the runway above us. Smearing the sky with carbon, it lifted toward a bombing range on one of the tinier islands to the north; or maybe this plane would head down to Australia, for a low-altitude, radar-evasive training run. The bats ignored it. A second B-52 came blasting out after the first. Meanwhile the bats slept and suckled and mated. The U.S. Air Force didn't worry them.

But at another moment, all at once, half a dozen animals were in flight. Others flailed their wings nervously, shifted their grips on the branches. Something was wrong. The whole colony showed signs of agitation. Had the breeze swung around to put us upwind of them? "I hope that's not us," Gary said.

If it was—if the stench of our humanity had reached them and set off a wave of alarm—we'd have to pack up our scopes and leave. Of course, we intended them no harm. We hadn't come to rake their colony with shotgun fire and gather dead bodies for the stew pot. In fact, these animals probably had no better friend and advocate than Gary Wiles. But the bats didn't know that, and the world was a dangerous and confusing place. It wasn't a misunderstanding that could be settled by smell.

EITHER OR NEITHER

Slime Molds, Binary Thought, and
the Breaking of Alan Turing

Before venturing into a welter of lurid and tragic ambiguities, I want to make three simple statements.

Statement one: This is an essay about the slime molds. What are the slime molds? Not, as you might suppose, a Seattle-based rock-and-roll band. The slime molds are creatures so robustly peculiar that they flout all the familiar biological categories. They aren't animals, they aren't plants, they aren't fungi. They aren't single-celled organisms (except on a part-time basis) and they aren't (except part-time) multicellular. Sometimes they're called the social amoebae, though they don't actually belong to the genus *Amoeba*. They're neither this nor that, but always something else—something whose identity is protean. They flow like spilled syrup across the ruler-straight lines of binary definitude. What do they look like, these slime molds? That depends. They shift shape, according to circumstance and mood. They transmogrify spookily. During one stage of life, a slime mold resembles a slug, smearing its way along on a linear migration; during another stage, it becomes sessile and efflorescent, taking roughly the form of a dandelion; during still another stage, it consists of thousands of discrete amoebae, all ignoring one another while they pursue their own appetites. A representative genus is *Acrasia*, named from the Greek word meaning "bad mixture." The slime molds are collective but individual, social but solitary, primitive but elaborate, inconspicuous but significant. In a word, paradoxical. They're slimy, yes, but not moldy, no. Although they don't fit within any of the standard pigeonholes for flora or fauna, they do have their own eerie charm. Did you ever see a movie called *The Blob*?

Statement two: This is also an essay about Alan Turing. Who was Alan Turing? Not, as you might suppose, a biologist who studied the slime molds. Turing was a brilliant English mathematician, a pioneer of computer theory, a Fellow of the Royal Society, and one of the chief cryptanalysts responsible for breaking the German naval code during World War II. Enigmatic himself, he helped solve Hitler's fancy machine-based cipher system, known as Enigma. He was a gentle nerd who buried his money in the woods instead of entrusting it to a bank, collected wildflowers and fir cones to study their anatomical patterns, took up long-distance running in his thirties, turned his hand to mathematical biology, made some trailblazing efforts in the field now known as artificial intelligence, and dreamed of building an electronic machine that could play chess. He was also a quiet but stubborn rebel against authority, an unsecretive homosexual at a time when homosexuality was illegal in Britain, and eventually a convicted perpetrator of forbidden acts, a victim of quackish "organotherapy" in the form of court-mandated hormone treatments, and a suicide. He died of cyanide poisoning in 1954.

Statement three: The connection between statements one and two, the link that I ask you to ponder between the slime molds and Alan Turing, is a process called morphogenesis.

Morphogenesis, defined in plain language, is the acquisition of form. In language less plain but equally valid, it's the biological miracle of becoming. An embryo within a womb, or within an eggshell, is engaged in morphogenesis. So are an adolescent girl, as her boyishly smooth chest begins showing breasts, and an adolescent boy, as his girlishly high voice cracks into a lower range. So are a butterfly as it emerges from a cocoon, a tadpole as it loses its tail, and a germinating seed as it sends out its first shoot. The slime molds and Alan Turing fall together into this discussion, a natural pair of complements, for several reasons—one of which is that, in both cases, the miracle of becoming seems especially extraordinary. Another reason is that Turing, late in his short life, transformed himself abruptly into a theorist on morphogenesis.

What makes a slime mold metamorphose from stage to stage? What made Turing into the wondrous, difficult man that he was? What are the factors that give any being its shape, its role, its destiny? Morphogenesis isn't an answer. But it's the label on the dark box that holds those questions.

I tell you this much in advance to minimize surprise and confusion, so that you can save your perplexity for where it counts.

THE FIRST thing worth knowing about the slime molds is that the term *slime molds* itself is a bit loose and slippery. It encompasses two major groups of organisms, superficially similar but fundamentally unrelated, of which the more interesting are the cellular slime molds. They're labeled cellular because they retain their individualized multiplicity (many cells, one nucleus to a cell) throughout their aggregative stages of life. Among the most famous of the cellular slime molds (a narrow distinction, admittedly) is a species called *Dictyostelium discoideum,* first described to the world sixty years ago by a scientist named K. B. Raper, who had found it among decaying forest leaves.

In the decades since, *D. discoideum* has become a special favorite of biologists who study morphogenesis. It's their equivalent to the fruit fly or the guinea pig or the white rat, an ideal small organism through which to explore big questions. The prominence of *D. discoideum* derives from several convenient traits: It thrives in the laboratory, its life cycle is brief, it lends itself well to experimental manipulation, and it manifests the process of morphogenesis in a particularly stark way, separated in time from the process of growth. That last point is important. In most species, growth and morphogenesis occur simultaneously and therefore seem inextricably entangled—the human embryo growing larger as it changes shape, the adolescent boy or girl getting taller and heavier while enduring those transformations of puberty. But in *D. discoideum* the two processes occur consecutively, not simultaneously. The amoebae stop eating, stop growing, and stop fissioning when they receive the signal to aggregate; from that point until the next generation, all changes are purely morphogenetic. "This is an ideal situation for those interested in biological form," according to John Tyler Bonner, an eminent evolutionary biologist at Princeton, "for here is a natural separation of the two form-producing factors which are ordinarily so closely connected that it is impossible to determine the roles of each." Bonner should know. He has studied *D. discoideum* and other slime molds for fifty years, combining profound conceptual work in developmental biology with laborious attention to the bizarre details of his pet group.

The life cycle of *D. discoideum* begins when a single spore lands in good habitat—some parcel of moist soil, fresh water, or dead vegetation containing an abundance of bacteria, which are its natural prey. From the spore hatches a hungry amoeba. The amoeba begins gobbling bacteria. With plenty to eat, it grows bigger, reaches a limit of size, and reproduces itself by cell fission, splitting into two independent amoebae. These two amoebae repeat the same steps—predation, growth, fission—as do the resulting four, as do the eight, as do the sixteen, and so on, until the habitat is dense with amoebae of *D. discoideum*. About this time, the supply of bacteria runs short. With the onset of famine, some of the amoebae release a chemical signal and others echo it, like a howling pack of coyotes. The exact molecular nature of the signal remained obscure for some years while Bonner and other slime mold researchers worked doggedly to identify it. Now it's known to be something called cyclic AMP, short for cyclic adenosine monophosphate. But the message content had long since been obvious. What the amoebae signal to one another with cyclic AMP is, Yo bubba, let's aggregate.

They come streaming together. They pile themselves into a central gloppy mound. Then the mound surges upward, rising erect like a little rounded tower of Babel, the first startling evidence of cooperative effort. But wait—the Babel analogy doesn't quite fit, because these gathered individuals all speak the same language. Matter of fact, they aren't even individuals anymore; they are now the cellular components of a multicellular organism. The tower topples over into a sluglike thing composed of thousands of amoebae, and then the slug starts to move as one body. This is collectivization as Lenin and Mao could only dream of it.

The slug migrates through the soil like an earthworm, abandoning its food-depleted habitat for a different sort of place, where a different sort of need can be met. With the purposefulness of a single sentient being, which it now is, it travels toward light and heat. Why light and heat? Because the sunlight and warmth of exposed surfaces coincide with locations that will be optimal, later, for spore dispersal.

Satisfied in a new place, the slug stops migrating. It anchors itself to the ground with a discoid (this presumably accounts for the species name) base of cells, like a suction cup; raises its body vertical again, this time into a thin cellulose stalk; and tops out the stalk with a spheroid knob. The knob consists mainly of spores. This is the culminating stage of *D. discoideum,* the stage with roughly the same shape and function as a dandelion blossom. When a splash of water or a passing insect dislodges the spores, those that travel far enough to land in good amoeba habitat (another patch of moist soil or dead vegetation, rich with bacteria) will start the process again. Eat, grow, fission, eat, grow, fission— until the food supply again fails.

The entire cycle is nicely adapted for accomplishing what the amoebae couldn't accomplish solitarily: long-distance dispersal from food-poor to food-rich locations. The species survives because some amoebae sacrifice themselves—becoming stalk cells and base cells, never achieving the status of spores—for the sake of others. The spores escape from oblivion by standing on the shoulders of their comrades.

What process controls that last invidious differentiation, separating the escapees from the self-sacrificial? It's not simply natural selection, the survival of the fittest based on genetic differences, because all the amoebae in a given slug may carry identical genes, having descended as clonal copies from one original amoeba. And it's not simply altruism among close relatives—that explains *why* some amoebae might sacrifice themselves for others, but not *how* the individual assignments of role are made. What, then? What chemical, physical, or accidental factors specify the final transformation of each amoeba?

This is one of the big slime-mold questions, and it resonates into larger contexts with no diminution of mystery: What determines an individual's character and fate?

ALAN TURING had a fractured, lonely childhood. His father was a gruff man who served as a British colonial functionary in the Indian Civil Service and returned to England only when he was on leave. Alan's mother had been born in India herself but raised with her uncle's family in Ireland. She was an unsentimental woman, it seems, who went back to India with her husband just a year after Alan's birth, leaving Alan and his older brother fostered out to a middle-aged couple. The middle-aged couple had four daughters of their own and took in still other children besides the Turing boys, on what seems to have been a boardinghouse basis. "This was not home," according to Alan's biographer, Andrew Hodges, "but it had to do." Alan's father had decided that the climate of Madras was risky for English children, and his mother satisfied herself with seeing the boys intermittently, year by year. When Alan was eleven, he and his brother were shifted to a different foster household. Then suddenly Mr. Turing resigned from the Indian Civil Service, in a funk about something or other, and set up residence as a tax-dodging exile on the coast of France. This wasn't home either, not for the boys; but again it had to do.

At age thirteen Alan went off to Sherborne School, one of those notorious English "public" schools that were decidedly private and grim. Sherborne, like the others, was a place of cold dormitories, cold showers, rote teaching, corporal punishment, hazing and bullying that enforced a rigid hierarchy among the students—picture *Lord of the Flies* within ivy-covered walls—and a high incidence of homosexual infatuations between older and younger boys. It could probably be argued that the last of those, the erotic schoolboy friendships, may have done more to ameliorate the general brutality than to degrade further the moral tone. Anyway, Alan spent a few miserable years at Sherborne, emotionally isolated and academically mediocre, before finding his solace and his focus through a fiercely romantic (but chaste) attachment to a boy named Christopher Morcom.

Then bad luck gave Alan Turing a thump from which, maybe, he never recovered. Just before Christopher Morcom would have left Sherborne in triumph, to take up a scholarship at Cambridge, he died suddenly of bovine tuberculosis. Alan was devastated.

He went to Cambridge himself, finding it a decent place for exploring his sexual identity and an excellent one for developing his math talent, which turned out to be great. He finished his undergraduate degree with distinction and got a research fellowship that allowed him to stay, delving deeper into mathematics and logic. He became slightly less shy, slightly more confident, capable even of humor, and not above affectation. At Christmas of 1934, when he was twenty-two, he asked his mother for a teddy bear, something he'd never had as a child. This teddy-bear business sounds like a plot device compounded from *Citizen Kane* and *Brideshead Revisited*, but his biographer reports it as fact.

"The axioms of his life were becoming clear by now," Hodges writes, "although how to live them out was quite another question." Alan didn't seek noisy confrontations. He wanted an ordinary existence, more or less. "But he found himself to be an ordinary English homosexual atheist mathematician. It would not be easy."

In 1937, he published an extraordinary paper. It appeared in the *Proceedings of the London Mathematical Society* under a longish title; history now knows it as "Computable Numbers." The paper's main subject was a notorious conundrum (Hilbert's *Entscheidungsproblem* to the cognoscenti, of which I ain't one) in the philosophy of mathematics. Incidentally it offered some other far-reaching ideas, including the notion of a universally adaptable thinking machine and the convention of using binary numbers to streamline automated calculations. One advantage of using binary numbers (expressing all numbers as sequences of zeros and ones) was that they could be represented by the slick either/or simplicity of electric switches. About the same time, Alan applied that idea in his design for an electric multiplier machine, part of which he actually built in a university machine-shop, using switches he made himself.

Ten years later, after his wartime experience with code machines, he would play a major role in a more ambitious project, a government-sponsored effort to create the Automatic Computing Engine, which drew newspaper attention as an "electronic brain." For a while he was at the center of that effort. But Turing was a cranky collaborator, a bad boss, a lousy administrator, and his personal participation was never so important as his indirect theoretical influence. He was the author of "Computable Numbers," after all. Andrew Hodges argues, and many authorities seem to agree, that Turing's 1937 paper was the conceptual origin of the electronic digital computer.

ONE OF the more striking facts about the cellular slime molds, to a biologist like John Tyler Bonner, is their capacity for what's called regulative development. This mode of development permits a certain flexibility in the fate of individual amoebae as morphogenesis proceeds. The essence is that, rather than having its eventual shape and role rigidly set, each amoeba is subject to chemical signals and physical forces that regulate its final transformation. If those regulating factors are somehow altered, the final transformation goes differently. In direct contrast to regulative development, there's mosaic development, which is more deterministic. With mosaic development, each part of a developing embryo is rigidly destined to assume a particular shape and role in the adult organism.

Regulative development, the flexible sort, shows vividly in D. discoideum. Every amoeba in the migrating slug retains its potential for transformation into any of the specialized cell types of the culminating stage—spore, stalk cell, or base cell. Opportunity remains fluid and democratic. That fact can be demonstrated experimentally by cutting a migrating slug into sections. Each section will still achieve culmination, blossoming into a complete (but miniature) version of the final dandelion structure. Slug sections can even be shuffled and patched back together. Such experimental rearrangements show that the position of an amoeba within the slug, not its inherent identity, is what settles its eventual shape and role.

Bonner himself has sketched the pattern of correspondence between position and fate. The fast, eager amoebae that assemble themselves into the slug's front tip, leading the migration, end up humbly as stalk cells. The caboose amoebae end humbly too, becoming base cells. Oddly, it's the amoebae of the slug's midsection that are privileged to become spores. So the last shall be last, the first shall be next to last, and the middling shall inherit the future. Then again, the slash of a dissecting tool can change everything.

Bonner's first major study of D. discoideum was published fifty years ago—in a journal of botany. Slime mold research has come a long way since then. Bonner himself has admitted recently, in a scientific autobiography titled Life Cycles, that whereas he once thought the slime molds were totally regulative, nowadays the point seems less clear. He sees some evidence of mosaic development too. Maybe there's a mixture. Maybe destiny is modulated by circumstance, and vice versa.

To me it sounds like part of a much larger discussion. Regulative or mosaic? Heredity or environment? Free will or determinism? Bootstraps or good fortune? Choice or chance?

What combination of chemical reactions and physical forces accounts for cell differentiation within D. discoideum? Bonner suggests that one small piece of the answer is cyclic AMP, the same substance that carries the earlier summons to aggregate. But how can a chemical signal be converted into an astonishing three-dimensional upheaval among a mass of genetically identical cells? Addressing that subject, so closely entangled with his own life's work, Bonner nods respectfully to an influential paper published in 1952. The title of this one, not needing abbreviation by history, is "The Chemical Basis of Morphogenesis." It was written by Alan Turing.

I won't even try to summarize "The Chemical Basis of Morphogenesis." Most of it flies over my head like a peregrine falcon. Anyway, I'm more interested in the person who wrote it.

Not long after finishing the paper, Alan Turing stood accused of being a sex criminal. By then he was living in the city of Manchester, a distinctly less tolerant milieu than Cambridge. He was charged with "gross indecency," under an 1885 law, for acts committed in his home with another man. The police had come stumbling into his personal life in the course of investigating a burglary he had reported, and without thinking much about his jeopardy or his options, Turing had poured out a set of startling admissions. He didn't act guilty or, apparently, feel guilty. But on March 31, 1952, before a judge and a prosecutor, he pleaded guilty.

A character witness, a man he had worked with on the Enigma project, described him as a national asset. Another witness called him "one of the most profound and original mathematical minds of his generation." He was put on probation, with the condition that he "submit for treatment by a duly qualified medical practitioner at Manchester Royal Infirmary." It wasn't quite like sentencing Oscar Wilde to the treadmill at Pentonville prison, but it was bad enough.

The medical practitioner began giving him organotherapy treatments of estrogen—sizable doses of female hormone—on the theory that this would eliminate sexual drive in a male. Chemical neutering was considered more effective, and maybe more humane, than physical castration. But the estrogen didn't have its intended effect. It had another effect, unintended: Within a few months, Turing complained to a friend that he was growing breasts.

He didn't kill himself during the treatments. He lingered for more than a year, then did it. People who knew him were caught by surprise. Even his friends had assumed that he'd passed through the worst of his emotional crisis and emerged beyond. They assumed wrong. More evidence of the ultimate unplumbability of the human soul . . . as though we need more.

And some people didn't care to plumb. His mother, for one, convinced herself that the fatal self-poisoning had been an accident, some little chemical experiment gone haywire. Alan always *had* been careless about washing his hands.

Several sad ironies are on display in the story of Alan Turing. The most obvious is that British penal pharmacology, imposed by a society so unrelentingly binary that it couldn't tolerate homosexuality between consenting adults, had the effect of making his sexual identity *more* intermediate, rather than less so. Related to that irony is another: that Turing himself, as father of the digital revolution, has played a paramount role in making binary numbers the fundamental language of our age. Largely because of him, most of the world's automated figuring and communicating is now done through neat little yes-or-no switches.

Still another irony, conscious on his part, appeared in his choice of a suicide method. From the evidence found in his house, it seems that he soaked half an apple in a solution of potassium cyanide. He lay calmly on his bed. He ate a few bites of the apple and died. What was he trying to say about the tree of knowledge of good and evil?

The connections I've been sketching here, between Alan Turing and the slime molds, might seem tenuous. I suppose they might seem worse than tenuous: either insulting or insufficiently judgmental, either moralistic or amoralistic, depending on your point of view. Those little risks are worth taking, I think, because to me the connections are intriguing and richly suggestive. What do they suggest? New grounds for being mystified at the multifariousness of biological forms and transformations; and new paths that might, or might not, lead toward understanding. I haven't raised the most obvious question, at least until now: What accounts for Alan Turing's morphogenesis? That one can be parsed into others. What made him a genius? Was his homosexuality a result of genetic destiny, determinative personal experiences, or free choice? Why did he transform himself from a theorist of digital computing into a theorist of biological form? Did English society of the 1950s in some sense cause his suicide, or did he alone bear the weight of responsibility?

Those are all ontological issues—that is, concerned with being and becoming. What interests me more is an epistemological issue—that is, concerned with knowing. The final question I'm getting at in this ungainly disquisition on Alan Turing, the slime molds, and morphogenesis is, Can we really *expect* to comprehend the factors that give any being its shape, its role, its destiny? Some people adamantly say yes. Others, also adamantly, say no. The answer I prefer might sound craven, but it's appropriate to the story of Turing, the story of *D. discoideum*, and maybe it's less craven than it seems: yes and no.

� IV ✴

NEAR SIGHT

BEAST IN THE MIRROR

Science Uncovers Another Chimpanzee

In 1699, more than a century before the birth of Charles Darwin, a London physician named Edward Tyson dissected a chimpanzee. The conclusion to which this exercise brought him was curiously foresightful. Probing in cold flesh with his seventeenth-century scalpel and his seventeenth-century frame of mind, Tyson anticipated not just *The Origin of Species* and *The Descent of Man* but also some of the most profoundly provocative work to appear in the *Journal of Molecular Evolution* during the late years of your century and mine.

The chimp in question had been taken alive and shipped from what is now Angola to England, where after just a few months it succumbed to English weather and other forms of desolation. It reached Edward Tyson as a cadaver. It wasn't the first of its species to be abducted by European explorers (a chimpanzee had been presented in 1640 to the prince of Orange), but it was among the earliest few. Other species of ape—the gorilla in Africa, the orangutan in Sumatra and Borneo—were still known only through breathless, inaccurate hearsay. Peeling away the skin and the muscles of the chimpanzee on his table, Tyson made elaborate, textured drawings in the ghoulishly beautiful style of Vesalius. He spackled those drawings with numerical labels. He compared certain features that were manifest in his specimen with the anatomical particulars of humans, on the one hand, and, on the other hand, of monkeys.

He counted thirty-four features in which the chimpanzee resembled monkeys more closely than it resembled humans; balanced against those, he found forty-eight other features in which it matched more closely to humans. (For instance, its brain was much larger in proportion to body size than the brain of any known monkey.) Tyson could only conclude that this beast fell somewhere between. Although it wasn't human, it appeared to be more like a human than like any other creature that he'd ever seen. Gropingly, without guidance from a theory of evolution by common descent, Tyson judged that an animal so similar deserved to be welcomed to the human genus, *Homo*. He wasn't making any revolutionary assertion about shared ancestry. He was just trying to give an orderly, logical name to a piece of God's creation as he found it. He called the chimp *Homo sylvestris*. Translated: man of the forest.

Nowadays, after decades of field study and museum work in comparative anatomy, the common chimpanzee goes by a different name: *Pan troglodytes*. In conventional textbooks and taxonomic encyclopedias, it's placed in the family Pongidae, which includes also the pygmy chimpanzee (a smaller species, formerly unrecognized but now designated as *Pan paniscus,* and sometimes known as the bonobo), the gorilla, and the orangutan. To understand the significance of that placement—and of striking new data that challenge it—you might need to know just a nickel's worth of taxonomy.

Pongidae is a family of apes, as distinct from monkeys; the gibbons, which are apes too but somewhat smaller and more gracile, comprise a closely related family, Hylobatidae; the Old World monkeys (a group that includes the colobus monkeys and the mangabeys of Africa, the langurs of Asia, as well as the baboons and the macaques) belong to another distinct family, Cercopithecidae; the prosimians (such as lemurs and lorises) and the New World monkeys all fall within various other primate families. And the conventional reference books list still another family, Hominidae, with *Homo sapiens* as its sole living species. This puts humanity in an honored position, all on its lonesome. But some recent work in molecular biology suggests that Edward Tyson's view— of a congeneric chimp-human relationship, one little genus for both them and us, slashing across the orthodox notion of placement in two separate families—was more accurate.

From the evidence of DNA and other complex molecules, it appears that we humans as a species have no closer living relatives than chimpanzees. That much might not seem surprising. It appears also that chimpanzees, God help them, have no closer living relatives than us.

THE RECENT molecular findings, which I'll describe presently, were prefigured not just by Tyson's anatomical insight but also by several significant discoveries in the realm of behavior. Chimpanzees, whatever the degree of anatomical or biochemical resemblance they may or may not bear to us, act in certain ways that seem—almost—uniquely human. For instance, humanity was once considered the only toolmaking species, until about 1920, when a pioneering ethologist named Wolfgang Kohler observed tool assembly and tool use among a colony of captive chimpanzees. Jane Goodall later witnessed toolmaking by wild chimps at her Gombe Stream site on Lake Tanganyika. The contribution of one Gordon G. Gallup, Jr., is even more intriguing, though less widely famed than the work of Goodall or Kohler. Gallup worked with mirrors.

He was an experimental psychologist, not a field primatologist, and his chimp-and-mirror studies were carefully contrived and conducted within a lab. In 1970, Gallup published a report of those studies in the journal *Science*. He had taken four juvenile chimpanzees, all born in the wild, and confined each within a small cage in an otherwise empty room. After giving them two days of isolation, he set up a full-length mirror opposite each cage. Then, for ten days, each chimp was left alone to acquaint itself with the animate image it saw. The question at issue: Would a chimp take the mirror image to be another chimp, or would it recognize its reflected self? To answer that, Gallup anesthetized each chimp, painted red marks on its face with dye, and let it wake up to another round of confronting the mirror. He found that the four chimps were fascinated (or possibly alarmed?) by the red marks that had appeared on their faces. They gazed in the mirrors while touching themselves on the marked spots. They probed and gaped, matching their tactile investigations with their visual ones. The attention they gave to the spots indicated that each chimp had made the conceptual connection between the beast in the mirror and the being that was itself. Monkeys of the relatively clever and adaptable genus *Macaca,* on which Gallup tried the same test, made no such connection. To a macaque, the beast in the mirror was just a splotchy-faced stranger.

The chimps' mirror-using behavior implied "a concept of self," Gallup wrote, and he claimed to have made "the first experimental demonstration of a self-concept" in a nonhuman species. "Our data suggest that we may have found a qualitative psychological difference among primates," he concluded, "and that the capacity for self-recognition may not extend below man and the great apes."

As used by Gallup in 1970, the phrase "great apes" referred exclusively to the Pongidae: chimpanzees, orangutans, and gorillas. The current usage, at least among some thinkers, is slightly broader.

"WE ARE human, and we are also great apes," write Paola Cavalieri and Peter Singer in the preface of a recent book titled *The Great Ape Project*. From that start, they proceed through an ambitious syllogism. "Our membership of the human species gives us precious moral status: inclusion within the sphere of moral equality. Those within this sphere we regard as entitled to special moral protection." Our membership in the great-ape category, on the other hand, gives us a crosscutting affinity. Why shouldn't *that* category serve as our encompassing moral sphere? "This book urges that in drawing the boundary of this sphere of moral equality, we should focus not on the fact that we are human beings, but rather on the fact that we are intelligent beings with a rich and varied social and emotional life. These are qualities that we share not only with our fellow humans, but also with our fellow great apes."

The Great Ape Project is a compendium of scientific, philosophic, and polemic essays by more than thirty researchers and writers (including Jane Goodall, the biologist Richard Dawkins, the ecologist Jared Diamond, the animal-rights philosopher Tom Regan, the best-selling intergalactic funnyman Douglas Adams, and the primatologist Geza Teleki) documenting the advanced social and emotional capacities of chimpanzees, gorillas, and orangutans, and exploring the ethical issues raised by the imprisonment and abuse of such creatures for human convenience.

Some of the contributors, such as Dawkins and Diamond, are known primarily as scientists, not as crusaders. Some, such as Goodall and Teleki, have made primates the focus of their professional lives, while moving gradually from field research to advocacy. Some, like Singer, have concerned themselves more broadly with human treatment of animals—all sorts of animals. They've joined in consensus for this project because, Cavalieri and Singer explain, the (nonhuman) great apes seem a bellwether case. If we can't revise our attitudes and behavior toward them, we probably can't revise our attitudes and behavior toward any part of the natural world.

But maybe, these experts hope, we can.

WHAT'S THE scientific background to this notion that humans belong in the great-ape category? Early evidence came from comparative anatomy. In the eighteenth century, Linnaeus classified humans and apes together in the order Anthropomorpha, arguing that although humans might be quite distinct morally and intellectually, they aren't very different physically from other anthropoids. He was only ratifying what Tyson had suggested. A century later the anatomist and evolutionist T. H. Huxley also agreed, using Darwin's theory of common descent to explain his own observation that humans resemble the higher apes more closely than those apes resemble other primates. With passing time, these anatomical judgments were supported by other clues from paleontology, biogeography, and eventually molecular biology.

As far back as 1904, a researcher named G. H. F. Nuttall recognized remarkable similarities between some of the complex molecules of humans and of apes. Nuttall gathered his evidence from immunological comparisons of serum proteins—in plainer words, he studied how the blood molecules of each species reacted to biochemical intruders. In Nuttall's day, of course, DNA was unknown, and its guiding role in the manufacture of proteins was a mystery not yet defined, let alone solved. The notion of shared genes between two distinct species could hardly have been imagined, because the notion of the gene itself was still taking shape. After Nuttall, the subject seems to have lain fallow for six decades. Then a biologist named Morris Goodman published a few papers, based also on immunological comparisons, in which he noted strong similarities among the blood proteins of chimpanzees, gorillas, and humans. On these molecular grounds, Goodman argued, the genera *Pan* and *Gorilla* belonged with *Homo* in the family Hominidae, rather than with the orangutan in Pongidae. The three African genera of apes, as Goodman saw them, are more similar to each other than any of them was to the red ape of Borneo and Sumatra.

But what's the pattern of relationship among these African genera? Which two of the three—*Pan, Homo, Gorilla*—are more closely related to each other than to the third? Comparative anatomy has offered guesses, but anatomical similarities can be misleading. Paleontology has also been unable to settle the question, because the requisite fossil evidence hasn't turned up. Even Goodman's early immunological data provided no answer.

In the 1980s came another big breakthrough, when Charles G. Sibley and Jon E. Ahlquist began publishing results from a method called DNA hybridization. Sibley and Ahlquist had focused first on birds; eventually they proposed a grandly revised classification of the living birds of the world, based on DNA-hybridization tests involving more than a thousand species. Although that was high-flying stuff so far as bird taxonomists were concerned, it didn't hoot with significance for the general public. But they also turned their technique to the delicate question of relatedness among the great apes. This was the provocative work reported in the *Journal of Molecular Evolution*.

What's DNA hybridization? Crudely summarized, it works as follows. You take a sample of DNA from one species (say, *Pan troglodytes,* the chimpanzee) and heat it to 100 degrees Celsius. At that temperature, the double-stranded helical molecule will split ("melt" is the metaphor that the practitioners favor) into two single strands. Let it cool slightly—but hold it on simmer. Add another sample of split-apart strands from another species (say, *Pongo pygmaeus,* the orangutan) to the same pot. If the two samples of DNA are reasonably similar, some of those mixed single strands will zip readily (but imperfectly) together, forming hybrid two-stranded helices. Now take the hybrids and heat them again toward the original melting point, watching carefully on your fudge thermometer to register the melting point this time. Lo and behold, the new melting point will be lower. How much lower will depend on the degree of molecular dissimilarity between the two samples of DNA. The differences that inevitably exist between a DNA strand from one species and a strand from another species cause a reduced split-apart threshold in the hybrids—and molecular wizards such as Sibley and Ahlquist can even chart the phenomenon numerically. It happens to be blessedly neat: Each one-degree reduction in melting point signals a one percent discrepancy between the two strands.

Needless to say, kids, don't try this at home. You could sublimate your temptation, perhaps, by watching a video of *The Fly*.

SIBLEY AND Ahlquist performed hybridization-and-melting trials on DNA from gorillas, orangutans, common chimps, pygmy chimps, humans, two species of gibbon, and seven species of Old World monkey. Their results are precise and telling. The average difference in DNA structure between the lineage of monkeys and the lineage of apes (including humans) was 7 percent. Between the gibbons and the great apes (again including humans) that difference was 5 percent. Orangutan DNA differed from DNA of the other great apes by just 3.6 percent. All of these figures are unsurprising, since they agree with the deductions drawn from anatomy and geographical distribution.

Now comes the newsy part. Gorillas differed from chimps and from humans by about 2.3 percent of their DNA. Based on the rate at which DNA structure is presumed to change during the course of evolution, that 2.3 percent difference corresponds to about nine million years of divergence. The two chimp species, so similar in appearance, differed from each other by just 0.7 percent. That corresponds to about three million years of divergence between them. And we humans—the closest living relatives that those chimps can claim, aside from each other—differed from both chimp species by just 1.6 percent of our DNA. That corresponds to about seven million years of divergence. By this molecular arithmetic, then, we're about two million years more closely related to chimpanzees than gorillas are.

It was Sibley and Ahlquist's work that gave birth to the informal statement, commonly heard nowadays, that humans and chimpanzees "share 99 percent of their genes." The precise figure seems to be more like 98.4 percent. Other teams of scientists, running similar tests in more recent years, have come up with virtually the same number.

A genetic difference of 1.6 percent isn't much. It's less than the difference between two species of gibbon. As Jared Diamond has pointed out in his contribution to *The Great Ape Project*, it's even less than the difference between *Vireo olivaceus* and *Vireo griseus,* two species of dinky gray bird that you and I couldn't tell apart without consulting a good field guide. "On this basis, then," according to Diamond, "humans do not constitute a distinct family, nor even a distinct genus, but belong in the same genus as common and pygmy chimps." The genus name *Homo* is older than the genus name *Pan*, Diamond explains, so by the rules of biological nomenclature that term should be preserved, and the revised species names should be *Homo troglodytes* for the common chimp and *Homo paniscus* for the pygmy chimp, both of them welcomed as congenerics with *Homo sapiens*.

In vernacular naming, on the other hand, there are no fixed rules. But since *Homo sapiens* is taxonomically outnumbered at a 2-to-1 ratio, Diamond offers the apt suggestion that we think of our own species, henceforth, as the third chimpanzee.

THERE'S AN ugly irony to the fact that the special similarity between chimpanzees and humans, long apparent in an informal way, has brought chimpanzees nothing but special persecution. Dressing them in pinafores and tuxedos for kitschy showbiz performances is only the least of it. Kidnapping chimpanzee infants from their native habitats, for sale to fatuous people who imagine that these babyish apes will make nifty pets, is also not the main problem. Even the vulnerability of the last wild populations of *Pan troglodytes* and *Pan paniscus*, already badly reduced and fragmented, facing further declines due to meat hunting and forest destruction, is only the second most thorny issue in this case. Their exploitation for medical research is arguably a more grievous matter, and certainly a more complicated one.

According to Geza Teleki, as many as five thousand chimpanzees are held in captivity throughout the world. Of that number, about three thousand languish in biomedical facilities, and more than half of those are in the United States. They serve as test subjects for hepatitis and HIV research, among other things. In this country, the minimum cage size allowed for their permanent confinement, under the Animal Welfare Act, was set by federal regulation in 1991: five feet by five feet by seven feet. A chimpanzee held in a cell of that size might survive for fifty years. Some sicken and die much earlier. Some become candidates for euthanasia, after their health has been broken and their scientific usefulness is exhausted. A few are retired to captive-wildlife facilities where their physical and social environment is not quite so bleak. The rest suffer out the slow and perplexing misery of their solitude.

These creatures aren't criminals, and they aren't medical-experiment volunteers. Possibly they don't know and can't comprehend that the species of tall bipedal apes dressed in white coats and armed with hypodermic needles—the species that imprisons and torments them—is also one of their two closest kindred species on the planet. Or maybe they do know, and still can't comprehend.

Medical research using chimpanzee surrogates is not just a hot issue, made hotter in recent years by the rise of the animal-rights movement and, in counterpoint, by the terror over AIDS. It's also, as Cavalieri and Singer realize, a central conundrum within the much larger issue of humanity's relationship to nature. It's bigger than AIDS; it's bigger than the enterprise of according legalistic "rights" to a few thousand species of vertebrates. By a sequence of almost syllogistically linked questions, it leads straight to the core of a very personal yet very global matter— whether we humans are really part of the natural world or not. It demands eventually that we ask ourselves, Is a human life sacred, or just valuable? And the corollary, If a valuable entity proliferates itself by a factor of six billion, is each unit still as valuable as it was?

Another question in the syllogistic sequence owes its sharp focus to Sibley and Ahlquist: Is it justifiable for humans to enslave and destroy creatures that, though preciously scarce, are each 98.4 percent as human as we are? If we'll allow ourselves license to do that, we'll allow ourselves anything.

Maybe one difference between them and us is perceptual acuity. Gordon Gallup showed that a chimpanzee, confronting its own reflected image, is capable of self-recognition. But humans look in a mirror and see only God.

PALPATING THE TUMOR

Cancer and Family, in Utah and Beyond

The closed geological basin that holds Great Salt Lake, just west of the mountains in northern Utah, is shallow and flat like a saucer. A small rise in lake level, therefore, can be accompanied by large changes. During wet eras, the lake grows huge, though never deep. Ten feet of vertical increase expands its area by hundreds of square miles. Briny water creeps out across the flatness, drowning plains and marshes, farmland and highways. Then comes a dry era, and it shrinks back. The cycles are natural, governed by rainfall and snowfall and rate of evaporation. The lake, as we all know, has no outlet. For rainwater and meltwater, it's a terminal destination. For dissolved salts, it's a sump. In autumn of 1982, after unusually heavy September rains, the level began rising. Not long afterward, Diane Dixon Tempest discovered a malignancy in her gut.

The lake level stood at 4,203 feet above sea level. Its historical average was 4,200, and as recently as 1963 it had dropped to a record low of 4,191. Mrs. Tempest's life, like the lake, seemed to be gripped by a cycle; she'd been through cancer before. Back in 1971, she'd endured a mastectomy, coming out of her treatment healthy and otherwise whole. The new problem, a dozen years later, was a Stage III epithelial ovarian tumor. It had metastasized. She would face surgery, then a year of chemotherapy involving an agent called cisplatin. The lake level would continue rising. We're privy to these details, you and I, we strangers, because Diane Dixon Tempest had a daughter and that daughter has written an extraordinary book.

The book is *Refuge: An Unnatural History of Family and Place,* by Terry Tempest Williams. It's a meditation on waterfowl and cancer. Its setting is Utah and it was published in 1991, but to anyone who has ever walked down the corridor of an oncology ward it will seem immediate and close to home.

Williams is a naturalist, a lover of birds, a forthright and graceful writer. She is also a fifth-generation Mormon with deep roots in the local landscape. She has known Great Salt Lake and its natural environs—the Wasatch Mountains, the Promontories, the alkali flats, the sage-covered hills, Stansbury Island, Antelope Island, and not least of all a small feeder stream along the northeast called Bear River—since her childhood. She has swum in the salty water and savored the torment of the brine flies. She views Great Salt Lake as a wilderness. It may be a homely and seemingly sterile sort of wilderness, to our unappreciative eyes, but it's hers. In particular, she has found pleasure (and at times consolation) in a certain wildlife reserve on the northeast shore, about fourteen miles west of Brigham City: the Bear River Migratory Bird Refuge.

This refuge is a low, marshy place, a brackish wetland where the river's fresh water comes into mix with the brine of the lake. The area supports cattails and bulrushes and grasses, burrowing owls on a nearby alkaline floodplain, ruddy ducks, egrets, avocets, pintails, pelicans, ibises, and herons. The ground-level elevation at Bear River is no more than about 4,206 feet. As the lake water rose to new heights, during the 1980s, the refuge became drowned and pickled. Brine shrimp and brine flies displaced frogs and muskrats and fish. The birds went away, the marsh died, leaving Terry Tempest Williams in mourning. She describes those losses in *Refuge.* But that's just the half of it.

She also describes the final four years of her mother's life, which were measured out simultaneously with the inundation. In a sequence of searingly personal glimpses, which seem to have come from a very private diary, she shows us a daughter's imperfect efforts to help her cancer-afflicted mother continue embracing life, right up to the moment of death. This wasn't precisely a struggle *against* death. Death is the foregone certainty, not just for Mrs. Tempest but for all of us, with only timing and mode at issue, and postponing it isn't always identical with continuing to embrace life. The mother's struggle, rather, was to preserve some bit of real vitality, some autonomy, some passion for the world, some spark of joy, notwithstanding the nearness of death. The daughter's struggle was to maintain connectedness. Cancer has traditionally been a lonely disease, but Terry Tempest Williams did her damnedest to violate that tradition.

One unforgettable episode stands emblematic of the rest. Just a few days before her mother's abdominal surgery, the extended family gathered for a summer's day of backyard visiting. Some played gin rummy, some sat on the lawn and talked. Diane Dixon Tempest planted marigolds. Then the sun set beyond Antelope Island. The lake mirrored twilight. They went inside for prayer. "After everyone left," Williams writes, "I asked Mother if I could feel the tumor. She lay down on the carpet in the family room and placed my hand on her abdomen. With her help, I found the strange rise on the left side and palpated my fingers around its perimeter."

CANCER is a malignant disease as distinct from an infectious one. Of all the things that we know and don't know about it, this is probably the most fundamental. Tuberculosis, bubonic plague, leprosy, and AIDS can each be passed directly from one person to another, even malaria can be carried between two humans by a single mosquito, but cancer is different. It's not directly transmissible. Some of the environmental factors that entail a heightened prospect of cancer can be shared, true enough: asbestos in the walls of a school, radon gas in a basement, Epstein-Barr virus (a microbe that's implicated in connection with Burkitt's lymphoma), aflatoxin in stale peanuts, cigarette smoke arriving from upwind. A genetic predisposition of vulnerability to cancer can also be passed—from parent to child. But these are all circumstances and risk factors, not the actual disease. The disease itself can't move laterally from person to person. A tumor is not contagious. That's a blessing for oncologists and family members but for an individual with cancer, I would guess, it makes the lonely situation even lonelier. Cancer, like night, is personal.

The fearfulness and mystery of cancer, the fact that for centuries it was almost inescapably fatal but no one knew why, have exacerbated the loneliness still further. Susan Sontag observed in *Illness as Metaphor* that cancer nowadays arouses the same sort of old-fashioned dread that TB once did. A sociologist of medicine named Arthur Frank, in a less-known book titled *At the Will of the Body,* agreed that cancer carries its own peculiar and illogical stigma: "dangerous, guilty, and unclean." These perceptions seem startlingly wrong-minded, of course, but real people have had to cope with them, while coping also with the real problems of their illness. Frank, a physically unfortunate man with a very healthy spirit, suffered a heart attack in early middle age and then, having recovered from that, contracted testicular cancer. A big differ-ence between those two travails, according to him, was the sense of stigma. Heart attack carried no dark resonance. Cancer did. Con-fronted by cancer, many healthy folk tend to take it for some kind of bad magic that, in Sontag's words, might be "morally, if not literally, contagious." Sontag herself, like Frank, survived a malignancy. So she may have been drawing on personal experience when she wrote that "a surprisingly large number of people with cancer find themselves being shunned by relatives and friends and are the object of practices of decontamination by members of their household, as if cancer, like TB, were an infectious disease." Sontag's book was published in 1978, just before AIDS broke on the scene and preempted cancer's role as the most perfervidly dreaded of diseases in Western society—but the AIDS phe-nomenon only underlines that curious, important point about cancer. AIDS is so scary partly because it *is* an infectious disease (though per-haps not an easily transmissible one); TB in the nineteenth century fit roughly the same profile. Cancer has always seemed ineffably scary, to physically healthy people who find themselves in its vicinity, despite the reality that it's *not* infectious.

This is all sadly ironic. The peculiarities of cancer should allow it to be less lonely than other diseases, instead of making it more so. Besides the fact that it holds no threat of contagion, there's the fact that it's, so common. Epidemiologists report that, in the modern Western world, about a quarter of the population gets cancer. A decade ago that frac-tion would have seemed to me shockingly high; lately, in light of the experiences of my own parents, my wife's parents, and their networks of contemporary friends, one person out of four sounds unrealistically low. Cancer may be a dreadful disease but it's certainly not a rare one. It's as ubiquitous and familiar as the winter wind. It strikes young people occasionally, dramatically, cruelly, and it strikes older people terribly often.

Nor is it new. Papyrus documents from the Old Kingdom of Egypt, almost five thousand years ago, discuss symptoms and treatments of various types of cancer, including cancer of the breast (which was dealt with by cauterization, a brutal procedure most likely dreamed up by some dark-hearted Egyptian man). Burial sites among the Pyramids at Giza contained mummies with bone tumors. Hippocrates, in Greece around 400 B.C., attributed cancer to an excess of black bile, and six hundred years later Galen reaffirmed the same theory, arguing that these unnatural swellings (*tumores,* in his Latin) were solidified black-bile clots. In 1838, Johannes Mueller advanced medical knowledge greatly by showing that a tumor consists of cells. Where did those cells come from? A few decades after Mueller, a scientist named Rudolf Virchow added the crucial insight that *omnis cellula e cellula*—all cells arise from other cells. In the case of cancer, we know now, they arise by uncontrolled replication of a cell whose genetic program has gone haywire. The individual cancer cells aren't inherently inimical to the body, they're not toxic or predatory, but they cause trouble by invasion and obstruction, as they ignore the body's physiological messages about maintaining order and proportion. Just what triggers the runaway replication is still, after five thousand years, not completely understood.

It isn't such a simple disease as malaria or the plague. It isn't even so simple as AIDS, which of course is hideously complicated but can at least be traced to the work of a single virus. Cancer seems to result from many different causes and circumstances, which operate singly sometimes, but more often in combinations. It involves genetic predisposition (in some cases, anyway) converging (in some cases) with causative environmental factors. Besides tobacco and radon gas and aflatoxin and asbestos, a large number of other nasty substances are incriminated, but with the right genes, it seems, a person might enjoy resistance to those carcinogens. Some forms of cancer, on the other hand, are directly inherited by way of one dominant gene: retinoblastoma, for instance, a malignant but usually curable tumor of the eye. Variables of geography, diet, and socioeconomic status also correlate (sometimes suggestively, sometimes confusingly) with cancer incidence. The same Epstein-Barr virus that's associated with Burkitt's lymphoma also causes mononucleosis (but not lymphoma) under some circumstances, and Burkitt's lymphoma in Africa seems to be somehow connected with malaria; in southern China, however, the Epstein-Barr virus is implicated as a cause of nasopharyngeal cancer. No one knows just what this means. Cancer of the esophagus is especially common in certain coastal areas on the Caspian Sea but, again, for reasons unknown. Some families, too, suffer an inordinately high incidence of cancer. One form of such familial affliction is Li-Fraumeni Syndrome, rare but devastating, which seems to result from a single genetic mutation (at the gene locus p53 on chromosome 17p) passed down among generations, and which manifests itself as a family epidemic of brain tumors, leukemia, bone cancer, lung cancer, and breast cancer. Some researchers suspect that p53 in its normal form is a tumor-suppressing gene, and that mutation to a new form destroys its suppressive value. Mutations of p53 have also been found in Burkitt's lymphoma. But the whole picture is still impossibly complicated—a mixture of eloquent patterns, zones of total obscurity, and puzzling exceptions to the eloquent patterns.

Cancer in general seems to share less with other forms of disease than with the inexorable phenomenon of aging. Our bodies do wear out. All our lives we depend on the miraculous process of controlled cell replication, and when the process develops just a momentary glitch, cancerous replication can begin. Maybe we carry the seed of jeopardy at p53. Maybe the carcinogenetic effects of tobacco tars, or asbestos, or aflatoxin, or sodium nitrite, or coffee, or God knows what else, are cumulative over a lifetime toward some critical threshold. Entropy and the mathematics of chance make it seem, though awful, unsurprising.

ALL OF this information might sound distant and clinical. To me it's not. I wish it were. Curious as I might be about the etiology of cancer, the subject has a special immediacy that I don't find in dark-matter physics or island biogeography or the dietary foibles of some Malaysian moth. I intrude here with the first-person pronoun only to avow that I belong to the mainstream: My family has known cancer before and we know it again now.

Probably yours has known it too. If not, I'm sorry to say, the odds are that you're overdue.

Not many families know it more thoroughly than the family of

Terry Tempest Williams. At age thirty-four, because of the death toll among her female relations, she became by elimination a matriarch. In the last chapter of her book, she elaborates: "I belong to a Clan of One-Breasted Women. My mother, my grandmothers, and six aunts have all had mastectomies. Seven are dead. The two who survive have just completed rounds of chemotherapy and radiation." She adds: "I've had my own problems: two biopsies for breast cancer and a small tumor between my ribs diagnosed as a 'borderline malignancy.'" This is her family history, she says.

She is aware of the complicated scientific hypotheses about how cancer happens. She has read about genetic predisposition and about the possible significance of such factors as fatty diet, childlessness, or becoming pregnant after age thirty. Her own hypothesis is that living in Utah—downwind from the Nevada Test Site during those years when American bomb researchers salted the clouds with fallout—may have been far more significant for the women of her family. The testing went on, above ground, setting the atmosphere crackling, between 1951 and 1962. Williams herself remembers a nuclear flash, which she witnessed personally and involuntarily. Sometime before dawn on September 7, 1957, it blanched the desert with its sudden unhealthy light, just as the Tempest family happened to be driving across Nevada. Terry, an infant, was on her mother's lap.

Just less than thirty years later, in January of 1987, her mother died. The level of Great Salt Lake was 4,211. The Bear River Migratory Bird Refuge had disappeared. It was buried under five feet of salty water. These facts were linked emotionally, for Terry Tempest Williams, if not scientifically or logically.

For all the poetic wisdom that she extracts from that linkage, though, and for all the rightness of her anger toward those winds of polity that brought radioactive nuclides to rain on the women (and men) of Utah, another aspect of her book strikes me more forcefully. This one is simpler. Figuratively and literally, she laid hands on her mother's tumor. It was a small act, but heroically indecorous.

She rejected the stigmatization, the fatalistic tendency to view persons with cancer as somehow branded with doom, the surrender to passivity, the obsessive and brittle hope for recovery as though "recovery" were the only state under which life could continue to be lived, and she seized the precious moments of connectedness. She internalized, in a sense, her mother's malignancy. "An individual doesn't get cancer, a family does," she writes. To some extent that's true and to some extent it may be an analgesic conceit of the healthy; her mother, judging from Williams's own honest testimony in *Refuge,* didn't necessarily agree. Still, no healthy person is more entitled to such a leap of presumption than Terry Tempest Williams.

Throughout the four years chronicled in her book, she tried (sometimes obstreperously, and not always in perfect harmony with her mother, let alone her father) to breach cancer's loneliness and share its terror and its pain and its teachings. She fought to maintain connectedness, daughter with mother, healthy person with ill. At one point in the narrative, she describes in fastidious detail the mechanics of changing her mother's morphine-solution intravenous drip. In another vignette, she recounts emptying a pan of her mother's greenish-black vomit, then vomiting after it into the toilet. A doorbell rang as she was bringing her mother a Percodan and, distracted, she swallowed the pill herself. She recalled a line from Auden: "Our dreams of safety must disappear." By the end, she had gone further in that direction than most of us can hope to manage.

But we'll have our own chances.

Refuge is not a cheering or comforting book. It's a stark, ambivalent record of hard-won wisdom and uncertain courage: the courage to hold, the wisdom eventually to let go. It reminds us that, though death may be a solitary experience, living with cancer needn't be. Cancer, as Sontag argued, isn't a metaphor for death. It's a condition that visits only the living.

These are tangled truths, and Terry Tempest Williams doesn't pretend to lay them straight. She tells a story of birds and family. The lake level eventually receded. The Bear River Migratory Bird Refuge came back to life but her mother didn't.

RETHINKING THE LAWN

Turf Warfare in the American Suburbs

There was a time, back in the late Fifties and early Sixties, when I was inclined to view the American lawn as part of a Communist plot. Thousands of square miles of valuable landscape, from Bangor to San Diego, were covered with useless swards of turf. Millions of man-hours (and, more pointedly, boy-hours) were squandered each year on its upkeep. Did that extravagant commitment of resources serve the national interest? Clearly not. Like the helpless GI in *The Manchurian Candidate,* so it seemed, the entire class of American suburbanites had all somehow been brainwashed to execute certain dronish tasks. Mow. Rake. Trim. Fertilize. Kill off the broadleaf invaders with poison. Mow again. It was ruinously stupid. Khrushchev, I figured, had to be chortling up his fat little sleeve.

I conceived and nurtured this theory during my own long boy-hours spent at the exhaust end of a mower—hours that, I believed, would have been far better devoted to more meaningful pursuits (such as baseball, or throwing cherry bombs at hornets' nests, or breaking my nose on the handlebars of a bicycle), if only the cabalists in the Kremlin hadn't managed to perpetrate this wholesale diversion of democracy's young talent into the soulless drudgery of lawn care. *Sputnik* and then Yuri Gagarin had gone into space, after all, while America remained earthbound and I stained my Keds green with grass clippings. I was the only son among three children, and therefore the designated mowist. We lived on a half-acre. Formerly farmland, and before that deciduous forest, amid the rolling hills and the humid breezes of southwestern Ohio, it was relentlessly verdurous.

Our yard was gracefully punctuated with trees, true enough, a smattering of maples and sweet gums and pin oaks planted with heartfelt zeal by my tree-loving father, but most of the area was given to a conventional carpet of grass. The grass, unlike the trees, lacked individuality, conviction, and stature. This was grass like the neighbors' grass, grass by conformity and default, grass maintained in the state of arrested development that distinguishes a lawn from a meadow or a prairie: always growing longer, always demanding to be coddled, never maturing into anything self-sufficient or useful. It would have been different if we'd sold hay.

My father, a reasonable man and a patriot, did most of the landscaping labor himself. He worked cheerily, with an innocent enjoyment of vegetal greenness in any form, from broccoli to sequoias, so I always assumed that he was unwitting to the conspiracy. Besides, why should he be expected to see through to the darker reality, the secret Marxian subtext of American turf warfare, when other suburbanites for a thousand miles in every direction did not? Then one day, decades later, finding myself an adult and a home owner, I bought a mower myself.

Nothing else that I'd ever done was quite so banally momentous. I had registered for the draft, I had voted, I had signed a mortgage, I had gotten a passport, I had once even cohabited with a television; but buying a lawn mower was the act that made me feel like a rock-solid American. Now I was co-opted. I mowed. I raked. I abandoned my conspiracy theory. I scowled at dandelions while they were still yellow and pretty, God help me. I even paid people to apply fertilizer and weed-killing chemicals. The national fetish for epicene lawns, I came to realize, was something more subtle and deeply rooted, not to mention more durable, than mere Communism.

Communism fell; lawnism continued. I began wondering, Why do we do it?

THE NUMBERS are sobering. Americans spend twenty-five *billion* dollars a year on the planting and maintenance of turf grass, including municipal and corporate lawns as well as residential ones. The residential component alone amounts to seven billion dollars in retail trade—that's seven billion spent for mowers and Weed Whackers and leaf blowers and other powered machinery, for fertilizer and seed, for pesticides and hoses and sprinklers and rakes and clippers. Bermuda shorts and plastic flamingos are tallied separately.

The grassy yards of American home owners cover a total of twenty million acres, roughly the same area as Ireland. Unlike Ireland, though, a great portion of the American lawn acreage is arid, or semiarid, or otherwise climatically inhospitable to those species (mostly exotics from Europe) considered seemly for a well-manicured yard. One consequence of the bad climatic match is a need for intensive watering. Roughly 30 percent of the urban water use on the East Coast, by one estimate, goes to lawn irrigation. On the West Coast, with its dry chaparral zone and its desert golf courses, the estimate is 60 percent. No doubt the preternaturally green lawns in Texas and New Mexico and Arizona, in Utah and Nevada, on the dry plains of eastern Montana and the Dakotas, are sucking away a similar share. Almost 800 million dollars' worth of grass seed is sold each year. The annual take by professional lawn-care businesses is about three billion dollars.

These figures reveal that the American lawn ethic, far from being a Commie ruse, is actually in the best tradition of rapacious capitalism. Most of the data I've just cited come from a gently iconoclastic book titled *Redesigning the American Lawn,* compiled by F. Herbert Bormann and some colleagues and grad students in the schools of forestry and art-and-architecture at Yale University. Bormann and company also report that lawn-happy customers account for 25 percent of the profits to the synthetic-fertilizer industry, and that we use up to ten times more chemical pesticides per acre than do American farmers. Pesticides, in this usage, encompass herbicides, fungicides, insecticides, rodent poisons, whatever—any chemical designed to kill a certain type of living creature that's unwelcome on a lawn. And the essence of a traditional lawn, of course, is that virtually *all* types of living creature—except the chosen species of narrow-bladed grass—are unwelcome. In one recent year, the lawn-pesticide market ran to 700 million dollars in sales, representing sixty-seven million pounds of variously lethal chemicals purchased for application to American parks, greenways, golf courses, cemeteries, ball fields, and yards. Any of us who buy organic vegetables or moan about industrial pollution while maintaining a chemically enhanced lawn can take these facts as a challenge to our intellectual coherence.

Redesigning the American Lawn outlines the ecological and environmental costs of all this watering and fertilizing and poisoning, then offers a spectrum of viable alternatives, only some of which will cause your neighbors to surmise that you've gone insane. If your yard lies in Iowa, for instance, you could let the inexorable process of ecological succession return it to tallgrass prairie. If you live in Tucson, you could restore it to crumbled rock decorated with paloverde and scorpions. These would be noble and sensible courses of action that, in the long run, would save money and water and leave your Saturdays open for tennis. But before any further discussion about alternatives to the American norm of lawn maintenance, I want to go back to a more basic question: Where did the norm come from?

HISTORY offers a partial answer. One branch of the historical explanation involves the developing profession of landscape architecture within the last two hundred years. A second branch involves the rise of middle-class suburbs, a phenomenon that began in America during the mid–nineteenth century. A third branch of the story is technological: In 1830, an English carpet manufacturer named Edwin Budding patented the first lawn mower. "Country gentlemen will find in using my machine an amusing, useful and healthful exercise," Budding told the British Patent Office, and he seems to have died without ever being called to account for that piece of egregious hype.

The phrase "country gentlemen" gives an important clue to the sociological context of Budding's invention: No one else, in that era, *had* a lawn. As known in England and continental Europe during the eighteenth and early nineteenth centuries, lawns were a luxury of the wealthy classes, associated with grandiose and carefully landscaped country estates. In France the landscaping style was formalized and geometrical, as ultimately exemplified at Versailles, with flat polygons of lawn interspersed among walkways and canals and mazes and topiary gimmicks and elaborate gardens. In England there was a bit of that too, but toward the end of the eighteenth century a man known as Capability Brown created a new fashion in landscape design by loosening the formality, trading crisp linearity for naturally curvy lines, allowing trees to be trees and bushes to be bushes, and emphasizing large undulant fields of grass. Part of what made Brown's style both appropriate and successful was the English climate—mild in the winter, cool in the summer, wet constantly. Grass *loves* England, and so England justly returns the compliment. But the only mowing performed on Capability Brown's aristocratic lawns was done by hungry sheep or peasant laborers working with scythes. Edwin Budding's nefarious invention came later.

Although the English climate wasn't transferable to America, the seeds of its grasses were, and so was the passion for lawns. That passion established itself here in new soil, with one difference—this was the land of democracy, and so lawns would be democratized too. About the same time as Budding patented his lawn mower, advances in transport technology (the steam railroad, the horse-drawn trolley, then the integrated mass-transit network including both) were expanding the margins of cities and making it convenient for middle-class people to relocate toward those margins. Row houses near the city center had formerly been the preferred dwellings for urbanites who could afford them; but now the preference shifted toward detached houses, each a little American castle, each on its own plot of land. This was the dawn of suburbia.

Meanwhile, several influential American landscapers of the mid–nineteenth century helped to popularize the notion that every residential lot should be upholstered with grass. That notion wasn't a logical necessity; we might just as well have fallen into the tradition of planting our yards full of ivy, or buttercups, or alfalfa. Among the earliest of those American trend-shapers was Andrew Jackson Downing, best known for his *Treatise on the Theory and Practice of Landscape Gardening, Adapted to North America, with a View to the Improvement of Country Residences,* which appeared in 1841. The book was appealingly written for a broad audience and laid strong emphasis on the element of the lawn. In 1853 Downing published another, *Cottage Residences,* encouraging middle-class suburban householders to want their own miniature versions of an Anglo-American country estate. "Quite an area, in the rear of the house, is devoted to a lawn, which must be kept close and green by frequent mowings, so that it will be as soft to the tread as a carpet," he decreed.

There were others who followed Downing's lead. Jacob Weidenmann published *Beautifying Country Homes* in 1870, arguing in its first sentence that such a beautified home "should be sufficiently back from the public road to afford ample room for an unbroken ornamental lawn." Frank J. Scott published *The Art of Beautifying Suburban Home Grounds* the same year, insisting that a "smooth, closely-shaven surface of grass is by far the most essential element of beauty on the grounds of a suburban house." A modern author named Michael Pollan, in his own excellent book of horticultural ruminations, *Second Nature: A Gardener's Education,* suggests that Frank J. Scott's volume "probably did more than any other to determine the look of the suburban landscape in America." May God have mercy on Mr. Scott's soul.

These guys, from Capability Brown to Frank J. Scott, can be seen as the founding ideologues—the Marx and the Engels and the Proudhon and the Fourier and the Trotsky—of American lawnism. And if that's so, then a man named Frederick Law Olmsted might be considered the Lenin. Pollan, for one, credits Olmsted with having virtually invented the American lawn. Although Olmsted is best known as the landscape architect who designed Central Park in Manhattan, he and his partner were also responsible for the prototypical grassy suburb—a development called Riverside, on a bank of the Des Plaines River eight miles west of Chicago. Laid out in 1869, served by railroad from the city, Riverside was intended to accommodate ten thousand people in an affordable middle-class parody of country living, with lots nestled side to side like keys on a piano and a continuous sweep of lawn uniting them all. It was bucolic escapism with a distinctly collectivist tinge, suggesting that maybe my adolescent conspiracy theory wasn't so wrongheaded after all.

ANOTHER partial answer to the mystery of lawnism comes from evolutionary biology. This is the savanna hypothesis, as proposed by a biologist named Gordon H. Orians.

Orians outlined his idea in several semi-obscure papers published during the 1980s, one of them titled "An Ecological and Evolutionary Approach to Landscape Aesthetics," and later expanded and tested the hypothesis in collaboration with a colleague, Judith H. Heerwagen. Orians himself had been drawn to the subject of landscape aesthetics by his studies of habitat-selection processes among birds, which led him to wonder how we humans select *our* preferred habitats. It's a crucial issue in the lives of most individuals belonging to most species, including *Homo sapiens*. "If a creature gets into the right place," according to Orians and Heerwagen, "everything else is likely to be easier." That "everything" refers to all the basics of survival and Darwinian success: finding food, finding water, finding ways to escape from predators and prevail against competitors, finding mates, finding the security and resources necessary for raising young. In the case of our own lineage, Orians figured, the crucial first few million years of evolutionary adjustment occurred in eastern Africa, where early humans and their hominid ancestors had diverged from the arboreal, forest-dwelling apes and adapted themselves to a new sort of life, prowling bipedally through sunny grasslands punctuated only sparsely by trees—the savannas.

For a creature like us, it was the right place. In a tropical forest, most of the edible biomass (animal flesh, fruits, leaves) exists in the canopy, beyond reach of a terrestrial primate. But in savannas, Orians noted, "trees are scattered and much of the productivity is found within two metres of the ground where it is directly accessible to people and to grazing and browsing mammals." There's much more meat on the hoof, in a savanna. There's much more edible vegetation within reach. Also, sight lines across the grasslands are long, so there's better chance for alert hominids to spot a dangerous predator that might turn *them* into meat. And the sparse clusters of trees with low-branching trunks offer emergency refuge—if a lion or a rhino threatens, a hominid can revert momentarily to the arboreal habit. One inconvenience of savannas is the scarcity of water, but even that scarcity becomes an advantage to hunters, by concentrating game around water holes during the dry season. For all these reasons, Orians argued, savannas would have been more hospitable for early humans than either wetter or dryer habitats.

He went a step further. If the fitness of a species to its habitat can be coded genetically in the form of landscape preference, and if a few million years of such coding can survive throughout just a few thousand years of civilization, Orians predicted, then "savanna-type environments with scattered trees and copses in a matrix of grassland should be highly preferred environments for people and should evoke strong positive emotions." The history of landscape architecture, not just in England and America but throughout the world, tends to suggest that he's right.

The spooky implication of Orians's hypothesis, as I read it, is that siting a house in the suburbs on a patch of lawn, with a few low-branching trees at the edges, might be one way of answering a hardwired genetic mandate that's almost as peremptory as hunger or sex.

THEN AGAIN, we don't eat raw zebra meat anymore, most of us. The average American suburbanite doesn't suffer much threat from lions or rhinos. So why should we otherwise prolong our retrograde adherence to a savanna lifestyle?

Besides, living amid grass is one thing; maintaining it in a state of impeccable, homogeneous primness is another. Anyone who has ever slacked off from the regimen of fertilizing and poisoning for a couple years knows that keeping a lawn free of crabgrass and dandelions and chickweed—let alone all those other invaders that waft their seeds through the suburbs, eager for a foothold—goes against all the rules of ecology and entropy. It's as futile as trying to organize a precision drill-team among stray cats.

Are there alternatives for the conflicted suburbanite?

There are always alternatives to nonsense. Bormann and his colleagues, in *Redesigning the American Lawn*, advocate shifting to what they label the Freedom Lawn, a slightly disheveled and heterogeneous plot of postmodern landscaping, as distinct from the Industrial Lawn, with its petrochemical inputs and its assembly-line conformity to convention. Michael Pollan's book describes his own gradual divergence from greensward orthodoxy: He grew bored with mowing and found that, the more serious he became about real gardening, the more dubious he felt about lawns. He planted a rough hedge of forsythia and other mixed shrubbery to break up the Olmstedian continuity between his lawn and his neighbors', and he converted a half-acre of grass into a meadow of daisies and black-eyed Susans. He also arrived at a keen understanding of the larger trend: "Lawns, I am convinced, are a symptom of, and a metaphor for, our skewed relationship to the land. They teach us that, with the help of petrochemicals and technology, we can bend nature to our will." He started letting his patch of nature unbend.

These folks have emboldened me toward a similar course of deviant behavior, which feels long overdue. I've been cutting grass for the past thirty-five years, off and on, but now there's a voice within me saying: No mow.

It's the right time for a radical change, because lately my wife and I have begun planning to build a new house on the same lot where we presently live. We love the location; it's just the old house itself, ramshackle and tiny and mostly held up by bookshelves, that's no longer adequate. So we'll raze the building, or give it away to whoever might want to move it, then cause a more suitable home to be built on our little patch of land. And now that we're imagining into existence precisely the house that will fit our needs and convictions, we've also started rethinking the lawn.

We don't feel the necessity, here in Montana, of mimicking a tropical savanna or an English manor. Beyond that general truth, there are ecological and aesthetic particulars to be settled: what to jettison, what to keep, what to add. The two large mountain ash trees will stay, though building around them may entail extra costs. Mountain ash is a native species hereabouts, thriving robustly through the long snowy winters, the long snowy springs, the scorching dry summers followed by frozen autumns. The riotous hedge of lilacs will stay too; I'm not sure they're native but they don't demand special treatment and no earthly smell is more cheery than blossoming lilacs in early June. The spruce in the southwest corner will stay and, perhaps, the four smallish maples that we planted eight years ago in a gesture of nostalgia to my Ohio roots. The raspberries will be offered room to expand. The lawn itself will go. If any grassy vegetation finds its way into our final collage, I suspect, it will be native species of the region—western wheat grass or blue grama, for instance. It will be welcome to grow tall and seedy, but it will have to get by on its own.

What else will we add? Sagebrush and wild rose and prickly pear might be nice. We don't play barefoot badminton out there anyway. A Douglas fir, a cluster of aspens, maybe a western larch, so we can watch its needles turn yellow in the fall and sprinkle down like shredded saffron. I'd love a big cottonwood, but this isn't a riparian neighborhood and I don't think we should commit to keeping its thirst slaked. Likewise with alder and water birch. But there should certainly be a chokecherry, so that I don't have to continue poaching fruit off the one across the alley. Anything that attracts bumblebees will be encouraged to blossom. We'll have crows and magpies if we have to hire them. And decorative statuary? Well, no plastic flamingos for this ecosystem, but maybe a nice discreet cast-iron effigy of a grizzly. It'll have to be in miniature, though, because ours is a very small lot.

There will be no mowing. There will be no whacking of weeds—the very concept of what a "weed" is or isn't will be thrown into question. There will be no semiannual visits by the chemically armed enforcers from Nitro-Green. There will be raking, OK, maybe, but only to clean up after the deciduous trees and the lilacs. So far as possible, this will be a low-maintenance landscape as well as an ecologically sensible one.

There will be a new meaning given to the notion of yard equipment. My wife may continue to plant wildflowers, but for that she needs little more than a trowel. As for the rest, I've got my own ideas. In place of the mower and the Weed Whacker and the rake and the sprinkler and the spray dispenser for pesticides, I see a folding aluminum lawn chair, an all-weather end table, a pair of sunglasses, a broad-brimmed hat, and a hardback copy of *Leaves of Grass*.

HALF-BLINDED POETS AND BIRDS

The Vision of Robert Penn Warren

Milton, we know, was totally blind. So he wrote about the ways of God. But leave a man with one good eye and he is liable to raise it skyward, squint it, focus it into the middle distance. In two dimensions he will see those animals that move in three dimensions, and what lacks to eyesight can be supplied by heart and imagination. He is liable to write about birds. I have in mind just a pair of cases. These two cases, though, are each imposing enough that together they loom as a pattern. It's a small pattern, more than coincidental and less than profound. I harbor no grand symbolist theory about the pattern and I don't want one. Half-blinded poets and birds: a mystery to be savored, not solved.

The pattern became vivid to me recently when I discovered a new poem by Jim Harrison. I was groping for some good poetry in the aftermath of a death, reading it like you'd take a painkiller, or maybe an antibiotic, when this particular poem made my mouth fall slack. Its title is "Counting Birds." Jim Harrison himself is a one-eyed poet, I knew. He lost the use of his left eye in a boyhood accident, I've been told. I haven't asked him about it directly, neither before nor after my little epiphany over "Counting Birds," because though I know his address I do not know his phone number, or whether he has one, and besides I don't like pestering poets with biographical questions that might help me get a grip on their work. I'd rather speculate recklessly. In any case, knowing the fact of that lost eye has no bearing on Harrison's merit (high, in my view) as a writer. But it does add a little something to this poem.

> *As a child, fresh out of the hospital*
> *with tape covering the left side*
> *of my face, I began to count birds.*
> *At age fifty the sum total is precise*
> *and astonishing, my only secret.*

I wish I could quote you the whole thing but there are laws and proprieties about that. You'll find it in a book called *The Theory & Practice of Rivers and New Poems,* from Clark City Press of Livingston, Montana. There you can read Harrison's proud confession of a lifetime measured, filled, validated by birds. You can see him call back to his mind's eye

> *. . . the twenty-one thousand*
> *snow geese and sandhill cranes at*
> *Bosque del Apache; the sky blinded*
> *by great frigate birds in the Pacific*
> *off Anconcito, Ecuador; the twenty-one*
> *thousand pink flamingos in Ngorongoro Crater . . .*

as well as the hallucinatory ones that fly through his troubled dream-life, those which he labels the "almost deadly birds of the soul." All of them have been counted. All of them count. Birds are important, says Harrison's poem; birds are vital, crucial, as essential to a person as breath and love. The seeing of birds (as distinct from the watching, since it would be perilous to call Jim Harrison a bird-watcher) stands for the very substance of a life richly lived. The seeing of one bird, in Harrison's sense, implies more than an observation distantly made; it implies paradoxically a seizure, a connection, a participatory relationship that nevertheless doesn't violate the bird's tetherless untouchability. And the numbering of birds is the cumulative record upon a man's soul of those acts of connection. The snow geese in his poem are real snow geese, yes, and the flamingos at Ngorongoro are real flamingos. Of course, the birds also represent something more—Lord knows, you might even call them symbolic—but let's not go into that. I'm trying to talk about poets and birds, not commit literary criticism.

> *On my deathbed I'll write this secret*
> *number on a slip of paper and pass*
> *it to my wife and two daughters.*

But even at that late moment may come, says the poem, a cheering possibility of one final bird glimpsed through the death-room window. And counted.

Jim Harrison has seen more birds with one eye than most of us will in a two-eyed lifetime. He has seen them sharper, more immediately, more consummately. This is not an ornithological distinction. It is not about life lists or Leitz binoculars, God forbid. (A one-eyed man, anyway, has only half the need for binoculars.) It's the phenomenon I mentioned. Half-blinded poets seem to appreciate, better than anyone, the import of the sight of a bird.

What does it mean? Maybe that's not an appropriate question. A poet's bird, like a poem, should not mean but be. A poet's bird should swim through the sky of our memory, hefty but weightless, and it should somehow profoundly matter. Harrison's birds do that. He is serious and he is good. We are lucky to have him.

Especially now, when American literary culture (not merely American poetry) has lost its most precious single eye.

THERE WAS a man named Robert Penn Warren. Maybe you haven't heard of him, if you've been trapped in a coal mine for the past fifty-five years or came through puberty into a world of MTV. He was born in Kentucky. He grew at the knee of a Confederate grandfather. He lived a long life of writing and teaching and giving. He received many prizes and honors—eventually, some honors even drew their own validation from the fact of being given to him. Many people thought of him as a novelist. He thought of himself as a poet who sometimes wrote novels. He had fine reddish hair, the chest of a longshoreman, and one blazingly clear eye. He wrote often about birds.

He wrote:

Their footless dance
Is of the beautiful liability of their nature.
Their eyes are round, boldly convex, bright as a jewel,
And merciless. They do not know
Compassion, and if they did,
We should not be worthy of it. They fly
In air that glitters like fluent crystal
And is hard as perfectly transparent iron, they cleave it
With no effort.

He began his writing life as a poet, and as a poet he finished. But his mental and self-conscious life had begun, slightly earlier, on a different course. He spent much of his childhood in the Kentucky and Tennessee woods. He was a "boy naturalist," in his own later words. He knew taxidermy. He kept snakes. Around the same time, age twelve, he took a passionate notion of becoming a painter. What he wanted to paint was animals. He was shipped off for one summer to a convent in Nashville, where a benign watercolorist named Sister Mary Luke gave the young boy instruction. Each day they would go out to the local zoo, Sister Mary Luke would sleep on the grass, and the boy would paint. "I painted the whole damned zoo, practically. And she'd snore and then wake up, then we'd eat all this great delicious feast that the nuns had sent out with us," he later told one interviewer. Also at that age he discovered real poetry in the form of "Lycidas," Milton's elegy to a dead friend. But notwithstanding the painting, the woods, and "Lycidas," he still was pointed toward Annapolis and a career as a naval officer, he thought, when at age fifteen he was blinded in one eye. An accident. Now he couldn't pass the Annapolis physical. So he went off to college at Vanderbilt, where he fell in with a crowd of young men who cared fiercely about making and reading poems. The world lost a naval cadet, small loss, and gained a towering lifetime of poetry.

He wrote:

Long ago, in Kentucky, I, a boy, stood
By a dirt road, in first dark, and heard
The great geese hoot northward.

I could not see them, there being no moon
And the stars sparse. I heard them.

I did not know what was happening in my heart.

It was the season before the elderberry blooms,
Therefore they were going north.

At age sixty-four he rounded to completion a circle that had begun with Sister Mary Luke, publishing a poem about America's first great painter of birds. This was the little book titled *Audubon: A Vision*, from which come the two fragments quoted above. He created a portrait of the historical Audubon in a few verbal strokes and a handful of narrative tableaux. Then through Audubon's eyes he viewed the unspoiled American landscape, the question of a man's destiny, and the trickier question of how a man might either escape his own destiny or align himself toward it like a sighted rifle. For instance, a man's destiny as a wandering painter on the frontier, or his destiny as a poet. Warren became John James Audubon and vice versa. Through his imagined Audubon, he

> *Saw,*
> *Eastward and over the cypress swamp, the dawn,*
> *Redder than meat, break;*
> *And the large bird,*
> *Long neck outthrust, wings crooked to scull air, moved*
> *In a slow calligraphy, crank, flat, and black against*
> *The color of God's blood spilt, as though*
> *Pulled by a string.*

And:

> *Moccasins set in hoar frost, eyes fixed on the bird,*
> *Thought: "On that sky it is black."*
> *Thought: "In my mind it is white."*

Thinking: "Ardea occidentalis, *heron, the great one.*"

And:

Wrote: "*. . . in my sleep I continually dream of birds.*"

The *Audubon* book was Warren's most sustained ornithological reverie. But birds appear frequently throughout his early and late poems. Herons, owls, geese, gulls, crows. These birds are not decorations. They are not merely symbolic. Most of them seem also, like Harrison's snow geese and flamingos, to be real—the carefully counted birds of a man's life, in all their actuality and larger resonance. His attention was especially captured by hawks. "I saw the hawk ride updraft in the sunset over Wyoming," one poem begins, and you feel positive that the poet actually did. "It rose from coniferous darkness, past gray jags / Of mercilessness, past whiteness, into the gloaming." That's from "Mortal Limit." Hawks are also sighted or imagined in "Picnic Remembered," in "Watershed," in "The Leaf," and often enough elsewhere that one critic discussed the fact in a review. Warren conceded that the man had a point, though not one to which he himself had consciously paid any mind, and in mischievous response wrote a fine poem called "Red-Tail Hawk and Pyre of Youth," dedicating it to that critic. The hawk in the poem possesses "Gold eyes, unforgiving, for they, like God, see all." The boy in the poem kills it, stuffs it, and then is never able to forget the cruel ambivalence of his own mock-heroic feat. Probably this one is autobiographical. Decades after his own days of taxidermy, decades before he wrote "Red-Tail Hawk," Warren published a long essay on "The Rime of the Ancient Mariner," that wonderfully lurid lamentation of guilt and consequence over the murder of a bird. Surely it wasn't coincidence.

The critics have theories about all this. Me, I don't have theories. Erudite books have been written, explaining in dry academic intricacy the meanings and secret sources of Warren's poetry. I haven't read them. Maybe I should have; maybe my time could have been better spent. I've only read and reread the poems, the words he put down so carefully, which as far as I am concerned are their own meanings.

My time as a reader of his work overlapped richly with my time as his student and protégé. I knew him first as a novelist, the way most of the world did, and came to his poetry late. I came to his acquaintance almost as late, with forty-three years of age and a chasm of respectful deference between us. The respect never dimmed, but the personal chasm narrowed considerably. He did me a great generosity: He took me to be a callow youth worth teaching, then a writer worth helping, and later a friend upon whom he could call. He'd had a Confederate grandfather and I, with no living grandfathers after childhood, had him. Early on, I lived with his family for a short period of time, shared a room with his son, played tennis with his wife, taught his daughter to drive a car. But I only sat with him once at a campfire in the woods of Vermont, near the mountainside home that he loved, while he suggested I think about (for a doctoral project, though in the upshot I followed his example not his advice, and never bothered to do one) the place of rivers in American literary history. I only walked with him once over the autumn-browned grass of the Little Bear Paw battlefield, in northeastern Montana, keeping my mouth shut while he shaped in his head the ending of *Chief Joseph of the Nez Perce,* his last major narrative poem. I only had one year of his teaching and twenty years of his friendship, and maybe my time during those precious moments could have been better spent. I was young, and clumsy as a colt. I squandered opportunities. I dashed in divergent directions. I treasured my talks with him, but I never took notes.

I scarcely noticed which of his eyes was the good one. I neglected to ask him about birds.

DURING his last decade of life, Warren wrote no further novels. He also renounced expository prose—the sort of criticism and sociocultural essays that he had produced in midlife and that, if he'd done nothing else, would alone have made him an important American writer. Toward the end, he became again and only a poet.

For this there were several plain reasons. Poetry was his first love. It was not a profession or a genre but a way of life, he said. It was a means of seeing and knowing the world. Poetry had helped him through a bad period in his young manhood, a stretch of years dark with depression and with the fear of going totally blind, after he had lost the one eye and when the other showed some signs of failing. Poetry was a means of accepting, or at least dealing with, the world. "It's a way of existing meaningfully as much of your time as possible," he said later. "And that's never much." He had an acute sense of time's remorseless passage, and a fierce unwillingness to tolerate any of life's finite span being squandered or wasted—which bears on the second point about poetry, especially as written in old age. Poems may be short. They may be spectacles of concision. His are. Poetry almost by definition is the wisdom of the epic done in miniature. You might say that a good poem is a shard of mirror reflecting the Milky Way, a cameo locket containing the face of God. I wouldn't say any such thing, because in my prosaic soul I'd be embarrassed. But I'd say this: A good poem is a one-eyed glimpse of a bird in flight. Poetry's special grace, special challenge, is compaction— the compaction of language and meaning and time. A novel might be left half-written on a dead man's desk. A poem more likely would be complete. Even at age eighty, Warren knew he had time, if the muse blessed him, to finish with the making of one more poem.

As he had grown older, he hadn't grown weaker as a poet. Instead, he had taken on the stiffened vitality of a bristlecone pine. Some of the poems from his final ten years are as good as any that he (or any other American, to my taste) ever wrote. One of these is called "Grackles, Goodbye."

Another personal note: If I were allowed just a single sheet of paper to take with me into some desolate exile, "Grackles, Goodbye" would be printed on it.

He wrote:

> *Black of grackles glints purple as, wheeling in sun-glare*
> *The flock splays away to pepper the blueness of distance.*
> *Soon they are lost in the tracklessness of air.*
> *I watch them go. I stand in my trance.*
>
> *Another year gone . . .*

It's a poem about time and mortality, death and love.

It's also a poem about grackles. Grackles are precious, grackles are fleeting, because grackles are part of the world. And this poet did love the world. Seeing those birds go—but I mean *seeing* them go—he recalls how the hand of his mother once held his own hand while he, a child, kicked through autumn leaves on a lawn. The child on the lawn was laughing. The child on the lawn, so innocent of time, was unaware then that some other autumn he would watch—*watch*—his mother's grave being filled with dirt.

> *Grackles, goodbye! The sky will be vacant and lonely*
> *Till again I hear your horde's rusty creak high above,*
> *Confirming the year's turn and the fact that only, only,*
> *In the name of Death do we learn the true name of Love.*

He died in autumn, as the grackles were leaving Vermont.

TIME-AND-MOTION STUDY

Summer Is Short but Bumblebee Economics Are Long

The summer ended here, in this coolish valley of south central Montana, last Saturday afternoon between two o'clock and five.

Saturday morning had been gorgeous, radiant with just the right sort of roasting, late-summer heat to dry the life jackets of vagrant kayakers (including me) on the clothesline and turn the fat northern tomatoes of assiduous gardeners (not including me) from orange to red. I had spent part of that morning in a lawn chair, beneath the mountain ash tree in the backyard, beside the raspberries, savoring strong coffee and reading a fat book very slowly, as though time were an infinite quantity. I was as happy as the tomatoes, since there is no sweeter portion of my day than that morning hour allotted, in good weather, to sitting tree-shaded with a cup of coffee, nose stuck in some hefty tome that has nothing at all to do with a week's narrow work and everything to do with the history of the world. My current choice was Ernst Mayr's *The Growth of Biological Thought*. I had been reading it all summer, nibbling at it daily, and I still wasn't more than halfway through. I had a deadline pressing at me like a sinusitis—the same deadline that came around every month, for delivery of a magazine column on some aspect of nature or science—but during these preciously tranquil moments on Saturday morning I did my best to ignore it. A couple hours past noon, then, the air changed its feel. The sky went gray. A cold, humid breeze came in from the west, canceling any notion of breaking the workday with a long bicycle ramble out toward the foothills. By mid-afternoon, when I went to the post office, folks down on Main Street were in jackets. A few hours later the barbecue grills of the neighborhood failed to be lit on schedule. Gin-and-tonics didn't get made. At dusk my mate and I went off to a Mexican restaurant, wearing corduroy and wool for the first time in months, and asked for a table away from the drafty entrance. At nine in the evening, when we stepped out, it was snowing.

Second week of September. The snow was wet, melting on contact, but it was eloquent nonetheless. By morning there were small drifts in the garden and a dusting across the lawn, so we resigned ourselves to the obvious and turned on the furnace. In some locales, I know, summer shrivels away gracefully like a wilting rose, but in Montana it falls dead like a bull elk shot through the heart.

As always, the event caught me feeling an utterly futile sense of regret and frustration about things left undone. There was a research trip to Tasmania that hadn't happened. Another research trip, to Texas, for communing with rattlesnakes. Trees that didn't get planted, vegetables that didn't get grown. Grown vegetables that didn't get picked. An essay on Dachau and ichthyosaurs that still wasn't written. A nonrefundable ticket to New York City that ended up not being used. Spanish grammar still unlearned, two-year-old correspondence unanswered, backcountry trails unhiked. There'd been not even one kayak getaway to a new river in Idaho. I had imagined I might finish Ernst Mayr and begin reading some other grand intellectual doorstop. I had intended to stay home more, though I had also intended to travel more. I had meant to accomplish more, though also to relax more. And for one other instance, an emblem of summer's sad finitude, take the matter of bumblebees.

DURING some perfect mornings back in June and July, I had watched bumblebees working the raspberry blossoms. I had studied their movements lovingly with my head empty of thought. Stealing time from more linear, more cerebral responsibilities—including a shelf of ecology and entomology books, self-assigned readings that hadn't yet advanced past the status of good intentions—I had paused more than once to contemplate the burly, comic unlikelihood of the bumblebee. Probably that was my single most astute use of the limited summer hours. Bumblebees had served me as a mantra, supplanting cognition, clearing the brain of hub-bub for a few moments of transcendent calm. At the same time, these very bumblebees were themselves another accusation of delinquency. They were my reminder of the paradox that time flows at two different speeds, both too quick and too slow to accommodate the trudging human rhythms of daily life. Even as I sat outside watching the bees lift themselves mightily, industriously from flower to flower, inside my office among the other unread books lurked a pointedly relevant volume by one Bernd Heinrich. It was titled *Bumblebee Economics.* I had owned it and ignored it, now, for six summers.

Of course anyone who truly loves books buys more of them than he or she can hope to read in one fleeting lifetime. A good book, resting unopened in its slot on a shelf, full of majestic potentiality, is the most comforting sort of intellectual wallpaper. For instance, I own a two-volume set of Da Vinci's notebooks, an *Encyclopedia of Papua and New Guinea,* and a biography of Attila the Hun. These are valuable assets just as they sit, making no peremptory claims for my attention. But in my mental card catalog there's another group of books, a small and exclusive group, each of which is tagged: HIGH INTEREST/READ IMMEDI-ATELY. New books enter that category rarely, and some old ones seem never to get out. I have a volume of Rousseau's *Émile* that's been classi-fied HI/RI since 1976. Jacob Burckhardt's *The Civilization of the Renais-sance in Italy* and a severe, intriguing volume called *Scientists Under Hitler* are others. Life is too short for an earnest plodder like me, who reads only as fast as his lips can mime the syntax. Bernd Heinrich's *Bumblebee Economics* falls in the same category. I had never stopped intending to read it—soon, any week now—and meanwhile six years had gone by in a blink.

But not a seventh, I decided. Read it, by God, or throw the damn thing away. So on Monday (call this the first Monday of autumn, fresh upon that weekend snow) I wrapped myself in a warm jacket and went out to the lawn chair with *Bumblebee Economics.* It was a cold after-noon, beneath a sky the color of freezer-burnt fish. One yellowed moun-tain-ash leaf fell into my lap like a bookmark. There were no blossoms left on the raspberries, which had long since died back, and not a living bumblebee in sight.

◉   ◉   ◉

QUICKLY I learned why I'm partial to these animals. "Bumblebees are tundra-adapted insects," writes Heinrich. They are especially suited by evolution, he explains, for life in the short glorious summers and long daunting winters of the high latitudes. Their anatomy, their physiology, and their life-history cycles are all shaped toward making the best of a climate so cold that most insects would find it intolerable. Other groups of bees, such as leaf cutters, are plentiful in the tropics; bumblebees are scarce in the tropics and dominant in the lands of deep winter. They can be found widely from the Arctic Circle to Tierra del Fuego, but they do best near the north and south extremities of that range, where smaller and less cold-hardy bees can't compete. Bumblebees have been seen flying through chilly wind and rain, even through snow, at temperatures as low as 25 degrees Fahrenheit—an unachievable feat for a honeybee or a grasshopper. In order to flourish in those frigid situations, they're adapted for practicing two types of frugality: They conserve heat, and they make good use of time.

We've all heard the canard (masquerading as scientific fact that someone remembered someone else having read somewhere, always untraceable and unconfirmed) that the flight of a bumblebee is aerodynamically inexplicable. Truth is, it's entirely explicable, but not according to the fixed-wing aerodynamics of a Boeing 747. Rather, a bumblebee holds itself airborne more as a helicopter does, its little thin wings moving like reverse-pitch, semi-rotary blades. To accomplish the trick, those wings must beat nearly two hundred times per second. And to support that pace of activity, the bumblebee (despite its lummoxy appearance) must maintain a frenetic metabolism. Its bodily heat-engine operates at high speed—higher than that of a shrew, higher than a cliff swallow, higher even than a toy poodle on uppers. During flight, the metabolic rate of a bumblebee is about twice (for its weight) the rate of a hummingbird.

The bumblebee generates this metabolism by burning sugar, derived from the nectar of flowers. Sugar, in fact, is the sole sustenance of an adult bumblebee (though the immature bees are fed pollen, containing protein for the growth of their tissues), and during summer, when its metabolism is running full speed, an adult held in confinement without food for as long as an hour is liable to die of starvation. This is a big animal—in relative terms, at the insect scope—with big needs. Its sugary nutriment is pumped through the bloodstream to a set of four muscles, which fill the bee's great husky thorax. Within the cells of those muscles, the sugar molecules are combusted, providing energy for beating the wings and, just as importantly, for heat.

Bernd Heinrich has watched bumblebees over a long span of years. He concludes that "a high temperature of the thoracic flight musculature is both a necessity and a consequence of the bumblebee's flight metabolism." By means of some ingenious lab experiments, involving both tethered and free-flying bees, Heinrich found that the thoracic temperature must be not just high, but steadily maintained within a high, narrow range: between 86 and 111 degrees Fahrenheit. When the thoracic muscles are cooler than 86, the bumblebee can't fly; above 111, those muscles suffer damage like an overheated engine. So how does the poor creature function in an Arctic environment—where summer temperatures between dawn and dusk fluctuate drastically, and where the wing muscles of an insect stand to be chilled or overheated far outside that range?

The bumblebee has an elaborate, multipurpose system of thermoregulation. On a cold morning it shivers, firing the thoracic muscles in rapid succession (without engaging the wings), and this shivering raises the muscle temperature to 86. The thick coat of fur on its thorax provides insulation to hold that temperature steady. The very size of the bumblebee, far bigger than other bees, also helps it retain heat, since heat retention correlates positively with the volume-to-surface ratio. Meanwhile a countercurrent heat-exchange system, built into circulatory conduits where they carry blood between thorax and abdomen, holds heat in the thorax while letting the abdomen stay cool. Then in the blaze of the afternoon that heat-exchange system is bypassed, allowing heat to flow back to the abdomen, from which it radiates away. This active heat-regulation mechanism gives the bumblebee worker a great advantage: temperature control of the internal anatomy, independent of external heat sources. That allows it to plow on through bad weather like a bear or a raven or some other bulky, endothermic animal.

A bumblebee queen uses the same two-mode thermoregulatory mechanism in springtime, during the colony-founding period when she nurtures her first offspring. She has emerged from hibernation, gravid but alone. Single-handedly, she must gather food, she must incubate her eggs and then the larvae that hatch from them, while conserving her nectar, her heat, and her time. So she holds heat jealously within her thorax when she needs those muscles warmed for flying; she releases heat generously through a bald patch on her abdomen when she sits warming her brood; and she makes no wasted movements. She memorizes the best path to the best flowers. She *walks* from blossom to blossom when that mode of travel is more energy-efficient than flying. She maximizes the return on her efforts by avoiding, somehow, those flowers that have already been drunk at by other bees. She cannot afford dithering, play, prodigality, or digression of any sort. In the brevity of an Arctic summer, wasted movements are what leave a bumblebee queen caught by first frost with a nest full of unripened heirs.

These are fiercely efficient insects. In some sense, they hear and heed every tick of the season's clock. A dawdling bumblebee is likely to die without passing on her genes. A successful bumblebee, a matriarch, a founder of rich bumblebee lineages, is one who sticks strictly to business. How terrible for her. Reaching that point in *Bumblebee Economics,* I was almost sorry I knew.

Then, in a chapter devoted to pollination behavior and the cost-efficiency of collecting nectar, I read this:

> Could the bees determine by scent whether or not a flower had been visited? I decided to take seriously the aphorism about sniffing the flowers. I lay back in the clover with my eyes closed, and a student held blossoms to my nostrils.

With almost 90 percent accuracy, Heinrich reports, he himself could distinguish by smell between clover blossoms containing nectar and clover blossoms without. His little experiment reveals that the careful flower-by-flower selectivity of bumblebee foraging may well have an olfactory basis. More importantly, it reveals also his grasp of the paradoxical truth that time flows at two different speeds, both too quick and too slow for a purely scientific approach to bumblebees.

The sun came low from the west by now, and the dregs of my coffee were like ice water. I was alone in a yard without bees. It was late on a cold, beautiful, autumn afternoon. I savored Bernd Heinrich's good example. Having converted this month's deadline into an opportunity to contemplate bumblebees, I wondered how I might also justify—about the same time next month, under the same pressure—sneaking off into Burckhardt's *The Civilization of the Renaissance in Italy*. Maybe an essay on Michelangelo and the geology of Carrara marble? A disquisition on hydrological turbulence as revealed in the drawings of Leonardo? Life in its richness goes by too quickly, I thought, for a person to do it all justice. And then I sat awhile longer, without thinking about anything.

❋ V ❋

TRICKS OF THE LIGHT

THE BOILERPLATE
RHINO

Nature as Concocted, Nature as Found

The black-footed ferret is now available at Blockbuster Video, yours on a three-evening rental for only two bucks. Also currently in stock are the orangutan, the polar bear, the leopard, the great white shark, the mountain gorilla, the American bison, the duck-billed platypus, and the wombat. The place has its own menagerie. Ignore the shelves labeled DRAMA CLASSICS and COMEDIES and ROMANTIC TEARJERKERS, ignore COPS & ROBBERS and SCHWARZENEGGER and HORROR and SUPER NINTENDO, proceed on toward the back of the store, and there you find it, categorically distinct and conveniently accessible: NATURE. You can pick out a handful of rare and prodigious species, tote them home in your grocery bag or your briefcase. On Tuesdays, take two for the price of one. Obviously I'm talking not about the actual flesh-and-blood creatures but about what passes in our age for the phenomenological equivalent: their images, expertly captured, potently edited, and preserved with the permanence of plastic, which surpasses the permanence of life.

The personnel at Blockbuster will even rent their wares (I have verified this experimentally) to a curmudgeonly Luddite who doesn't own so much as a television, let alone one of those VCR contraptions, and who can therefore only watch *The Mysterious Black-Footed Ferret* in an audiovisual cubicle at his local library, wearing headphones, feeling like a time-spy from the eleventh century. The clerks don't care; they want cash and two ID cards, but actual television-ownership isn't mandatory. They offer also *The Smile of the Walrus,* from Jacques Cousteau, to warm your den at the touch of a few buttons. They provide *Lions of the African Night,* from National Geographic, to roar at you on command. And, sure, they've got rhinos if you want rhinos. You can go birdwatching in Botswana without suffering the jet lag or the shots. You can get a zoo-visitor experience without even crossing town to the zoo. It's the age of takeout, and now the zoo comes to you, each beast caged tractably in a plastic cassette.

This phenomenon, the mass-marketing of video nature, carries an ambivalent mix of implications. The positive ones are straightforward. People learn a fact or three about those endangered ferrets. People enjoy the sense of spectacle. People witness amazing processes and behaviors that they never otherwise could, and as witnesses they acquire, maybe, a certain vested concern for the preservation of wild places and wild beings. The negative implications are less patent and more complicated. Among them: People are lulled, pandered to, hypnotized, and misled. They learn to take nature for granted, as just another form of human amusement, like C-Span or Monday Night Football. They become spoiled to the small natural wonders in their local woodlands, since the bigger wonders of Malaysia or Peru are served up more vividly on the tube. They accept the video entertainments as substitutes for, not just reflections of, real living leopards or bears or gorillas. Worst of all, they are enticed to believe that nature as they have seen it—concocted expertly from flickering photographic images—represents nature as it exists.

Of course it doesn't. Images can lie, even photographic images. Time is always compressed, context is often concealed or altered or flouted, in a filmic composition. Nature in reality is more diffuse, more tedious, less satisfactorily dramatic, and often more perishable than a video documentary of some marvelous ecosystem or species, plus in reality there's no heart-filling musical score. Drama is artifice—and natural-history drama no less so than other sorts. Nature as commonly found (without the telephoto lenses, without the cutaway nests, without the editing) is *not* very dramatic. The drab truth is that you could stand under the Amazon canopy for a month, with a good set of binoculars,

while the microbes ate your feet, and never catch a single glimpse of cop-
ulating monkeys or a snake in the act of swallowing a bird.

Charles Siebert highlighted this truth in a recent issue of *Harper's*.
In an essay titled "The Artifice of the Natural," Siebert noted that
nature documentaries on television are unnaturally "rapid, focused, and
framed," whereas an actual forest is "wide, old, and slow," sublimely
indifferent to any human on the lookout for zoological drama. In fact,
Siebert argued, the average nature show is actually less like a forest than
like a city, "both entities being elaborate human constructs: fast-paced,
multi-storied, and artificially lit."

What are the historical roots, Siebert wondered, of the nature-show
phenomenon? Where did the mass-market packaging begin? Scanning
old tapes at the Museum of Television and Radio, he traced back to the
early efforts of Jacques Cousteau, Marlin Perkins, and a few others.
Even before the infamously campy Mutual of Omaha's *Wild Kingdom*,
as it turns out, Perkins had a TV show called *Zoo Parade*. That was in
1955. And still earlier, in the Thirties, Perkins did a radio show about
nature from a station in St. Louis—until a mishap one day with an electric eel, which sent a jolt through him and into his microphone and
thereby blew out the station's power.

Siebert's historical search could have gone back even further, if he
hadn't chosen to limit himself to such electromagnetic media as television, radio, and eels. One of the first mass-market images of nature was
produced almost five centuries ago in the medium of wood. It was part
of Gutenberg's revolution, not McLuhan's. It came out of Nuremberg,
Germany, in the year 1515.

ON MAY 20, 1515, a rhinoceros arrived in the port of Lisbon, as
dolefully and terminally displaced as King Kong in New York. Good
lord, what is it? people wondered. No such zoological marvel had been
seen in Europe within recent memory—possibly, not since the exotic
menageries of imperial Rome. The animal had been sent as a gift from
Sultan Muzafar II of Gujarat, in western India, to King Manuel I of
Portugal. The king, finding himself in no particular need of a live rhinoceros (which, taxonomy aside, he probably considered a white elephant), saw fit to pass along this unwieldy item to Pope Leo X, but in

the course of being shipped onward to Italy it died. Details of its death are sparse and not fully reliable: One account says that the ship sank but that the rhino's corpse was recovered, which sounds somehow more simple than it should. How do you dredge up a drowned rhinoceros from the floor of the ocean? Anyway, instead of a live rhinoceros, the pope received a stuffed (and perhaps soggy) carcass. This was the beast on which the great German artist Albrecht Dürer, up in Nuremberg, based a pen-and-ink drawing that he titled *Rhinoceron*.

Dürer's drawing survives in the British Museum. But that one-of-a-kind artifact isn't what concerns us.

From the drawing, Dürer produced a woodcut, probably executed in pear wood. The carving itself was most likely done by a specialist artisan, a *Formschneyder,* under Dürer's close supervision. From that woodcut block, multiple prints were taken—no one can tell us the exact number, but many—and in this form the image spread across Europe. The dead rhino had intersected with European culture at just the right historical moment to become a pop icon. If it had arrived a hundred years earlier, before Gutenberg's invention and the development of cheap mass-produced paper and the consequent rise of the printing trade, it might have been painted in oils by a medieval allegorist, it might have been memorably drawn in ink or in charcoal, but neither a painted nor a sketched image would have been *published*. Its portrait would have hung in the house of some burgher or in the castle of some prince, precious and singular on its wall, seen by not many eyes. And if the animal had arrived a hundred years later, it would have come too late to inspire one of the prototypic images in the foundational phase of graphic printing. In that case, its likeness would have been just one among hundreds in the published bestiaries of the seventeenth century, exerting no extraordinary force. But instead of being too late or too early, it arrived when it did, perfectly timed to achieve international fame.

Dürer himself never saw the pope's rhinoceros, either while it was alive or as a carcass. He concocted his image secondhand, from a sketch and a description sent to him by letter from Lisbon. Dürer was a consummate draftsman—with a genius hand, a precise eye, and a hungry curiosity toward the natural world that, among Renaissance artists, was second only to Leonardo's. Given his drawing skill and his passion for accuracy, it's only natural to assume that his woodcut would have looked different, and possibly much different, if he had inspected the rhino personally. Probably he'd have drawn the animal as he saw it, and no doubt he'd have seen it pellucidly. Instead he produced a stunning cartoon, a tendentious bit of surrealism with a presciently modern zing, centuries before the birth of, say, Ralph Steadman.

Having heard that the rhinoceros was plated protectively with panels of stiff skin, he gave it a suit of armor. And not just any armor, but armor closely analogous to what a German knight would have worn in the feudal scuffles of Dürer's own era, complete with a gorget at the throat, a breastplate around the midsection, pauldrons for the shoulders, faulds skirting the thighs, and nicely aligned rivets along the plate edges. He canted back the angle of the horn, making it more dangerous as a weapon for hooking and ripping. He applied arabesques of detail, and no small amount of gnarly menace, to the face. For good measure he added a second horn, smaller, pointing forward from the back of the neck. The lower legs he wrapped in chain mail. As Dürer imagined and portrayed it, the rhinoceros was a magnificent aggressor, surly, invulnerable, built to cause terror wherever it strode: a war rhino. His vision, misleading as it was, may have done much to set the tone of European perceptions of rhinos for the next four hundred years.

At the top of the woodcut, in Gothic lettering, Dürer placed an inscription. "After Christ's birth, the year 1513, on May 1, this animal was brought alive to the great and mighty King Emmanuel at Lisbon in Portugal from India," he wrote. "Its color is that of a freckled toad and it is covered by a hard, thick shell. It is of the same size as an elephant but has shorter legs and is well capable of defending itself. On the tip of its nose is a sharp, strong horn which it hones wherever it finds a stone." He further declared that it's the deadly enemy of elephants, which it tears open at the belly with its horn, and that the rhino itself is impervious to being stabbed by a tusk, thanks to its armor. When an elephant lies disemboweled and helpless, the rhinoceros finishes it off by strangulation, Dürer claimed, though he didn't explain how. Amid all the other items of misinformation, his 1513 date was two years too early.

"They say that the Rhinoceros is fast, cunning, and daring," he added. Dürer's rhinoceros, anyway, was forevermore all of these things, even if the pope's rhinoceros hadn't quite been.

One piece of evidence tells us that Dürer himself intended this image for mass-market publication: the decision to make it a woodcut, as distinct from a copperplate engraving. Both those techniques had come into use for graphic printing at Dürer's time, and he was a master of both. His father, a Nuremberg goldsmith, had taught him as a boy to inscribe delicate patterns onto metal with a fine-pointed burin, and some of Dürer's mature engravings, such as *Knight, Death, and Devil* and *Melencolia I,* are among the most gracefully spooky images of the German Renaissance. Generally, engraving technique offered the advantage of allowing finer lines and more intricate detail than a woodcut. But an engraving also had to be inked and wiped separately for each print, and its finely incised lines tended to wear out rather soon; woodcut prints, on the other hand, could be run off more quickly, using the production-line capacities of a Gutenberg press, and the coarse but sturdy lines of the woodblock held up throughout many repetitions. When an artist chose the woodcut technique in preference to engraving, that choice implied a willingness to compromise the delicacy of each individual print for the sake of producing more copies. It was a familiar trade-off: popular appeal versus subtlety. A woodcut print was a democratic form of art, in those days, cheap enough to be bought and enjoyed by the folks in the humble cottages. Dürer himself was a man of expensive middle-class tastes, with a good head for business, and large-edition woodcuts were one of the ways he made his money.

His rhino woodcut—the carved block itself, not just the image—far outlived him. At least nine separate editions were eventually run from it, each edition comprising unknowably many prints. By the time of the eighth edition, produced by Dutch printers in the seventeenth century, the block showed a crack that slashed through all four of the rhino's legs, plus wormholes in the neck, eyelid, and horn. That it was still being printed, wormholes and crack and all, suggests the exceptional graphic power of Dürer's image. And that image carried even beyond the nine editions; Dürer himself inserted the same rhino as a decorative touch in a huge composite woodcut, *The Triumphal Arch,* done as a commission for the emperor Maximilian. It was also copied by other artists. One of the knock-off versions appeared, soon after Dürer's death, in Konrad von Gesner's volume *Historia Animalium.* Another close copy showed up in a collection of animal and plant drawings assembled by Ulisse Aldrovandi at the end of the century, and still another in the Reverend

Edward Topsell's *Historie of Foure-footed Beastes,* published in 1607. When Europeans of that era imagined a rhino, either as a real animal or as a fabulous one, they imagined it according to Dürer. Still later, of course, there were not just plagiarizations but many respectful reprints in books about Dürer's life and work, about the art of the woodcut, about artistic representations of nature in general. From the year 1515 until now, it has probably been the single most familiar image of a rhinoceros among people who have seldom if ever laid eyes on the real thing. In fact, its broad popularity tends to overshadow Dürer's whole body of diverse, wonderful work. Toss the name Albrecht Dürer at a person with some interest in art, ask for a memorable example, and that person is likely to mention the boilerplate rhino.

A similar image even appears—fleetingly, in connection with an old text on Chinese folk medicine, including the uses of rhino horn—in a National Geographic documentary titled *The Rhino War,* now available at Blockbuster Video.

DÜRER was fascinated by the natural world, at least as a source of visual images. He created some striking portraits of animals and plants. In most of those cases, he seems to have worked either from live models or from dead specimens, not from imagination or hearsay, and he rendered the real creatures with passionate exactitude. During his first visit to Venice he found things to interest him at the city's fish market, producing a watercolor of a crab so minutely specific that it could stand as a scientific illustration. He also did a splendid lobster. Later he painted a young hare, its eyes bright, its ears erect, its fur textured with such fastidiousness as to anticipate photo-realism, crouching self-consciously as it must have in Dürer's studio. At the height of his powers he did a dead duck, a dead roller (a bird of the family Coraciidae, with iridescent wing feathers of brilliant blue and green), and, still more striking, the wing of a roller, as a disjointed study, sedulously realistic in its treatment of every feather. Even his conventional religious scenes were sometimes festooned with fauna—for instance his *Virgin with a Multitude of Animals,* in which the madonna and child sit surrounded by two owls, two swans, a parrot, a fox, a crab, a frog, and a stag beetle. Not all of his animals, though, were impeccably lifelike. In his early woodcut of Saint Jerome (that's the fellow who, according to pious legend, pulled a thorn from a lion's paw), Dürer's lion is too small, too skinny, with too tiny a head; it looks like a cocker spaniel with an embarrassing summer haircut. But later in life Dürer saw his first living lion, at a zoo in Belgium, after which his lions were vastly more leonine.

Probably his finest work in this vein is a watercolor-and-gouache painting called *The Great Clump of Turf,* which features dandelions and ribwort and meadow grass and a few other herbs, all seen up close and from ground level as though they're a hummock of sizable trees. At first glance it seems a humdrum, uninteresting image, but more careful inspection reveals that Dürer made these little plants into something profound—a world, an ecosystem—by treating them with profound respect. How exactly did he do it? Well, he used a trick of perspective to give them stature, but that wasn't all. He also paid them the compliment of precision.

IT MIGHT seem incongruous that the same man who painted *The Great Clump of Turf* and the roller's wing and the hare—each one a singular image showing fervent concern for anatomical accuracy—could have also accounted for those nine editions of cartoonish rhino. It seemed incongruous to me, especially after my hour in that library cubicle watching *The Rhino War,* which turns out to be a compelling and clear-sighted film, full of real animals bearing not much resemblance to Albrecht Dürer's notional beast. Matched against those photographic images, Dürer's woodcut looks like fantasy. But hold on, there's another line of sight onto this matter. *The Rhino War* deals only with poaching against the black rhino, *Diceros bicornis,* an African species brought to the verge of extinction by gangs of horn hunters within the past twenty years. Four other rhinoceros species survive elsewhere in the world. Three of those, native to various regions in Asia, are also severely endangered but were beyond the purview of this particular film.

Africa's rhinos have two prominent horns. Dürer's has one. So I consulted a photo in a mammal encyclopedia.

Specifically, I looked at *Rhinoceros unicornis,* the one-horned Indian species, since that's what Muzafar II must have sent from Gujarat to the king of Portugal. Although I had seen *R. unicornis* in the flesh (some years ago, at a reserve in Nepal), I had managed to forget its appearance. What I found now was a peculiar-looking animal, even by rhinoceros standards. It differed drastically from the two smooth-flanked African species. Its stiffened skin seemed to be gathered in slabs—like a suit of armor, yes, complete with breastplate and paul-drons and faulds—and pocked with dermal protuberances resembling rivets. It was surprisingly similar, by God, to the Dürer image. Considering that Dürer worked from hearsay, it was shockingly similar.

This bit of elementary research obliged me to recognize what I should have already known: that the least accurate aspect of Dürer's woodcut is the inscription. His date is wrong; his dermatology is right. His artwork is reasonably faithful, compared to that business about a toad-colored animal in a "thick shell," big as an elephant, cunning and deadly, honing its horn on a stone. His rhinoceros is better than it reads.

That constitutes a chastening reminder for someone like myself, with a bias in favor of the written page and a sour prejudice against mass-market video: a reminder that, although images can be deceptive, they don't stand convicted alone. Writing is just another form of con-coction. Words can lie too. You can trust me on this, probably.

LIMELIGHT

The Little White Octopus on the World Stage

In the future, Andy Warhol predicted, everyone will be world-famous for fifteen minutes, even marine biologists who study octopus behavior. A woman named Janet Voight has grounds to believe he was right.

Dr. Voight is a curator of invertebrate zoology at the Field Museum of Natural History in Chicago. She has a strong character and a good sense of humor, which no doubt have proved useful recently. After twelve years of careful research, much of it published in scientific journals but inconspicuous to the larger world, she found herself suddenly flash-fried by the limelight of international fame. It happened for reasons having little to do with the substantive themes of octopus biology or her own work; it happened because the world loves to think about kinky sex. On October 13, 1994, the British journal *Nature* published a one-page report, by Voight and her colleague Richard A. Lutz, a respected deep-sea ecologist at Rutgers, describing an extraordinary sexual encounter between two octopuses.

This particular encounter had occurred in December of the previous year, at a site on the bottom of the eastern Pacific, along an active ridge of tectonic spreading known as the East Pacific Rise. The depth there, hundreds of miles off the coast of Central America, was more than eight thousand feet. By a wild stroke of luck, the two octopuses had been noticed by scientists (including Lutz himself) aboard the *Alvin,* a deep-diving research submersible, which was passing nearby. The tropical Pacific at eight thousand feet down is a limbo of sunless darkness, as well as extreme pressure and near-freezing cold, but the submarine carried floodlights and strobes. Before the *Alvin* was obliged to resurface, its high-resolution video camera had shot a vivid sixteen-minute sequence of tape, capturing the octopuses in an act of copulation.

One of the two octopuses was small, graceful, and white. Its eyes stood forward strangely from its head, dark dots at the ends of protrusive, fleshy tubes, presenting a profile unlike anything in the known octopus gallery. The second octopus was large and dark. The slender white octopus embraced the big dark octopus from above, shifted position, and then delicately inserted its copulatory arm into the big octopus's body cavity. The big octopus acquiesced.

What made their encounter extraordinary? Three things. First, it involved two different species. Second, both individuals were males. Third, it occurred in the vicinity of a hydrothermal vent, a bizarre sort of ecosystem based on hot water and lava rock and hydrogen sulfide and bacteria, undiscovered by science until 1977. Having documented the interaction on tape, Lutz shared the document with Voight because he knew she was capable of helping him identify—and maybe understand—what he had seen. They wrote their joint paper and sent it to *Nature* without foreseeing that it would trigger an international fit of giggles. Needless to say, the part about the hydrothermal-vent ecosystem was not what inspired the world's media to come clamoring for sound bites from Janet Voight. Even the different-species aspect seemed secondary. *Homosexual octopuses on videotape* was the high concept that took the story global.

As published in *Nature,* the report also included a color still from the videotape. It shows a little white shape enwrapping a big rosy-gray shape. The photo is mildly interesting at first glance. On a second or third inspection, when you know what you're looking at, it's amazing.

THE EDITORS of *Nature* release an advance press packet for each issue, held under blackout until the day before publication. Promptly when the press blackout lifted, Voight's phone started ringing. It kept ringing, crazily, for days. CNN called. *USA Today* called. The *Daily Telegraph* and the BBC called from England, the CBC from Canada, the Australian Broadcasting Corporation from down under, *Der Spiegel* from Germany, *Libération* from France, and a gay- and-lesbian newspaper known as the *Windy City Times* from right there in Chicago. The magazines *New Scientist, Discover, Omni,* and *Self* contacted Voight, and the *Donahue* show requested a copy of the videotape for the direct edification of its audience. The Associated Press put out a story on its wires, derived from an interview with Voight, that would be reprinted in local newspapers under such headlines as "Weird Science: Sex and the Single Octopus." Some of the calls came from reporters with no clue what the original *Nature* paper said, let alone what it might or might not mean; they had seen the skimpy but prominent *USA Today* article and merely wanted a quote or two for themselves. A few reporters did get some scientific substance into their stories—Usha Lee McFarling wrote a sensible piece for the *Boston Globe*—but they were exceptions. Then, with another ring of the telephone and before she knew what was afoot, Janet Voight found herself on a talk radio show out of West Palm Beach, Florida, facing a host with a homophobic edge.

Isn't it true, the man wanted her to confirm, that these animals had retreated to the dark depths of the Pacific because they were *so ashamed of what they were doing?* Well, no, Voight explained civilly, that notion was not scientifically supportable. "I talked about depth distribution and species limits," she recalls, and when the host went back to his preferred theme, she persisted stubbornly with hers. "I was not to be shut up." But the experience travestied her professional expertise and, still more importantly, violated her personal sense of liberal tolerance. "I mean, this really upset me," she says.

The media whoop-de-do continued through October and November. By the middle of December it had tapered away, and in January she got only a few calls. Though it amused her to see both *Playboy* and *Esquire* taking notice, she was "terribly tired of the whole thing."

The glare of the limelight having dimmed, Voight's working life is now back on track. She has papers to write, specimens to dissect and analyze, while she continues pondering broad issues in marine biology. Lately she has been reading up on the ecological communities associated with hydrothermal vents, and has expanded the scope of her attention from shallow-water octopus species, her specialty, to include the creatures of the deep. She can look back on her moments of notoriety not just with amusement, but with some generosity.

Was all the media interest, and all the public appetite for it, merely idle and prurient? No, she doesn't think so. "A lot of people are really fascinated," she says, "by the thought of life in this completely alien environment." Voight shares that fascination, and finds herself wanting to go deeper.

IN THE early nineteenth century, the ocean depths were believed to be *azoic*—that is, utterly lifeless. The word was coined by a British naturalist named Edward Forbes, who surveyed the Aegean in 1842 and found no signs of life below three hundred fathoms. Although a careful researcher, Forbes suffered the disadvantage of never having *seen* what goes on at three hundred fathoms; he did his dredging and made his deductions from the surface, as any prudent Victorian air-breather would.

Almost a century later, that disadvantage was overcome by William Beebe, the intrepid soul who developed the bathysphere. Beebe's bathysphere was a steel ball with a tiny window, in which a person could be lowered by cable from the side of a ship. His record descent to 3,028 feet was eventually topped—or rather, bottomed—by deeper dives, and Beebe's bathysphere gave way to Auguste Piccard's bathyscaphe, which could travel down and back up without need of a cable. The bathyscaphe worked by regulated buoyancy, like a hot-air balloon. James Hamilton-Paterson, in a book called *The Great Deep,* reports these developments and also the fact that, by 1960, an improved bathyscaphe had plumbed the Marianas Trench. The trench bottom is almost 36,000 feet down, and the oceans don't get any deeper.

These are the pioneers—Forbes, Beebe, Piccard, among others—who probed the way for the deep-diving submersibles of our own era. The vehicles of today are better equipped with scientific gear, and more mobile horizontally, and presumably safer, if not more roomy. Still, there can't be many earthly experiences scarier than dropping into the deep in a gizmo as cramped as the backseat of a Volkswagen while knowing that, in case of breakdown, you can't call the AAA. Anyone who remembers the *Thresher* (a U.S. Navy submarine, lost in deep water in 1963 with 127 men aboard) is bound to shudder at the thought of what could happen. But no doubt the thrills of such a descent match the terrors. And the most thrilling of all must have been the deep dives made in early 1977, aboard the *Alvin,* by a team of scientists led by John B. Corliss, which yielded the first direct human glimpses of a hydrothermal-vent ecosystem. Until then, no one had suspected the existence of gigantic blood-red tube worms and the other strange species associated in vent communities.

Further research over the years since has revealed a fair bit about vent biology, though plenty of mystery remains. At the core of what's been learned is one fact: These communities thrive despite the absence of sunlight and, therefore, despite the absence of photosynthesis. Elsewhere on Earth, photosynthesizing plants serve as the primary producers on which all other creatures depend, either directly or ultimately, for metabolic fuel. But not at the vents. At the vents, primary production is accomplished through a completely different process—chemosynthesis. Seawater circulates underground through the lava rock of tectonic ridge zones; it emerges at high temperatures from scattered vents along the ridge, carrying strong concentrations of hydrogen sulfide; specially adapted bacteria metabolize the hydrogen sulfide, which allows them to proliferate in the surrounding water and to form mats and clumps on the bottom. Other species feed on the bacteria, or else on something that eats them, or else on something that eats something that eats them. The whole food chain includes tube worms, bristle worms, acorn worms, whelks, barnacles, limpets, sea anemones, mussels, clams, shrimp, fish, crabs, and Poseidon only knows what else. At the top of that chain stand such large-bodied predators as octopuses.

One other fact about these vent communities, too fundamental to be omitted from even the barest summary: They're highly localized. A typical community might cover no more than an acre, with the nearest other community a mile away. The gradient of water temperature drops off fast with distance (from perhaps 650 degrees Fahrenheit at a vent down to 36 degrees nearby), and so does the gradient of bacterial concentration. The gradient of general biological hospitableness follows roughly upon those. Because the vent communities are so limited in area and so circumscribed, some researchers call them oases. Outside the perimeter lies a zone of frigidity, starvation, and solitude.

Solitude in excess is a serious problem for any lineage of sexual creatures, with dire implications for their perpetuation and evolution. And octopuses, it's clear, are decidedly sexual creatures.

THE LITTLE white octopus seen on the videotape belongs to a species unknown to science. He's so distinctly peculiar that he can't easily be assigned even to a known genus. "The smallness of the head and the slenderness of the entire body are outstanding," according to Janet Voight. The arms are exceptionally long. The skin is delicate. And those tubular eyes are very odd. "The shape of the eyes . . ." Voight says, and lets her syntax dangle. Speaking by phone from her lab on the fourth floor of the Field Museum, she continues, "I'm looking at some of the video stills right now—and God, it's just so weird. There are characters that I've seen in the video image, and that have been captured on these stills, that are unique in the family." Voight herself may be the person to whom falls the gratifying chore of describing and naming the species.

She has a preserved specimen in her lab, partly dissected and awaiting further study. Her specimen is not the same individual whose perplexing act of outreach appears on the tape. That animal receded quickly into obscurity when the lights and the camera were shut off. Probably he's dead by now too, like her specimen, since octopuses are generally short-lived. He may even have been dead by the time the *Alvin* bobbed up into daylight, eight thousand feet overhead, if the big octopus turned on him for a meal. Then again, maybe not. Maybe the little white animal of video stardom is still alive and well at this moment, and still searching for a partner who can give him some offspring. Voight's specimen was collected for her, during a later dive, by Richard A. Lutz. As shown in a photograph taken on shipboard before it went into preservative fluid, says Voight, "the skin is literally see-through." And not just the skin, but also the musculature of the mantle, the main body chamber, is amazingly thin. The internal organs stand forward visibly through those transparent layers. Is that trait unique to the species? Voight can't say—not enough data—but "this guy is really different in terms of apparent physiology, because the thinness of that mantle musculature suggests he could essentially be using his skin to gain oxygen."

The coloring is also notable. The eyes are black, the branchial hearts (one for each gill) are deep purple, but virtually everything else is ghostly white, which suggests to Voight that maybe "it's eating only animals that are getting their energy from a diet that's free of the carotenoid pigments that plants produce." The absence of those plant pigments would be understandable in a species restricted to an ecosystem in which photosynthesis doesn't occur. Whether the little white species is found solely in vent communities of the eastern Pacific, though, is another question that can't be answered yet.

Beyond these matters of physiology and biogeography, Voight has of course been thinking about the behavioral anomaly on the videotape. Posing to herself the question that all the reporters posed to her— "What's going on with this male who's attempting a copulation?"—she starts judiciously into an answer.

"There are various things you have to know about octopus biology to understand the potential *risks* here," she says. The first is that cannibalism is common among at least some species of octopus, practiced opportunistically along with less intimate forms of predation. A big female octopus might well gobble a small male in the aftermath of a copulation, just as a female black widow might gobble her mate. "So if you're close enough to interact with an animal who's much larger than you, you're risking a lot," says Voight. But there's a countervailing risk faced by a male octopus, in its confinement within a small oasis of hydrothermal habitat: the risk of dying without issue. If he never succeeds in locating a receptive female during his brief months or years of potency, he ends as a loser by the terms of evolutionary score keeping. And females of the little white species may indeed be hard to find; based on human observations, anyway, they seem either disproportionally rare or exceptionally elusive. If that rarity or that elusiveness is real, then a little white male might well behave desperately, making a reckless attempt to put his sperm into play—at least once!—before dying of predation or old age.

Yes, the little white octopus in the video was incautious—but who's to say he hadn't weighed these respective risks? Yes, he was undiscerning—but remember, it was pitch-dark down there until the *Alvin* came along, whereas octopuses as a group (the shallow-water species, anyway) tend to be highly reliant on their eyesight.

This possibility of a severe shortage of females harkens back to earlier work that Voight herself has done on shallow-water octopus species. Ten years ago, among a population of the Pacific pygmy octopus in the Gulf of California, she found that the sex ratio appeared to be strongly biased toward males, at least during most months of the year. Why? Possibly because the females practice a life-history strategy that's drastically different from the males' strategy. A female lays only one clutch of eggs in her lifetime and defends those eggs dotingly (in an abandoned shell or some other protective recess) until they hatch; then she dies. A male, on the other hand, can mate repeatedly in his short lifetime, provided he finds any females to mate with. His limiting factors are opportunity and time, not the energy cost of any one act of procreation. And the older a male gets, the more urgent his dilemma will be. "As senescence approaches," Voight wrote in a journal paper reporting this work, "the fitness cost of being preyed upon is less than that of not mating." Fitness cost, a term biologists use in connection with that ineluctable Darwinian standard, the survival and procreation of the fittest, is what regulates the evolution of behavioral instincts. And the fitness cost paid in a hasty, unproductive copulation—*whoops, wrong species, wrong gender, SORRY!*—may also be less than the cost of not mating at all.

This other Voight paper, discussing sex ratios and strategies among the Pacific pygmy octopus, was published several years ago in the *Journal of Zoology*. It was a nice piece of science, rich in field data and in meticulous analysis of the risks and imperatives of octopod life. But for some reason it slipped past the notice of *USA Today*, and the Associated Press, and *Playboy*, and Phil Donahue's people. Even *Discover* didn't call. That was just as well, as Voight knows from experience now.

Life has returned to normal on the fourth floor of the Field Museum, and there's work to be done. Among the ambitious but not especially lurid tasks that presently tempt her are a revision of the phylogeny of octopuses and further study of their biogeographical distribution. These efforts will demand tranquil concentration. Having had her fifteen minutes of Warholian fame, Janet Voight seems to be glad that it wasn't an hour.

Gardening on Mars

Cosmic Loneliness Confronts
a Universe of Possibilities

There's a part of the human heart that desperately yearns for Martians. It's a matter of cosmic loneliness, I suspect, roughly the same character trait that makes itself so eagerly susceptible to religion, ghost stories, UFO sightings, cryptozoology, Shirley MacLaine, and news of higher communication among dolphins. We clutch at these giddy distractions because, partly, we dread to think that we're alone. We don't want to believe that our visible, quotidian life is the whole shebang. Mortal existence on this one little planet seems a cold and small thing; therefore it must be just the tip of an iceberg. We crave metaphysics, transport to new realms after death, paranormal companionship. In the extraterrestrial arena, that trait has manifested itself in particular over the last dozen decades as a poignant, incurable hope of discovering life on Mars.

Civilized life would be preferable; great Martian cities populated by an advanced race of benevolent beings would be ideal. But even an advanced race of malicious louts, even sand worms and space bugs, even a smear of microbial life would do. Even some indisputable fossil evidence of ancient and now-vanished microbes (as distinct from the highly disputable evidence we got in 1996, when a NASA-funded team led by David McKay found what looked *possibly* like traces of bacteria in a Martian meteorite, now famed as ALH 84001) would do. In our minds somehow there exists an empty slot for this hypothetical fact, Martian life, and that slot is a vacuum imagination abhors. The novelists (beginning with Edgar Rice Burroughs and H. G. Wells, forward through Bradbury and Clarke to hundreds more) have been eager to help us fill it. But our loneliness needs more than the consolation of fiction. We want our extraterrestrial beings to inhabit the actual world also.

If not Mars, then where? Earth and Mars seem to be siblings, after all—numbered three and four from the sun, similar in age, similar in rate of rotation, each with a tilted axis and therefore a similar cycle of seasons, not drastically different in size or volcanic activity or (at some periods of their history, anyway) climate. But they are two sibling planets that, then again, are not siblings, because the differences are as striking as the similarities. It might be more apt to say: Life on Mars is the older brother that Earth never had.

Is he nonexistent, that brother, or long since dead? Or is he simply in hiding?

Mars has recently been haunting the eastern evening sky, red and provocative as a bloodshot wink. It has been closer to Earth, more vividly visible, than at any time in decades. The Russians have launched a new Mars probe, and now American public sentiment, rattled and wary since the *Challenger* incident, seems also to be focusing toward a revived interest in Mars exploration. Walter Cronkite, Steven Spielberg, Johnny Carson, and a litany of other famous folk have signed a "Mars Declaration" that urges national commitment to a series of Mars missions. Senator Spark M. Matsunaga of Hawaii has published a book on the subject. *Omni* magazine polled a group of its readers, 54 percent of whom favored an immediate effort toward Mars. All these people agree that Mars is the place, that now is the time, and that the American space program badly needs some goal more lofty than shuttling telephone equipment into position for MCI. As far as that proposition goes, even a crank like myself can agree—especially insofar as the early stages of Mars exploration are done with scientifically sensible and cost-effective robotics (such as the miniature dune buggy known as *Sojourner* that amused us during late summer of 1997), not by platitude-spouting human astronauts who plant American flags. But there's a danger involved in sending scientific missions to Mars. I don't mean the possibility of bad O-rings. I don't mean bankruptcy of the national treasury or runaway competition with the Russians, who aren't much in the planet-grabbing business anymore, anyway.

The danger of Mars exploration is that it may deprive us, definitively, of Martians.

SOMETIMES you can see a lot just by looking, as the philosopher Yogi Berra has remarked, and in precisely that willful spirit the Italian astronomer Giovanni Schiaparelli, back in 1877, caught sight of something funny on Mars.

It was a network of strange, straight lines crisscrossing the planet's surface.

Schiaparelli called the lines *canali* and published a map. Within the world of astronomy, this was a modestly titillating development. Outside that narrow world, it was resoundingly ignored. Almost ten years passed and then, as professional interest endured, as equipment improved, some other astronomers began seeing Schiaparelli's lines. And some didn't. Neither the people who saw, nor the people who didn't, knew just what to make of these observations, and so the elusive Martian *canali* remained merely an intriguing, ambiguous matter of science. The subject didn't burst garishly into the popular consciousness until Percival Lowell took it for his own.

Lowell was a wealthy businessman from the same blue-blood family in Boston, that city of beans and cod, who spoke only (so goes the old doggerel) to Cabots, who spoke only to God. Percival was the exceptional Lowell, destined to speak to the masses. Inspired by the findings of Schiaparelli, he bought himself a world-class observatory for the study of Mars. With the autonomy of a rich dilettante, but also with prescient good sense, he sited his observatory not in the lap of a great urban university but on a mesa above Flagstaff, Arizona, amid the thin clear desert air. This was in 1894, when Lowell himself was almost forty. Although he had been a lifelong amateur astronomer, he wasn't a trained scientist. (Then again, neither was young Darwin.) Lowell had traveled widely in the Orient, served as a special counselor to Korea, and published several books, one of them titled *The Soul of the Far East*. He began work at Flagstaff, using a high-quality eighteen-inch refractor, state-of-the-art gear, and within a very short time there was news for the world.

"When the great continental areas, the reddish-ochre portions of the disc, are attentively examined in sufficiently steady air," Lowell wrote in *The Atlantic Monthly* of July 1895, "their desert-like ground is seen to be traversed by a network of fine, straight dark lines. The lines start from points on the coast of the blue-green regions (the darker areas of the Martian surface), commonly well-marked bays, and proceed directly to other equally well-marked points in the middle of the continent." Several things about these lines were peculiar, but one especially: "All the lines, with the exceptions of the few that are curved in a regular manner, are absolutely straight from one end to the other."

Percival Lowell had found the *canali*. To his eye, assisted by superior equipment in a superior location, the lines were more numerous and more regular than even Schiaparelli had claimed. Lowell took the Italian term at its most literal and announced that these dark lines marked the paths of artificial canals. He found them by the hundreds. He drew elaborately reticulate global maps. He labeled his map features with erudite classical names. In a sequence of four articles for *The Atlantic,* and later in a series of books, Lowell hypothesized that the canals were part of a vast irrigation system by which an advanced Martian civilization watered huge round oases of cropland, down in the Martian equatorial desert. Also in those articles he offered some off-the-cuff calculations. Blessed with gravity only one-third as strong as on Earth, Lowell's Martians could be three times as large as a human in every dimension, and therefore twenty-seven times (by geometric upscaling) as massive but only nine times (in the lesser gravity) as heavy, with twenty-seven times (again the geometric increase) our muscular force and eighty-one times (factoring back in that lower gravity, which would make lifting and other such work easier) our efficaciousness at civil engineering. Whew. Clearly, any such race of Mongos would have no trouble carving a few hundred thousand miles of canals.

The oases, where most of the agriculture would be done, showed up on the Martian surface as large disks at the points of intersection among canals, nexus for the Martian green revolution. Those disks showed up even more vividly on Lowell's maps. The canals themselves were visible at such distances, from forty million miles away on a mesa in Arizona, he hypothesized, because their immediate channels were bordered with wide belts of dark vegetation—possibly indicative of forestry, or of additional riparian gardens. This explained why the lines disappeared for months at a time even from Lowell's eye, and reappeared, when they did, only slowly—not at the rate water flows down a ditch, but at the rate vegetation leafs out in springtime. The canals were not visible, ever, to some other watchers on Earth (for example, E. E. Barnard of Lick Observatory and G. E. Hale of Yerkes Observatory) because of inadequate equipment and bad air. So claimed Percival Lowell, anyway. You can imagine the warm colleagueship felt by veteran astronomers for this rich, condescending newcomer.

The most unexpected thing about Lowell's career is that he did turn himself into a good scientist, eventually, and he did make some valuable contributions to astronomy. For instance, he pioneered the search for a ninth planet, which is now known to us as Pluto. And he was right about the wisdom of siting observatories on desert hilltops. But those valuable contributions did not include his theory of irrigation canals on Mars. That theory is what made him famous in his day, and that's what today makes him look famously wrong.

It was a mistake as translucent as the emperor's new suit. When modern spacecraft (such as *Mariner* 4 in 1965 and *Mariner* 9 in 1971) began arriving at Mars, with high-resolution cameras that could broadcast images back to Earth, those cameras showed no sign of vast irrigation works spread out across the desert. They showed nothing remotely similar. The canals and oases did not exist—not where Lowell had plotted them, and not anywhere else. There were no straight lines of any sort. The surface of Mars turned out to be pocked with craters, bulged up by huge volcanoes, scoured with deep and irregular canyons that seemed to have been cut by flowing water, but utterly innocent of precise linear artifice. No canals. No oases. No evidence of gardening.

The whole *canali* phenomenon, from Schiaparelli down through the decades, must have been some sort of infectious optical mirage, a trick played by eye and brain upon the human observer, and by one human observer upon the next, as each observer (but in particular, Percival Lowell) strained unconsciously to impose shape upon randomness at the dim threshold of visibility.

"The canals of Mars are probably due to the eye's penchant for order," the late Carl Sagan once speculated. "It is much simpler to draw disconnected fine detail as a few lines, joining them up, than to put down all the irregular mottlings observed in an instant of good seeing. There is no question that the straightness of the lines is due to intelligence. The only question concerns which side of the telescope the intelligence is on."

IN THE decades since those early *Mariner* cameras refuted Lowell, the search for Martian life has continued—of course it has, who could stop it?—along two very different lines. Those two might be thought of as 1) the Biochemical Sieve School, and 2) the Face-of-Jesus-in-the-Tortilla School.

The Biochemical Sieve School includes David McKay's team, scrutinizers of the celebrity meteorite, ALH 84001. It also includes those scientists who designed and conducted the life-search experiments of the *Viking* mission, America's next look at Mars after the *Mariner*s. This group included such impeccably sober scientists as Gerald Soffen, Gilbert Levin, Norman Horowitz, Vance Oyama, and Harold Klein, as well as Sagan himself and Joshua Lederberg and others who had been rigorously but hopefully exploring the subject they called exobiology (the science of extraterrestrial life) for many years. These people had applied their brains to a pair of fundamental questions. First, what exactly constitutes a living creature? Second, how do we detect such a creature with remote technology at a distance of forty million miles? Their best answers to those questions went into the design of three life-search experiments, and a miniaturized lab for the performance of all three was aboard each of the two *Viking* landers, which touched down gently on the Martian surface in late summer of 1976.

One of the three, known as the protolytic-release experiment, was intended to detect any plantlike metabolic activity by which carbon dioxide or carbon monoxide was synthesized into other compounds. Another, the labeled-release experiment, involved a nutrient solution marked with radioactive carbon, which would yield traceable carbon dioxide if any of the nutrients were metabolized. The third, called the gas-exchange experiment, monitored any change in the atmosphere of the test chamber as a response to either water or nutrient. The total amount of Martian soil scooped up by each lander and processed through these experiments could be measured in thimbles. The results were elaborately ambiguous. There were some odd, surprising fluctuations inside the test chambers, but whether these fluctuations reflected biological processes—or, alternately, chemical reactions—couldn't be known. The scientists found some grounds for doubting that life could exist on Mars; but they found other grounds for doubting their doubts. If the planet did not support life, they concluded, then it certainly was the scene of some very bizarre chemistry.

Possibly that bizarre chemistry is enough to explain the ropy structures in ALH 84001. Or not. The debate over that meteorite, and over similar clues in another hunk of Martian shrapnel now known as EETA79001, is still fiercely unsettled as of this writing.

The Face-of-Jesus-in-the-Tortilla School is decidedly less rigorous, decidedly less sober, but by a nice bit of irony this school also argues from data produced by the 1976 *Viking* mission. Specifically, the Tortillists have fixated upon two photographic frames among the thousands taken by *Viking* cameras from orbit. The frame officially coded as 35A72 was snapped on July 25, 1976, above the Cydonia region of northern Mars, and it supposedly shows a monumental human face gazing upward at the camera. The face is a great sphinxlike structure, roughly one mile from forehead to chin, carved out of rock or somehow otherwise fabricated down there on the Martian desert. The second frame is 70A13, taken five weeks later over the same spot but with a different angle of sunlight, which supposedly proves that the first image was no two-dimensional illusion cast by shadows. Majestic and humanoid, a product of artifice, this face obviously stands as evidence of a lost civilization. Yes? Clearly it's the face of a Martian Ozymandias, hearkening to Shelley's line, "Look on my works, ye mighty, and despair." Yes? Maybe you've read about this in the checkout line of your supermarket.

The face was first noticed by two computer scientists named Di-Pietro and Molenaar, who had access to the *Viking* photos in the course of their work at a NASA office in Maryland. They did some computer enhancement of the image. The more they enhanced it, the more symmetrical and facelike it seemed. Here was the mouth, here was the nose, here was a pair of matched eyes, and whoa, down in one of the eye sockets was an eyeball with a pupil. Of course if you enhanced a lifetime's worth of tortillas in a lifetime's worth of hot skillets, eventually there might come a day when, by a holy miracle, or by chance, you beheld an image every bit as facelike as the one in 35A72. But never mind. According to *Omni*, DiPietro and Molenaar went so far as to "doubt that nature was totally responsible" for the face in their planetary tortilla. Then a breathlessly credulous science writer named Richard Hoagland got hold of the photos.

Hoagland didn't see just a face. Several miles from the face along a sight line that can be made to seem tenuously Pythagorean, Hoagland also saw a huge five-sided pyramid; he saw a pattern of rectilinear markings; by God, he saw a city.

"It was at this point that I decided I needed major help," Mr. Hoagland has written. "Either I was crazy, or I was onto something so amazing that it was going to occupy a major portion of the rest of my entire life (to say nothing of the lives of all the rest of you)." Or, a third possibility he didn't mention: He wasn't crazy, he wasn't onto something, he was merely susceptible to the delicious delusion of seeing nonexistent patterns that were bigger and more exciting than reality. You can find Hoagland's account in a back issue of *Analog Science Fiction/Science Fact,* and decide that one for yourself.

It's an old complaint: Society, ever myopic, persecutes the visionary with its indifference. Sometimes the complaint is valid. Another thing society does with its indifference is to drive fringe thinkers further fringeward, to make mildly loopy people even loopier. From the tendentious prose of Richard Hoagland, you might take an impression that Gerald Soffen and other space scientists—who have been willing to sift the sands with fastidious biochemical experiments but who hold Face-of-Jesus-in-the-Tortilla zealots at arm's length—are secretly biased against the possibility that somebody might indeed find life on Mars.

Percival Lowell made the same complaint. Back in 1895, feeling defensive, he argued that the seeming outlandishness of his Martian-canal hypothesis was just a subversive reaction, arising from "the instinctive reluctance of man to admit the possibility of peers." In Lowell's view, "To be shy of anything resembling himself is part and parcel of man's own individuality. Like the savage who fears nothing so much as a strange man, like Crusoe who grows pale at the sight of footprints not his own, the civilized thinker instinctively turns from the thought of mind other than the one he himself knows. To admit into his conception of the cosmos other finite minds as factors has in it something of the weird." A human reluctance to share the world with "other finite minds"—this much sounds accurately diagnostic. In fact, our disinclination to face the implications of our sibling-species relationship with chimpanzees (see "Beast in the Mirror," page 153) tends to confirm Lowell's point. But he continued: "Any hypothesis to explain the facts, no matter how improbable or even palpably absurd it be, is better than this."

The canals were his first mistake. That statement was his second. Truth is, we'd all love it, at least while the novelty lasted.

IMPERSONATING
HENRY THOREAU

Solitude, Wilderness, and the Myth of Walden

I met a man who impersonates Henry Thoreau. This is a young fellow with a laconic, severe manner behind his oldfangled whiskers. He wears an orange Day-Glo sweatshirt for riding airplanes and a Victorian coat and vest onstage. Dressed in costume, he speaks Thoreau's words; he offers a plausible version of what must have been Thoreau's own laconic, severe manner. He travels to schools, conferences, wherever a group will sit still for his performance, and in summer he takes up residence at the very shrine of memory, Walden Pond. At Walden during those months, if I have it straight, he is employed officially as a Thoreau impersonator (although *dramatic interpreter* might be the preferred term) by the Massachusetts Department of Parks. I met him in the Syracuse airport. We had both come to address the same conference, and neither of us, now that I think of it, was who he seemed.

Myself, I was there to lecture on biology, practicing scientific explication without a scientist's license. But at least I was free to wear my own clothes. I talked about the evolution and extinction of giant flightless birds, and the other fellow talked about spending two years in a cabin beside a lake.

The real Henry David Thoreau went to Walden in July of 1845. At that point he was a twenty-seven-year-old with a Harvard degree, a high sense of self-esteem, and an uncrystallized identity. He had been out of college eight years, living mainly at home or with his patron Ralph Waldo Emerson, back in the village of Concord where he'd been born. During that time he had founded an unconventional school with his brother, John, closed the school when John became fatally ill, served as a handyman for Emerson, made no great splash as a poet, and taken one modest camping trip on a couple of local rivers. Concord was a small town, especially for a young man of large but unfocused aspiration. People there knew the Thoreau family, and after eight years, those townspeople may have begun arching their eyebrows condescendingly at the mention of Henry's name. Probably he looked to them like a well-educated layabout. Now in 1845 he decided to build a tiny cabin out on the edge of this nearby pond. He lived in the cabin for two years and two months. Later he wrote a book about it. The book was published in 1854 and sold very damn few copies between then and 1862, when Thoreau died. This is the framework of cold fact; the human reality is much more complicated.

But then the human reality is always more complicated than anything that can be put down on paper. You might seek out a fuller account of Thoreau's life in *The Days of Henry Thoreau,* by Walter Harding, which seems to be the best of the biographies; but the human reality is certainly more complicated than Harding's 469-page version also. You might speculate endlessly about Thoreau's intellectual dependence on Emerson or his emotional dependence on his own mother. You might get curious about his truncated romance with a young woman named Ellen Sewall. You might crave a better understanding of his famous one night in jail, or of his admiration for the murderous abolitionist John Brown. You might very well ask yourself why exactly he moved out to the cabin at Walden Pond. You might question what his daily existence was like during that period. Why he stressed some parts of the experience, in writing *Walden,* and why he omitted others. Why he left the pond when he did, moving back to town for the rest of his life. You might trace your questions through a great haystack of printed sources—the various Thoreau biographies, the personal memoirs, the dozens of tweezing scholarly studies, not to mention the fourteen volumes of Thoreau's own private journal—and still you might find no pointed answers. In fact, the case of Henry Thoreau stands as proof for the whole notion of human inscrutability. This man told us more of himself than perhaps any other American writer, and still he remains beyond fathoming.

Notwithstanding those complications, *Walden* captured imaginations all over the world and eventually took its place as a landmark of literary history or (some would say) legend. It became one of those few books that all of us know—more accurately, that all of us claim cognizance of, whether we've read them or not. It became a temple more bowed toward than entered. Thoreau's little pond was transformed into a symbol of all those wilderness places into which a person might escape from civilization, and his *Walden* came to be seen as, in one critic's words, "the first and best example of that literary product especially identified with America, the 'nature book.'" John Muir and other genuine wilderness explorers took Thoreau as their patron saint. It was a phenomenon beyond literary explanation.

While I sat on the floor of a comfortable gathering-room at that conference in upstate New York, listening to the young man in oldfangled whiskers, surrounded by the raised faces of a hundred other attentive listeners, I wondered about all this. I wondered about the disparity between Henry Thoreau as he was and Henry Thoreau as we have chosen to know him and use him.

THE YOUNG man's performance was good. The words were better than good—the words were Thoreau's own, after all, and the one sure point in this whole muddle of motive and character is that Thoreau was, at his best, a fine writer. But I harbored ambivalence about the enterprise itself: doing homage to Henry Thoreau by impersonating him. It seemed self-contradictory. Near the end of *Walden,* for instance, Thoreau says:

> It is remarkable how easily and insensibly we fall into a particular route, and make a beaten track for ourselves. I had not lived there a week before my feet wore a path from my door to the pondside; and though it is five or six years since I trod it, it is still quite distinct. It is true, I fear, that others may have fallen into it, and so helped to keep it open. The surface of the earth is soft and impressible by the feet of men; and so with the paths

which the mind travels. How worn and dusty, then, must be the highways of the world, how deep the ruts of tradition and conformity!

Hear me out, he says, but for Christ's sake don't imitate me.

So I wondered about a certain paradox: the paradox that here we all sat, moon-faced, like pious acolytes to a religion of which the dogma was . . . faithless individualism. Huh? What would Henry think? Or was this particular paradox inherent in his own life and work? I didn't know.

The young man with the oldfangled whiskers finished his bit, and with the others, I clapped politely. I gave my talk about giant flightless birds, and came home.

Several months later, still wondering, I tracked down an essay titled "The Mystery of Walden Pond." You won't find it on the Thoreau shelf at your library, amid the biographies and the reverent scholarly rehashes. You won't find it in *Thoreau: A Century of Criticism*. This piece is buried away as one chapter in a far-ranging book by the critic Leon Edel, a book ominously titled *Stuff of Sleep and Dreams: Experiments in Literary Psychology*. "The Mystery of Walden Pond" is a tendentious but interesting essay, and it raises a question that transported me suddenly back to that evening in upstate New York. Was Henry Thoreau a Thoreau impersonator himself?

LET'S PROPOSE a hypothetical statement. *Henry David Thoreau went off into the wilderness and lived alone for two years in a cabin beside a remote lake.* Is this statement true or false? If you say true, you probably agree with a large majority of the American reading public—or at least a large majority of that portion of the reading public who have any clear sense of who Thoreau was at all. If you say false, you are correct.

In "The Mystery of Walden Pond," Leon Edel argues that not only is our hypothetical statement an American myth, widely held and utterly bogus, but it's a myth Thoreau himself strived cunningly to create. Henry Thoreau, the wise hermit of the woods, was an invention of Henry Thoreau the writer—this is Edel's view, though he doesn't make the following comparison—in much the same way that a later character known as Lawrence of Arabia was invented (with the collusion of Lowell Thomas, among others) by a shifty adventurer and memoirist named T. E. Lawrence. It is written.

Leon Edel is hard on Thoreau. He twists evidence to make it point toward his thesis. But there do exist some interesting bits of evidence that don't need any twisting by Edel. These are not well-kept secrets, merely items of inconvenient fact that have no place in the sleek mythical framework; they have been known but mainly ignored by the biographers and the literary scholars, and have lain just beyond view of the broader myth-honoring public.

To begin with, the woodland around Walden Pond was not, by any stretch of the word, wilderness. It was bordered along one side by a railroad line, frequented by picnickers and stray dogs and woodcutters, riddled with human presence. Likewise, the pond itself was not remote. It was a two-mile stroll from downtown Concord and a mile from Thoreau's family home. Thoreau did build a cabin there and sleep in it for two years, but during that time he seems to have been only dabbling at solitude. He had regular visitors, a steady flow of them, sometimes big friendly parties of as many as thirty people (by his own account) packed into the cabin at once. His mother and sisters came out to the pond every Saturday, bringing dishes of food. And Henry himself walked into town often—some sources say every day—to look in on his family, raid the cookie jar in his mother's kitchen, or stop for a meal at the Emersons' or some other house. What kind of solitude was this? asks Leon Edel. "By no definition of the word—and certainly not in terms of the traditional isolation and contemplation practiced by philosophers and visionaries throughout history—can Thoreau be said to have lived a solitary or even contemplative life at Walden. He was a sojourner in civilized life; he was an observant suburbanite; he was simply a man who had at last acquired a room of his own, and in a way which attracted the town's attention." That final phrase is important. Edel makes his most telling point on the subject of Thoreau's uneasy relationship with the town of Concord.

Going the mile out to Walden, setting up a cabin, camping there for two years, was an unmistakably public act. Thoreau could have disappeared for two years into the true wilderness of Maine, which he admired, at least in smaller doses; but he chose otherwise. He could have gone off on some great adventurous journey through the natural world, as William Bartram had done before him, as Alfred Russel Wallace did at his own time, as John Muir did later; but that didn't suit Thoreau's homebody disposition. (On the verge of his graduation from Harvard, Thoreau reportedly asked his mother what career he should follow. "You can buckle on your knapsack," she answered, "and roam around abroad to seek your fortune." Upon hearing this—so Edel tells us, anyway, without citing his source—sensitive young Henry broke into tears.) Throughout his adult life, Thoreau preferred to experience "the tonic of wildness," as he called it, mainly right there in his own neighborhood. "Solitude is not measured by the miles of space that intervene between a man and his fellows," he argued in *Walden,* a half-truth that Thoreau could succeed in believing only because he had never known the sort of absolute solitude that *is* measured in miles of isolation. Despite his short trips to Maine, to Cape Cod, to as far afield as Minnesota, he never seems to have felt that moment of sublime terror that you may have experienced, and I certainly have, when night falls around an emergency campsite and a person realizes: *I'm alone. I'm on my own. If I break a leg here, I'm finished. If my appendix goes bad, or my eyesight, I'm finished. If I die right now, no living soul will know where or how it happened—or even* that *it happened—for weeks, maybe months. I might be a pile of bleached bones before they find me. I'm alone.* Thoreau's dismissive comment notwithstanding, that sort of solitude does open the sinuses and dilate the eyes in a special way.

Thoreau's sojourn at Walden was something different. Edel is right to say it was less a way of life than a gesture.

It was a gesture to the people of Concord. For evidence of that, we need only go as far as the first page of the manuscript of *Walden.* In the author's own small handwriting:

> *Walden or Life in*
> *the woods by Henry Thoreau*
> *Addressed to my Townsmen*

Not only the book but also the two-year experiment in forest dwelling itself were in some sense a gesture directed toward Concord. Edel proposes a potent explanation for why that gesture came when it did.

Just one year before moving out to Walden, Thoreau had accidentally set fire to the woods. About three hundred acres were burned. It was a disaster to his already inglorious reputation, and possibly a blow to his lofty self-esteem. The book *Walden* contains only an oblique and cryptically self-exculpative reference to this forest fire. But six years after the event, Thoreau confides matter-of-factly to his journal: "I once set fire to the woods." He describes his own carelessness, the spreading flames, the run into town for help, the collective firefighting effort. Then he adds unconvincingly: "It has never troubled me from that day to this more than if lightning had done it." It certainly troubled the townspeople, some of whom (as Thoreau himself admits in the journal) called him a "damned rascal." The fire cost local landowners about two thousand dollars, big money in 1844. There was talk, ultimately inconclusive, of legal prosecution. Meanwhile, the Concord newspaper noted: "It is to be hoped that this unfortunate result of sheer carelessness, will be borne in mind by those who may visit the woods in future for recreation."

Visit the woods for recreation—those words may have galled Henry Thoreau. He asks in his journal: "Who are these men who are said to be the owners of these woods, and how am I related to them? I have set fire to the forest, but I have done no wrong therein. . . ." Less than a year after the fire, he began building his cabin at Walden.

From this episode, Leon Edel concludes:

> Thoreau's decision to move to Walden seems to have been, on one level, a way of withdrawing from a Concord hostile to him, while at the same time remaining very close to it; a way of asserting himself as an active "employed" man by embracing the career of a writer and philosopher; an act of defiance which would demonstrate that his was a better way of life than that practiced by his fellows. Deeper still may have been the petulance of the child saying, in effect, to the town and to Emerson, See how homeless I am; you have forced me to live in a shanty away from all of you. He would arouse pity; he would also arouse interest. Some such jumble of motives lay behind his decision to give an impression of "hermiting" while not being a hermit.

Hard as it is on the image of Henry Thoreau as most of us prefer knowing him, Edel's view seems to me neither implausible nor unfair.

⊚   ⊚   ⊚

BUT IT doesn't matter. To me, anyway, it doesn't matter what tangle of motives pushed Thoreau, or drew him, out to the shore of that pond; it doesn't matter what mixture of shame and courage kept him there for two years and two months; it doesn't matter that he was an emotional Peter Pan, refusing to conform (and maybe incapable of conforming) to conventional definitions of adulthood; it doesn't matter that he walked into town for Momma's cookies; it doesn't matter that he was, like other great prophets, more human than saint. It doesn't matter that he wasn't William Bartram or John Muir because, according to my reading of Thoreau (which differs in this regard from Leon Edel's reading), he never claimed to be. It doesn't matter which pond he went to, where it was located, or how long he stayed. What matters—to me, anyway—is not Walden but *Walden*.

"I went to the woods because I wished to live deliberately, to front only the essential facts of life, and see if I could not learn what it had to teach, and not, when I came to die, discover that I had not lived," the voice of the book tells us. Nothing in this straightforward statement seems less valid in light of the fire or the two-mile proximity to Concord or the cookies. Thoreau's reasons for refocusing his life at the cabin may have been complicated, but they aren't especially mysterious. We can find most of them right there on his pages. "My purpose in going to Walden Pond was not to live cheaply nor to live dearly there, but to transact some private business with the fewest obstacles; to be hindered from accomplishing which for want of a little common sense, a little enterprise and business talent, appeared not so sad as foolish," the voice says. It says: "In the midst of this chopping sea of civilized life, such are the clouds and storms and quicksands and thousand-and-one items to be allowed for, that a man has to live, if he would not founder and go to the bottom and not make his port at all, by dead reckoning, and he must be a great calculator indeed who succeeds. Simplify, simplify." Much later, the voice says: "In proportion as [a person] simplifies his life, the laws of the universe will appear less complex, and solitude will not be solitude, nor poverty poverty, nor weakness weakness." Of course, *Walden* is also sprinkled with loving descriptions of owls, and red squirrels, and thunderstorms, and of the pond itself—its waters that seemed to shift color according to weather and light, its pickerel, its unusual depth, the intricate patterns in its winter ice. But to file this white-hot and challenging jeremiad away on the mind's shelf as a nature book is to succeed in missing the point.

In its most familiar single sentence, *Walden* declares, "The mass of men lead lives of quiet desperation," but it continues less familiarly, more interestingly: "What is called resignation is confirmed desperation. From the desperate city you go into the desperate country, and have to console yourself with the bravery of minks and muskrats." While consoling himself with exactly that, Henry Thoreau's fundamental project was nothing less than reimagining and reinventing the way a human, not an owl or a muskrat, might conduct his life.

Walden is not nor ever was intended to be a book about how to live in the woods. It's a book about how to live in town. The muskrats and the patterns in pond ice are incidental. The careful attention to squirrel behavior is a means to an end. My own view is that *Walden* represents a great leap of ethical imagination and a precious touchstone in American intellectual history. But my own view is biased, arguably, by the fact that *Walden* is a precious touchstone to me. It would be braggartly to declare that this book above all others took a hold on my life and has never let go—so I'll simply say that I suspect and I hope that's the case. I suspect and I hope that *Walden* has affected me more than anything else I've ever read. But now we have come back again to the tricky subject of public and private selfhood, the same trail of spoor that made Leon Edel's nostrils flare wide.

We have come back to the subject of impersonation.

For instance: In late February some years ago I made a certain trip into the woods. This trip involved skis and a tent and coyotes and bison. It involved being alone in the snow for three days. It involved my fortieth birthday, and the recollection of my thirtieth, which had also been spent on skis in the same mountain drainage. It involved a deliberate effort to simplify, simplify, to front only the essential facts of life—for a brief time, at least—and to see if I couldn't learn what that simplification had to teach. It involved a desire to do something mildly irregular (welcoming middle age gladly, sitting alone on a snowdrift) without being self-consciously eccentric. But I sensed that the simplification was undermined, that self-consciousness was already intruding, as soon as I had admitted my birthday plan to more than one other person. Therefore it also involved a promise to myself that I would not write about this particular trip. I was not doing research; I was not on assignment; I was merely and solely living. That promise was made from fear of contaminating one purpose with another—contaminating conviction with gesture. It was made because I wanted to try to maintain a divide between the essence of Henry Thoreau's teaching and the impersonation of Henry Thoreau.

As of the paragraph above, that little promise has been broken. My ski retreat, undertaken for very private purposes, has been called into public use. And I'm more than ever aware that maintaining the divide between conviction and gesture, between essence and impersonation, is difficult. Maybe it was difficult even for Henry.

GOD'S WEAKNESS FOR BEETLES

An Amazon Apparition Carries Its Own Light

There is no dusk in the central Amazon, and there is no cocktail hour. Night falls abruptly, *whump,* and on this particular evening it catches me seated chest-deep in a coolish blackwater stream, under the doubled darkness of black sky and thick canopy, soaking away the day's insect repellent and sweat. I'm at a field camp in the forest, three hours north along a bad red-clay road from the city of Manaus, Brazil, where the Rio Negro meets the mainstem Amazon River. The field camp exists for ecological research. It's a well-designed outpost, relatively luxurious, with tin roofs on the huts and mosquito nets for the hammocks, plus a small handmade dam that gathers the blackwater stream into a bathing pool, but its luxuriousness does not extend to felicities of potation. There is no ice in the camp kitchen. There is no whiskey. There is no beer. The Brazilians have a wonderfully treacherous national drink called *cachaça,* Amazon moonshine, and alas there's none of that stuff around either. The water of the blackwater stream, rinsing my skin, seems almost as limpid and beatific as chilled Beefeater, but *almost* isn't close enough to transmogrify it into a martini. Besides, there's no vermouth and no olives. Point is, I am cold sober at the moment when the apparition occurs. Furthermore, I have corroborative witnesses, two men of unimpeachable clearheadedness, soaking their feet in the pool beside me.

The apparition is this: A large glob of orange light comes zigzagging through the trees. It moves slowly, flying a gracefully sinuous path, as though under command of Steven Spielberg. It's inexplicably weird, though pretty.

"Uh. Bbb-duh. Did you see that?" I say.

"Yes!" says Scott McVay.

"What?" says Tom Lovejoy.

McVay and I fall silent. He is a foundation executive from New Jersey, a man of charming and varied enthusiasms who serves on the board of the World Wildlife Fund. Lovejoy is a tropical biologist, guiding figure of what may be the world's most intriguing ecological experiment, a long-term study of fragmentation effects, population extinctions, and ecosystem decay as displayed in isolated rainforest patches, including the one within which we presently sit. Between them, McVay and Lovejoy own a pair of open but critical minds. Neither is the type to be caught reading *UFO Journal,* not even at the barbershop.

"*That,*" I say.

The spooky orange light has come wobbling back for another pass. It's ten times as large and ten times as fast as a firefly. It might be a hummingbird carrying a small kerosene lantern, but who knows. Only the light is visible.

"Yes!" says Lovejoy.

Again it disappears. Now we are all very puzzled. The list of possible explanations would seem to begin with the unlikely and proceed to the preposterous, or maybe to the frightening, and meanwhile here we are, not only out in the jungle but naked and pink and wet. Tom Lovejoy at this point does a smart thing. He puts on his clothes and climbs the dirt trail back to camp, where dinner is ready, leaving McVay and me at the scene of the visitation.

"You did see it. Correct? You saw."

"I saw. Yes, absolutely."

"It was big. Am I right?"

"Very big. Inexplicably big. And bright orange. Very bright."

"And it came winding through here. Right down through here. In and out, right along the stream. Like a Japanese monorail with an orange headlight."

"Absolutely. What on earth could it be?"

"Scott. Turn around quick."

This time it cruises past us, crosses above the dam, and then suddenly stops in midair. The orange light continues to shine. Motion alone has ceased. The light seems to hover. Oh good, I think, here comes the part where the intergalactic ultimatum is delivered to a couple of haphazardly chosen earthlings.

"It landed," I whisper. "On a tree limb. Or something." Scott and I squint. Just enough starlight leaks through the canopy to show us that no tree, no limb, occupies that particular space. So I pull on my shorts and tiptoe over there, barefoot, a freshly washed package of foolhardy curiosity in patterned boxers, and lo the mystery is solved.

A two-inch-long beetle, with an organ of luminescence, has flown into one of the mist nests spread open for trapping bats.

The creature glows vehemently when I touch it.

THIS IS NOT an essay about luminescent insects. If it were, I would probably tell you something about luciferin and luciferase, two substances involved in the chemical reaction that's capable of producing high-intensity and virtually heatless light within a living cell. I would mention the Lampyridae family, more familiar as the fireflies and glowworms, and explain the ways they use bioluminescent signals, in the great dark lonely world, to bring individual males and females together for mating. I might describe the fiendish ingenuity of females of the species *Photuris versicolor,* who mimic the flash patterns of other lampyrid species, luring horny male beetles in to be eaten. I might even quote from the observations of the Italian entomologist Marcello Malpighi, who dissected and studied glowworms back in the seventeenth century. But I won't. Luminescence among insects may be a mildly interesting subject, I suppose, but truth be known I don't care a damn about it.

The deeper question raised by that flying orange light, to my mind, is, Why are there so many different species of beetle?

For years I've been wondering. For years I've been hoping that some clever biologist would offer a good explanation. So far, no luck. Here we have what may be the most puzzling and possibly even the most significant (another possibility is that it's the most insignificant, though I doubt that) riddle in evolutionary biology, yet a person would be hard-pressed to find it answered in the pages of *Science* or *Ecology* or even the

Annual Review of Entomology. In fact, a person would be hard-pressed to find it asked. Why are there so many species of beetle? To grasp the depth of that mystery, you need a few numbers.

Modern biology now recognizes about one million known species of animal. What a biologist means by a "known" species is one that has been collected, formally described, and given its own binary Latinate name, a rigorous taxonomic procedure that demands time and painstaking labor. Because taxonomists are few and the workload is large, they have only gotten around to knowing, in that sense, a small fraction of Earth's diversity, and the big-bodied species have generally been attended to earlier and more thoroughly than the others. Still, the big-bodied groups don't put up the big numbers. Of that million known species, mammals account for just four thousand, a trifling minority. About nine thousand of the total are birds, and about 10,500 are reptiles and amphibians. Of the remainder, a huge portion are insects and other arthropods—roughly 874,400 species, according to one source. Within that 874,400 majority, about 290,000 species are beetles. In other words, more than one in every four species of known animal on Earth is a beetle.

If you estimate unknown species of animal, the percentage only goes higher. A coleopterist (that is, a beetle guy) named Terry Erwin, with the Smithsonian Institution, has published field results suggesting there might be ten or twelve million species of beetle still undiscovered in the tropical canopies.

It was this numerical imbalance that inspired a famous remark (possibly apocryphal, but very much in character) by the geneticist J. B. S. Haldane. Besides being a great scientist, Haldane was also a wit, an apostate from the British ruling class, and a dialectic materialist. On a certain occasion he found himself faced by an imperious clergyman, goes the story, who asked him what might be deduced about the character traits of the Creator from a study of the natural world. Haldane reportedly answered: "An inordinate fondness for beetles."

The mystery of beetle diversity can be looked at two ways. First, there's the narrow coleopterological perspective. A beetle by definition is an insect showing that pattern of anatomical and physiological adaptations unique to the order Coleoptera: a wormlike larva, a pupal metamorphosis, chewing or biting mouthparts, and (most important?) a front pair of wings modified into elytra. These elytra are a pair of hard coverings that fold neatly over a beetle's back, like cabinet doors, to protect a more conventional pair of rear wings that do the actual flying. Of this pattern—full metamorphosis, chewing mouthparts, elytra—science knows 290,000 variations. Nature knows millions more. So the pattern is extraordinarily successful. It's also extraordinarily flexible, as reflected in the fact that our biosphere isn't infested by just one dominant species of beetle (as it is by one dominant species of hominid), but instead supports that staggering wealth of variations—beetles of all crazy shapes, all gorgeous colors, all strange habits, all tiny and monstrous sizes, from one extreme to another and on into as-yet-uncounted myriads. Why? Nobody can say.

So much for the coleopterological approach. The other way of addressing the mystery of beetle diversity is by subsuming it within a larger mystery. Call this one the speciation approach. From this broader perspective, the question is, What factors produce new cases of reproductive isolation among populations of animals and plants? In more familiar words: What is the origin of species? Despite his book title, not even Charles Darwin knew the answer to that one.

Even today, it's a famously intractable conundrum among evolutionary biologists and ecologists. Why is the structure of a natural community as complex, in terms of species diversity and interactions, as it is? Why are there four thousand species of mammal? Why 18,800 species of fish? Why 248,400 species of higher plants? What factors have divided the coleopteran gene pool into as many as ten million landlocked puddles? What drives speciation?

IN 1958 one of the patriarchs of modern ecology, G. Evelyn Hutchinson, delivered a lecture that was destined to echo down through three decades of veneration and dispute. It was Hutchinson's inaugural address as president of the American Society of Naturalists, later printed in *American Naturalist,* and it dealt with the matters of speciation, niche-splitting, and competition among similar species within a single ecological community. The title was "Homage to Santa Rosalia *or* Why Are There So Many Kinds of Animals?" As a footnote to the published version, Hutchinson told the story (and this is the earliest recorded source for it, as far as I can determine) of J. B. S. Haldane's comment about God's weakness for beetles.

Rosalia was the name of a saint near whose shrine, on a mountain-side in Sicily, Hutchinson had made what became the most famous collection of water bugs in the history of biology.

A water bug is a hemipteran, not a beetle at all, and the word *bug* is technically accurate as applied to this and only this group of insects—water striders, backswimmers, water boatmen, that sort of thing. The Santa Rosalia water bugs would have looked very ordinary to you or to me. But Hutchinson saw something. Or, at least, he suspected that he did. Although his sample of specimens came from a single small pond, it included two distinct but closely related species. They were virtually identical, except that *Corixa punctata* was 1.46 times larger than *Corixa affinis*. Hutchinson happened to be a naturalist of the restlessly conceptual type and so, studying the specimens later, he asked himself two things. First, why did the pond hold just two species instead of, say, three or twenty or two hundred? Second, why did it hold two species instead of one?

His answer to the first question: competition. His answer to the second: reconciliation of competition by difference in size. The two similar species were able to coexist in one pond, Hutchinson surmised, because one was almost half-again bigger than the other. This alone, he guessed, gave them different enough needs, different enough habits, different enough niches, to circumvent the problem of incompatibility. Competition with each other had induced a gap in size, and that gap held their competition within mutually tolerable levels.

It sounds like a small point. But three decades later, you can sort ecologists into two distinct schools according to whether they think G. Evelyn Hutchinson was profoundly right or profoundly wrong about those water bugs. In the years since "Santa Rosalia," there has come an abundant and heated literature concerning the role played by competition in producing species diversity within ecological communities. Frustratingly, that debate (some would call it a feud) says almost nothing about the mystery of beetles. These arguing ecologists, both the competitionists and the anticompetitionists, are very much concerned with why a small plot of Amazon forest might include ten thousand species of plant and animal—as well they should be. Less haunting to them is the matter of why one order of insects, Coleoptera, might include ten million species scattered around the world.

I suppose that's just another reason (added to math anxiety and a love of rhythmical adjectives) that I'm not an ecologist myself. My curiosity works cross-grain to the serious questions.

FOR A moment, I stand at that mist net in the Amazon, trying to guess whether the beast with the orange light is ferocious or harmless. Most likely it's harmless. With even my skimpy entomological knowledge I can place it unmistakably as an elaterid—more commonly, a click beetle—by the body shape, the false eyespots on its thorax, and the snapping hinge between thorax and abdomen, which is no help at all in a mist net but will allow the beetle to somersault off its back from a flat surface. This elaterid, unlike any I've ever seen, has luminescent eyespots that glow green. It's also much larger than any click beetle I ever collected as a boy in Ohio. On the underside of the abdomen, that other luminescent organ continues pulsing orange.

I drag Tom Lovejoy back down the trail for a look. Together we get the beetle untangled from the mist net and carry it gingerly up to camp. While he and I and Scott McVay and a few other folk eat our fish stew, the talk ranges over conservation politics and bird-banding experiences, research funding and poetry, while the beetle sits before us on the rough wooden table, resting sedately inside a Ziploc bag.

I don't know it at the time, but I will later learn from reference books that this Amazon elaterid almost certainly belongs to the genus *Pyrophorus,* also called the fire beetles. A bit more research will tell me that fire beetles have been collected by Indians in tropical America for as long as four hundred years. The sixteenth-century scholar Ulisse Aldrovandi, an Italian like Malpighi, writing of the natural wonders of the new world, described why those jungle tribes might have valued *Pyrophorus.* "At home, it is useful to the Indians in two ways: it both catches mosquitoes and takes the place of a candle. It is allowed to fly about freely in the house within closed doors, and its light is no less than that of a candle. The Indians read, write and occupy themselves in other ways by its light." Exaggerating only a little, Aldrovandi added: "In the forest, the beetles shine so brightly that it is impossible to lose one's way."

The genus *Pyrophorus,* like other coleopteran genera, may include dozens or even hundreds of species. Science has only begun nibbling at the biological intricacies of the central Amazon, and most of those species are presumably undiscovered. Still, a two-inch-long click beetle with green luminescent eyespots and an orange luminescent belly makes a vivid impression. Gaping at the thing, I assume that it must be a familiar and maybe even celebrated denizen of the local forest. What species? I ask Tom, expecting him to toss off an answer.

He looks at me blankly. "I've never seen it before," he says.

Our gaudy elaterid may be a new species, unknown to science. Is that important? The answer depends on your perspective. To some people this whole business is a bit of amusing statistical trivia; to some people it's a bunch of bugs; to me it's the Parable of Coleoptera. Nature is vastly complex, that parable says, and human knowledge is small. After dinner, we let the beetle go.

LIMITS OF VISION

Dark Matter As Seen from Afar

The house is quiet. The backyard is quiet. The night sky is partly obscured with thick, wet summer clouds. The clouds move against one another, then apart, like grazing sheep. The moon is new and therefore has already set. The lights of the town too, because it's a small town, unafflicted with the more obvious forms of nocturnal excitation, are mainly doused at this hour. Only a pale glow, like watercolor yellow stroked onto gray paper, reflects from the undersides of the clouds. As those clouds slide apart, spangles of starlight appear in the deeper blackness of the gaps. The house is darkened. The backyard is small. There are two mountain ash trees, a wall of lilacs, a rotting old wooden shed full of kayaks, a weeping birch near the alley, several maples, one clump of rhubarb gone tall and seedy. Feral asparagus, dandelions, this is no horticultural showplace, but it's tranquil and private. A man lies on a narrow strip of grass between the raspberries and the wildflower garden, positioned to look at the sky. Although he has been sleeping intermittently, his glasses are still on his face. If he rolls over again, he's liable to smash them.

Stirring awake, he raises a pair of binoculars toward a patch of open sky. The patch comes alight with smeared flecks of brightness. He focuses. The smeared flecks become glittering dots. The dots represent stars and—for all he knows—galaxies, nebulas, superclusters. The dots are of course awesomely numerous. Their numerousness would be a matter of delight, ordinarily, but tonight another matter engages him more. Suspiciously, with newfound interest on this particular evening, he inspects the dark spaces surrounding those dots.

In the dark spaces he sees just what they'd see from Mount Palomar: nothing.

The man is alone. His wife has gone off to a gathering of musicians. He has lurked all day in his office, refusing to answer the phone, more stubbornly incommunicado than usual. He has been reading: *The Dark Matter,* by Wallace and Karen Tucker; *The Shadows of Creation,* by David Schramm and Michael Riordan; *Ancient Light,* by Alan Lightman; *Origins,* a compendium of interviews with cosmologists, edited by Lightman and Roberta Brawer; a handful of related books; a file folder of clippings; and several articles by an astronomer named Vera C. Rubin. This stuff has him pacing and mumbling. He has consulted his field guide to the constellations. Browsed his beautiful big *Atlas of Galaxies,* a gift from Dr. Lightman himself. Then at midnight he has locked the cats indoors, reserving the backyard for adults. The cats would torment him with play. Now he gapes skyward. He would like to catch sight of the Big Dipper. He is thinking about M101, the spiral galaxy just off the upper side of the Dipper's handle. M101 may not be apparent through binoculars, but at least he knows where to envision it: at the point of an equilateral triangle formed with the handle stars Mizar and Alkaid. He wants to lay eyes on the dark halo of invisible matter that—so he has been instructed—surrounds the luminous part of that galaxy. *Halo* is not his word. It's a word chosen by experts, a consensual label for the enormous spherical aggregation of nonradiant mass that has been deduced, from gravitational evidence, to encompass each spiral galaxy. The notion of a dark halo is oxymoronic, he knows. But then so is the notion of a wildflower garden.

Distinguished astrophysicists have persuaded him that the universe as we see it is simply a metaphor for reality.

Starlight is the bow tie on the Invisible Man. Everything else, which amounts to most everything, is what they call dark matter.

SOME HINTS came early and were largely ignored. In 1933 a Swiss-American astronomer named Fritz Zwicky studied the dynamics of a cluster of galaxies in the constellation Coma Berenices. Basing his calculations on the motions of those galaxies in orbit around one another, Zwicky was able to estimate their combined total mass. The estimate was perplexing. The visible mass as represented by starlight, he concluded, could account for less than a tenth of what must be there. The rest was somehow hidden. Without that huge hidden increment of hypothetical mass exerting its gravitational pull, the cluster would not remain cohesive. Its member galaxies, instead of orbiting mutually, would fly apart.

Coma Berenices is named for the missing hair of a bald-headed Egyptian queen. It's located out past the Virgo cluster on a line with the northern galactic pole of our own Milky Way, roughly three hundred million light-years away. Even with binoculars by Leitz, the man in the backyard can't find it.

He has a headlamp, powered by two double-A batteries. An elastic-strap headlamp is always useful outdoors, he has found, for such tasks as setting up tents after dark or reading star charts or flattening his hair beneath the strap into dippy configurations. He has a water bottle and a ground cloth and a self-inflating pad. This guy is prepared. He can't remember just how long it's been since he camped out in his own backyard.

Sometime within the next few hours the Big Dipper should swing out toward the northwest, clearing itself from behind the mountain ash tree that stands near the shed. With luck, by that time, the clouds will be gone. With greater luck, he'll still be awake. There are many impediments to a full cosmological perspective.

In 1940 the Dutch astronomer Jan Oort made an astute comment that went unappreciated for decades. Oort had examined the structure and dynamics of an unspectacular galaxy known as NGC 3115. Something seemed wrong here, just as something had seemed wrong in Zwicky's cluster. "It may be concluded," Oort wrote, "that the distribution of mass in the system must be considerably different from the distribution of light." Gravitational effects indicated that the galaxy was far heftier than it looked. "The strongly condensed luminous system appears embedded in a large and more or less homogeneous mass of great density." Oort had discovered that NGC 3115 possessed a dark halo.

Back in those days, it did not constitute a fruitful provocation. Most astronomers were focusing their eyes and their minds elsewhere. An exception among them was Vera Rubin, of the Carnegie Institution in Washington. Even as late as the 1970s, when Dr. Rubin decided to measure the rotational velocity of the Andromeda galaxy, she felt she had chosen a research subject that was peripheral, obscure, and not terribly interesting to other astronomers; that was just how she wanted it. By 1983, she and her collaborators had looked at the patterns of rotational speed within sixty different spiral galaxies. Drudge work, in the view of others. The strange thing about these patterns was that the rotational speed did not decrease as the inverse of radius. In English: Stars far out at the tips of the arms were orbiting as fast as stars near the spiral's hub.

The pinwheel shape of each spiral galaxy results from distal stars lagging behind proximal ones. That much had always been assumed. But the measurements by Rubin and her coworkers added an unforeseen insight. Those distal stars lagged only because the circumferential distance they traveled was greater; the speed at which they traveled turned out to be no slower than the speed of a star near the center.

The law of gravity would seem to say this is impossible. Gravity should be weaker (and therefore the gravity-driven rotation of an orbiting body should be slower) the greater the distance from a central concentration of mass. How could the arm-tips of a galaxy maintain such speed? One possible explanation was that the law of gravity, as enunciated by Newton and refined by Einstein, was drastically wrong. Another explanation, slightly less troublesome, was that luminosity (meaning not just visual radiation but also infrared, ultraviolet, X-ray, and every other known sort) did not give an accurate picture of the real concentration of mass. Maybe the farthest luminous arm-tips, which seemed to mark the galaxy's outer fringe, were actually well within the concentration of mass. Maybe the whole galaxy, including the tips, was contained within a huge sphere of invisible matter. "Observations of rotational curves which do not fall," Rubin wrote in the journal *Science,* "support the inference that massive nonluminous halos surround the spiral galaxies. The gravitational attraction of this unseen mass, much of it located beyond the optical image, keeps the rotational velocities from falling." Roughly 80 percent of the mass in a spiral galaxy, by her calculations, is invisible.

This was about the same as results arrived at by other scientists working with other modes of measurement on other aspects of the same mystery. Somewhere along the way it came to be called dark matter. Dark matter is not to be confused with antimatter, which consists of contrarian twins to the familiar subatomic particles—antiproton matched against proton, positron against electron, and so forth. Antimatter has been detected experimentally but is rare in our universe; upon contact with matter, it vanishes in a poof of high energy. Dark matter has been detected too—by Dr. Rubin, among others, through the indirect means of recording its gravitational effects—but dark matter is hardly rare. Also, it doesn't vanish so shyly as antimatter. It lurks. It abides. It embraces whole worlds, like a grizzly bear embracing a jar of mayonnaise. Dark matter, says the modern consensus, seems to account for as much as 90 percent of the mass of the universe.

But nobody has ever seen it. Nobody knows what it is. Hidden planets? Maybe, but probably not. Black holes? Maybe, but probably not. Brown dwarfs? Naw. Neutron stars? Naw. Vast hazy conglomerations of neutrinos, each neutrino redefined so as to possess a mass barely greater than zero? Probably not. Exotic new particles never yet detected by science?—axions, photinos, gravitinos? The ad hoc invention of new particles to fit new observations seems discomfortingly close to metaphysics. Besides, *gravitino* sounds too much like a type of rich, hefty pasta to be taken quite seriously. Each of these hypothetical answers has its merits and its drawbacks. Dark matter has helped put astrophysics into such a crisis of confusion that even the most cherished tenets are now being questioned—the big bang theory, the inflationary-universe variant of that theory, the law of gravity itself. Doubt is ascendant. Obscurity is manifest everywhere. The uncertainty principle looks positivist by comparison. "The enormity of our ignorance can be measured," according to Vera Rubin, "by noting that there is a range in mass of 10^{70} between non-zero-mass neutrinos and massive black holes." Seventy orders of magnitude, that is, between one dark-matter candidate and another. What she was saying, though more politely, is that we don't know our ass from a hamburger. On top of all that, at about three in the morning it starts to rain.

The man pushes his gruesomely costly binoculars into a plastic grocery bag. He wraps the ground cloth up over his shoulder. He goes back to sleep.

But at 4 A.M. there's a pageant of silent lightning. The rain is now serious. Thwarted and blinded and ignorant and wet, he stalks inside.

THE NEXT night is clear. With help from a lawn chair, he climbs onto the roof of the shed. This opens his view to the low northern sky and gives him an angle around the mountain ash. He'll stay here as long as it takes. Getting enough observational time, as Vera Rubin herself has testified, is always the hard part. Astronomers are obliged to compete for the use of the big telescopes; a handful of evenings per year, according to Rubin, and a person might count herself lucky. But he's got his binoculars, his headlamp, his star guide. The Big Dipper is aglow in the northwestern sky, out toward the Seventh Avenue overpass. Deep in the void beyond its handle, somewhere, resides M101.

Rubin began her career with a master's thesis on large-scale motions. Big bang theory (as originally supported by the observations of Edwin Hubble, and much modified since) describes a universe in which everything is flying apart, but this young woman wondered whether there might also be other vast patterns of motion, occurring within or across the great universal expansion. Weren't some galaxies streaking *toward* each other? Weren't some swinging this way or that, ignoring the general trend, ignoring Hubble's law, as though they'd been absent from class on the day of the bang? She put her ideas into a paper under the title "Rotation of the Universe." It was considered impertinent, overambitious, if not a bit ditzy. It was rejected by *Astronomical Journal*. No, we can't publish a paper titled "Rotation of the Universe," they said, and certainly not one by an obscure twenty-two-year-old student. Rubin abandoned the subject of large-scale motions. Almost forty years later, Alan Lightman asked her why.

Two reasons, she told him. "First of all, the only real contribution would have been observational. What would have been required would have been more galaxies and better velocities and magnitudes. I had two children by then. I think the honest answer is I knew that I just couldn't do things like that. There was no way I could get myself to an observatory and gather data. It was totally out of the question." The second answer was that she disliked controversy. She didn't care to provoke and contend, to fight the acrimonious battles between fashionable heresy and venerated orthodoxy. She simply wanted to do science, quietly and well. She turned to other questions and then, years later, became curious about the rotation of spiral galaxies. The centers of those galaxies were already attracting a lot of attention; she focused on the arms. How fast did those arms rotate? How did the speeds decline with distance from the center? At the time, it seemed an obscure little question, with which she'd be blissfully remote from the hot intellectual epicenter. At the time, astrophysics was not yet obsessed with defining and solving the problem of dark matter. Rubin went to the periphery, and the hot intellectual epicenter eventually followed her.

The man on the roof raises his binoculars to the vicinity of Mizar and Alkaid. About here, he thinks. A patch of darkness, dusted with starlight like mica. The binoculars are 7x35 Trinovids, excellent for birds in a jungle, virtually worthless for astronomy. If the galaxy M101 falls within their field, he doesn't see it. Flecks, dots, unsteady hands, who the hell knows. He sweeps toward the northeast. All right, out here somewhere, past Cassiopeia, low to the horizon, should be the Andromeda constellation, with its M31 galaxy. M31, he knows, was the first spiral that Vera Rubin studied. Where is it tonight? Obscured behind the Bridger Mountains, evidently. But at least he has looked. At least he has tried. And even if he did get a glimpse of either M101 or M31—with his Leitz lenses, or perhaps with the five-meter telescope at Mount Palomar, or even with the ten-meter monster on Mauna Kea—he would see but a small fraction of what was actually there. The true shape of the universe is not given to human eyes. We all knew that, from the murmured warnings of Plato and Hume and Heisenberg and Faulkner and Lawrence Durrell, but nowadays it's on record in such confident organs as *Astronomical Journal*.

The wonderful thing about this dark-matter business is that it offers something for everyone. Agnostics can say, See how little we know. Bible-thumpers can say, See how little science knows. Astrophysicists can say, We are now able to put a numerical figure upon the limits of our vision of the universe: uh, about 10 percent. What the man on the roof likes about dark matter, personally, is that it promises everything and delivers nothing. It combines all the best aspects of belief and unbelief. Dark matter informs us that the universe as we see it is a scrawny approximation of the universe as we don't see it. It reminds us that the weightiest truths, though invisible, can be detected by feel. It proclaims that the real shape of our world is not . . . Oh, stop it, he thinks. Go to bed, he thinks, before you hurt yourself.

He crawls down to the eave. The lawn chair has treacherously disappeared. Or anyway, he can't see it. He flops on his belly, lowers his bottom half tentatively, dangles a leg this way and that, but the window ledge has vanished also. Should he let go, dropping blindly? No. A bad idea for a mid-fortyish guy with a desk job. Things could get broken. Clutching at shingles, he struggles back up. Now he's stuck on his own rooftop at midnight. What a fool. No one can see him. People are asleep. It's a metaphor for reality, or something.

BIBLIOGRAPHY

A BRIEF DISCLAIMER: The editions cited below are the ones to which, in my haphazard, groping, and sometimes frantic research efforts (see "The Dope on Eggs"), I happened to have access. They are not necessarily the first editions, or the most familiar, of the works in question. Therefore some of the dates will seem historically incongruous; you and I both know, for instance, that Henry Thoreau did *not* publish *Walden* in 1965. Since this bibliography is intended primarily as a guide to your further reading and a way of giving credit to other authors where credit is due, rather than as a manifest of my (amateurish and risible) scholarship, I have refrained from ferreting out and supplying all that first-edition information. Also, there's the fact that it would have made me crazy.

RATTLESNAKE PASSION

Klauber, Laurence M. 1982. *Rattlesnakes: Their Habits, Life Histories, and Influence on Mankind.* Abridged by Karen Harvey McClung. Berkeley: University of California Press.

McKann, Belva. 1985. "Texas Serpents." *Texas Parks and Wildlife,* Vol. 43, No. 5.

Tennant, Alan. 1985. *A Field Guide to Texas Snakes.* Austin: Texas Monthly Press.

THE NARCOTIC OF EMPIRE

Ashley, Maurice. 1971. *England in the Seventeenth Century,* Vol. 6, *The Pelican History of England.* Harmondsworth, Middlesex, England: Penguin Books.

Hannas, Willard A., and Des Allwi. 1990. *Turbulent Times Past in Ternate and Tidore.* Banda Naira, Moluccas: Yayasan Warisan dan Budaya Banda Naira.

Lawson, Philip. 1993. *The East India Company.* London: Longman Group.

Muller, Kal. 1990. *Spice Islands: Exotic Eastern Indonesia*. Lincolnwood, Ill.: Passport Books.

Parry, John W. 1969. *Spices*. New York: Chemical Publishing Company.

Purseglove, J. W., E. G. Brown, C. L. Green, and S. R. J. Robbins. 1981. *Spices*, Vol. 1. London: Longman Group.

Ricklefs, M. C. 1993. *A History of Modern Indonesia Since c. 1300*. Stanford, Calif.: Stanford University Press.

Rosengarten, Frederic, Jr. 1969. *The Book of Spices*. Wynnewood, Pa.: Livingston Publishing Company.

Schivelbusch, Wolfgang. 1993. *Tastes of Paradise: A Social History of Spices, Stimulants, and Intoxicants*. Translated by David Jacobson. New York: Vintage Books.

Wallace, Alfred Russel. 1962. *The Malay Archipelago*. New York: Dover Publications, Inc.

Weil, Andrew T. 1965. "Nutmeg as a Narcotic." *Economic Botany*, Vol. 19, No. 3.

HARD PARTS

Bolton, Barry. 1994. *Identification Guide to the Ant Genera of the World*. With scanning electron microscope photography by Laraine Ficken. Cambridge, Mass.: Harvard University Press.

Clarkson, Euan N. K., and Levi-Setti, Riccardo. 1975. "Trilobite Eyes and the Optics of Descartes and Huygens." *Nature*, Vol. 254 (April 24, 1975).

Conway Morris, Simon, and H. B. Whittington. 1979. "The Animals of the Burgess Shale." *Scientific American*, Vol. 241 (July 1979).

Eldredge, Niles. 1986. *Time Frames: The Rethinking of Darwinian Evolution and the Theory of Punctuated Equilibria*. New York: Simon & Schuster.

Eliot, T. S. 1980. *The Complete Poems and Plays 1909–1950*. New York: Harcourt Brace & Company.

Fortey, Richard. 1991. *Fossils: The Key to the Past*. Cambridge, Mass.: Harvard University Press.

Glaessner, Martin F. 1984. *The Dawn of Animal Life: A Biohistorical Study*. Cambridge: Cambridge University Press.

Gould, Stephen Jay. 1989. *Wonderful Life: The Burgess Shale and the Nature of History*. New York: W. W. Norton.

Haeckel, Ernst. 1974. *Art Forms in Nature*. New York: Dover Publications, Inc. Originally published as *Kunstformen der Natur* (Leipzig and Vienna, 1904).

Hauff, Bernhard, and Rolf Bernhard Hauff. 1981. *Das Holzmadenbuch*. Privately printed.

Horner, John R. 1992. "Cranial Morphology of *Prosaurolophus* (Ornithischia: Hadrosauridae) with Descriptions of Two New Hadrosaurid Species and an Evaluation of Hadrosaurid Phylogenetic Relationships." Illustrated by Kris Ellingsen. Bozeman, Mont.: Museum of the Rockies Occasional Paper No. 2.

Levi-Setti, Riccardo. 1993. *Trilobites*. Chicago: The University of Chicago Press.

Ludvigsen, Rolf, and Stephen R. Westrop. 1983. "Franconian Trilobites of New York State." Albany: New York State Museum Memoir 23.

Pinna, Giovanni. 1990. *The Illustrated Encyclopedia of Fossils.* Translated by Jay Hyams. New York: Facts on File Publications.

Rudwick, Martin J. S. 1985. *The Meaning of Fossils: Episodes in the History of Paleontology.* Chicago: The University of Chicago Press.

Shaw, Frederick C. 1968. "Early Middle Ordovician Chazy Trilobites of New York." Albany: New York State Museum and Science Service, Memoir 17.

Simpson, George Gaylord. 1983. *Fossils and the History of Life.* New York: Scientific American Books.

Speyer, Stephen E. 1991. "Trilobite Taphonomy: A Basis for Comparative Studies of Arthropod Preservation, Functional Anatomy and Behaviour." In *The Processes of Fossilization.* Edited by Stephen K. Donovan. New York: Columbia University Press.

Stanley, Steven M. 1987. *Extinction.* New York: Scientific American Books.

Towe, Kenneth M. 1973. "Trilobite Eyes: Calcified Lenses in Vivo." *Science,* Vol. 179 (March 9, 1973).

Walker, Cyril, and David Ward. 1992. *Eyewitness Handbooks: Fossils.* New York: Dorling Kindersley.

Whittington, Harry B. 1977. "The Middle Cambrian Trilobite *Naraoia,* Burgess Shale, British Columbia." *Philosophical Transactions of the Royal Society of London,* Ser. B, Vol. 280, No. 970.

———. 1985. "*Tegopelte gigas,* a Second Soft-Bodied Trilobite from the Burgess Shale, Middle Cambrian, British Columbia." *Journal of Paleontology*, Vol. 59, No. 5.

CERTAINTY AND DOUBT IN BAJA

Alexander, Charles E., and Walter G. Whitford. 1968. "Energy Requirements of *Uta stansburiana.*" *Copeia,* No. 4.

Gans, Carl. 1979. "Momentarily Excessive Construction as the Basis for Protoadaptation." *Evolution,* Vol. 33, No. 1.

Herbers, Joan M. 1981. "Time Resources and Laziness in Animals." *Oecologia,* Vol. 49.

Hertz, Paul E., Raymond B. Huey, and Eviator Nevo. 1982. "Fight Versus Flight: Body Temperature Influences Defensive Responses in Lizards." *Animal Behaviour,* Vol. 30.

———. 1983. "Homage to Santa Anita: Thermal Sensitivity of Sprint Speed in Agamid Lizards." *Evolution,* Vol. 37, No. 5.

Hertz, Paul, Raymond B. Huey, and Theodore Garland, Jr. 1988. "Time Budgets, Thermoregulation, and Maximal Locomotor Performances: Are Reptiles Olympians or Boy Scouts?" *American Zoologist,* Vol. 28.

Huey, Raymond B., Albert F. Bennett, Henry John-Alder, and Kenneth A. Nagy. 1984. "Locomotor Capacity and Foraging Behaviour of Kalahari Lacertid Lizards." *Animal Behaviour,* Vol. 32.

Huey, Raymond B., and Paul E. Hertz. 1982. "Effects of Body Size and Slope on Sprint Speed of a Lizard *(Stellio [Agama] stellio.)*" *Journal of Experimental Biology,* Vol. 97.

————. 1984. "Effects of Body Size and Slope on Acceleration of a Lizard *(Stellio [Agama] stellio)*." *Journal of Experimental Biology*, Vol. 110.

Huey, Raymond B., and Joel G. Kingsolver. 1989. "Evolution of Thermal Sensitivity of Ectotherm Performance." *TREE*, Vol. 4, No. 5.

Huey, Raymond B., and Montgomery Slatkin. 1976. "Cost and Benefits of Lizard Thermoregulation." *The Quarterly Review of Biology*, Vol. 51, No. 3.

Huey, Raymond B., W. Schneider, G. L. Erie, and R. D. Stevenson. 1981. "A Field-Portable Racetrack and Timer for Measuring Acceleration and Speed of Small Cursorial Animals." *Experientia*, Vol. 37.

Tinkle, Donald W., Don McGregor, and Sumner Dana. 1962. "Home Range Ecology of *Uta stansburiana stejnegeri*." *Ecology*, Vol. 43.

PHOBIA AND PHILIA

Adams, K. A. 1981. "Arachnophobia: Love American Style." *Journal of Psychoanalytic Anthropology*, Vol. 4.

Bowd, Alan D., and Colin R. Boylan. 1984. "Reported Fears of Animals Among Biology and Non-Biology Students." *Psychological Reports*, Vol. 54.

Buss, Arnold H., E. Neil Murray, and Edith Buss. 1968. "Stimulus Generalization and Fear of Snakes." *Journal of Personality and Social Psychology*, Vol. 10.

Caras, Roger A. 1977. *Dangerous to Man: The Definitive Story of Wildlife's Reputed Dangers*. South Hackensack, N.J.: Stoeger Publishing Company.

Freud, Sigmund. 1953. *The Interpretation of Dreams*. Translated from the German and edited by James Strachey. London: Hogarth Press.

Geer, James H. 1965. "The Development of a Scale to Measure Fear." *Behaviour Research and Therapy*, Vol. 3.

Hardy, Tad N. 1988. "Entomophobia: The Case for Miss Muffet." *Bulletin of the Entomological Society of America*, Vol. 34.

Harrison, Jim. 1989. "Cobra." In *The Theory & Practice of Rivers and New Poems*. Livingston, Mont.: Clark City Press.

Hugdahl, Kenneth, and Ann-Christine Karker. 1981. "Biological Vs. Experiential Factors in Phobic Conditioning." *Behaviour Research and Therapy*, Vol. 19.

Joslin, J., H. Fletcher, and J. Emlen. 1964. "A Comparison of the Responses to Snakes of Lab- and Wild-Reared Rhesus Monkeys." *Animal Behaviour*, Vol. 12.

Kellert, Stephen R., and Edward O. Wilson, eds. 1993. *The Biophilia Hypothesis*. Washington, D.C.: Island Press.

Klorman, Rafael, Theodore C. Weerts, James E. Hastings, Barbara G. Melamed, and Peter J. Lang. 1974. "Psychometric Description of Some Specific-Fear Questionnaires." *Behavior Therapy*, Vol. 5.

Marks, Isaac M. 1969. *Fears and Phobias*. New York: Academic Press.

Mineka, Susan, Mark Davidson, Michael Cook, and Richard Keir. 1984. "Observational Conditioning of Snake Fear in Rhesus Monkeys." *Journal of Abnormal Psychology*, Vol. 93.

Mundkur, Balaji. 1983. *The Cult of the Serpent: An Interdisciplinary Survey of Its Manifestations and Origins*. Albany: State University of New York Press.

Murray, Edward J., and Frank Foote. 1979. "The Origins of Fear of Snakes." *Behaviour Research and Therapy,* Vol. 17.

Ohman, Arne. 1986. "Face the Beast and Fear the Face: Animal and Social Fears as Prototypes for Evolutionary Analyses of Emotion." *Psychophysiology,* Vol. 23, No. 2.

Ohman, Arne, and Joachim J. F. Soares. 1993. "On the Automatic Nature of Phobic Fear: Conditioned Electrodermal Responses to Masked Fear-Relevant Stimuli." *Journal of Abnormal Psychology,* Vol. 102.

Sabath, Michael D., Laura E. Sabath, and Allen M. Moore. 1974. "Web, Reproduction and Commensals of the Semisocial Spider *Cryptophora moluccensis* (Araneae: Araneidae) on Guam, Mariana Islands." *Micronesica,* Vol. 10, No. 1.

Seligman, Martin E. P. 1970. "On the Generality of the Laws of Learning." *Psychological Review,* Vol. 77.

Ulrich, Roger S. 1993. "Biophilia, Biophobia, and Natural Landscapes." In *The Biophilia Hypothesis,* edited by Stephen R. Kelert and Edward O. Wilson. Washington, D.C.: Island Press.

———. 1971. "Phobias and Preparedness." *Behavior Therapy,* Vol. 2.

White, E. B. 1980. *Charlotte's Web.* New York: HarperCollins.

Wilkins, Wallace. 1978. "Imagery Values of Fear Items." *Behavior Therapy,* Vol. 9.

Wilson, Edward O. 1984. *Biophilia.* Cambridge, Mass.: Harvard University Press.

———. 1985. "In the Queendom of the Ants: A Brief Autobiography." In *Leaders in the Study of Animal Behavior: Autobiographical Perspectives.* Edited by D. A. Dewsbury. Lewisburg, Pa.: Bucknell University Press.

Wolin, Lee R., J. M. Ordy, and Arline Dillman. 1963. "Monkeys' Fear of Snakes: A Study of Its Basis and Generality." *The Journal of Genetic Psychology,* Vol. 103.

WHO SWIMS WITH THE TUNA

Anderson, Ian. 1988. "Millions of Dolphins Butchered in Tuna Nets." *New Scientist,* March 17, 1988.

Brower, Kenneth. 1989. "The Destruction of Dolphins." *The Atlantic Monthly,* July 1989.

Conner, K. Patrick. 1990. "The Conversion of StarKist." *This World/The San Francisco Chronicle,* June 17, 1990.

Herald, Earl S. 1961. "Mackerels, Tunas, Marlins, and Their Relatives." *Living Fishes of the World.* New York: Doubleday.

Phillips, David. 1990. "Breakthrough for Dolphins: How We Did It." *Earth Island Journal,* Summer 1990.

Steiner, Todd, David Phillips, and Mark J. Palmer. N.d. "The Tragedy Continues: Killing of Dolphins by the Tuna Industry." San Francisco: Earth Island Institute.

TROPICAL PASSENGERS

Dawood, Richard. 1989. *How to Stay Healthy Abroad*. Oxford: Oxford University Press.

SPATULA THEORY

Bateson, Patrick, ed. 1983. *Mate Choice*. Cambridge: Cambridge University Press.

Batten, Mary. 1992. *Sexual Strategies: How Females Choose Their Mates*. New York: G. P. Putnam's Sons.

Berglund, Anders, Gunilla Rosenqvist, and Ingrid Svensson. 1989. "Reproductive Success of Females Limited by Males in Two Pipefish Species." *American Naturalist*, Vol. 133, No. 4.

Campbell, Bernard, ed. 1972. *Sexual Selection and the Descent of Man*. Chicago: Aldine Publishing Company.

Darwin, Charles. N.d.; reprint of 1871 edition. *The Descent of Man and Selection in Relation to Sex*. New York: The Modern Library.

Eberhard, William G. 1985. *Sexual Selection and Animal Genitalia*. Cambridge, Mass.: Harvard University Press.

———. 1990. "Animal Genitalia and Female Choice." *American Scientist*, Vol. 78 (March–April 1990).

Halliday, Tim. 1980. *Sexual Strategy*. Chicago: The University of Chicago Press.

Parkes, A. S., ed. 1956. *Marshall's Physiology of Reproduction*. London: Longmans, Green and Co.

Smith, Robert L., ed. 1984. *Sperm Competition and the Evolution of Animal Mating Systems*. New York: Academic Press.

Thornhill, Randy. 1983. "Cryptic Female Choice and Its Implications in the Scorpionfly *Harpobittacus nigriceps*." *American Naturalist*, Vol. 122, No. 6.

THE GREAT STINKING CLUE

Corner, E. J. H. 1949. "The Durian Theory or the Origin of the Modern Tree." *Annals of Botany*, New Series, Vol. XIII.

———. 1954. "The Evolution of Tropical Forest." In *Evolution as a Process*. Edited by J. S. Huxley, A. C. Hardy, and E. B. Ford. London: Methuen.

———. 1964. *The Life of Plants*. Chicago: The University of Chicago Press.

Eiseman, Fred, and Margaret Eiseman. 1988. *Fruits of Bali*. Berkeley: Periplus Editions.

Herrera, Carlos M. 1981. "Are Tropical Fruits More Rewarding to Dispersers Than Temperate Ones?" *American Naturalist*, Vol. 118.

Howe, Henry F., and George F. Estabrook. 1977. "On Intraspecific Competition for Avian Dispersers in Tropical Trees." *American Naturalist*, Vol. 111, No. 981.

Janzen, Daniel H., and Paul S. Martin. 1982. "Neotropical Anachronisms: The Fruits the Gomphotheres Ate." *Science*, Vol. 215 (January 1, 1982).

Loveless, A. R. 1983. *Principles of Plant Biology for the Tropics*. London: Longman Group.

Morten, Eugene S. 1973. "On the Evolutionary Advantages and Disadvantages of Fruit Eating in Tropical Birds." *American Naturalist*, Vol. 107, No. 953.

Piper, Jacqueline M. 1989. *Fruits of South-East Asia: Facts and Folklore*. Singapore: Oxford University Press.

Popenoe, Wilson. 1974. *Manual of Tropical and Subtropical Fruits*. New York: Hafner Press (Macmillan Publishing Co.). A facsimile of the 1920 edition.

Rick, Charles M., and Robert I. Bowman. 1961. "Galapagos Tomatoes and Tortoises." *Evolution*, Vol. 15.

Snow, D. W. 1971. "Evolutionary Aspects of Fruit-Eating by Birds." *Ibis*, Vol. 113.

Wilson, Mary F. 1983. *Plant Reproductive Ecology*. New York: John Wiley & Sons.

THE DOPE ON EGGS

Bell, Graham. 1978. "The Evolution of Anisogamy." *Journal of Theoretical Biology*, Vol. 73.

Burton, Robert. 1987. *Eggs: Nature's Perfect Package*. Photographs by Jane Burton, Kim Taylor, and others. New York: Facts on File Publications.

Charlesworth, Brian. 1978. "The Population Genetics of Anisogamy." *Journal of Theoretical Biology*, Vol. 73.

Ghiselin, Michael T. 1974. *The Economy of Nature and the Evolution of Sex*. Berkeley: University of California Press.

Hoekstra, Rolf F. 1980. "Why Do Organisms Produce Gametes of Only Two Different Sizes? Some Theoretical Aspects of the Evolution of Anisogamy." *Journal of Theoretical Biology*, Vol. 87.

Knowlton, Nancy. 1974. "A Note on the Evolution of Gamete Dimorphism." *Journal of Theoretical Biology*, Vol. 46.

Lewin, Roger. 1986. "Egg Laying Is for the Birds." *Science*, Vol. 234 (October 17, 1986).

Margulis, Lynn, and Dorion Sagan. 1986. *Origins of Sex: Three Billion Years of Genetic Recombinations*. New Haven: Yale University Press.

Parker, G. A. 1978. "Selection on Non-Random Fusion of Gametes During the Evolution of Anisogamy." *Journal of Theoretical Biology*, Vol. 73.

―――. 1982. "Why Are There so Many Tiny Sperm? Sperm Competition and the Maintenance of Two Sexes." *Journal of Theoretical Biology*, Vol. 96.

Parker, G. A., R. R. Baker, and V. G. F. Smith. 1972. "The Origin and Evolution of Gamete Dimorphism and the Male-Female Phenomenon." *Journal of Theoretical Biology*, Vol. 36.

Peterson, Roger Tory. 1979. *Penguins*. Boston: Houghton Mifflin Company.

Romanoff, Alexis L., and Anastasia J. Romanoff. 1949. *The Avian Egg*. New York: John Wiley & Sons.

Sokolov, Raymond. 1983. "About Eggs." *Natural History*, Vol. 92 (September 1983).

THE CATS THAT FLY BY THEMSELVES

Beadle, Muriel. 1977. *The Cat: A Complete Authoritative Compendium of Information About Domestic Cats.* New York: Simon & Schuster.

Clutton-Brock, Juliet. 1993. *Cats: Ancient and Modern.* Cambridge, Mass.: Harvard University Press.

Darnton, Robert. 1984. *The Great Cat Massacre and Other Episodes in French Cultural History.* New York: Basic Books.

Darwin, Charles. 1892. *The Variation of Animals and Plants Under Domestication.* New York: D. Appleton and Company.

Kipling, Rudyard. 1982. "The Cat That Walked by Himself." From *Just So Stories* and collected in *The Portable Kipling.* Edited by Irving Howe. New York: The Viking Press.

Kitchener, Andrew. 1991. *The Natural History of Wild Cats.* Ithaca, N.Y.: Cornell University Press.

McDonald, Donald. 1960. "How Does a Cat Fall on Its Feet?" *New Scientist,* Vol. 7 (June 30, 1960).

Serpell, James A. 1988. "The Domestication and History of the Cat." In *The Domestic Cat: The Biology of Its Behaviour.* Edited by Dennis C. Turner and Patrick Bateson. Cambridge: Cambridge University Press.

Shesgreen, Sean, ed. 1973. *Engravings by Hogarth.* New York: Dover Publications, Inc.

Todd, Neil B. 1977. "Cats and Commerce." *Scientific American,* Vol. 237, No. 5.

Turner, Dennis C., and Patrick Bateson. 1988. "Questions About Cats." In *The Domestic Cat: The Biology of Its Behaviour.* Cambridge: Cambridge University Press.

Vesey-Fitzgerald, Brian. 1957. *Cats.* Harmondsworth, Middlesex, England: Penguin.

Whitney, Wayne O., and Cheryl J. Mehlhaff. 1987. "High-Rise Syndrome in Cats." *Journal of the American Veterinary Medical Association,* Vol. 191, No. 11.

Zeuner, Frederick E. 1963. *A History of Domesticated Animals.* New York: Harper & Row.

LOCAL BIRD MAKES GOOD

Bakker, Robert T. 1971. "Dinosaur Physiology and the Origin of Mammals." *Evolution,* Vol. 25.

———. 1972. "Anatomical and Ecological Evidence of Endothermy in Dinosaurs." *Nature,* Vol. 238 (July 14, 1972).

———. 1975. "Dinosaur Renaissance." *Scientific American,* Vol. 232, No. 4.

———. 1986. *Dinosaur Heresies: New Theories Unlocking the Mystery of Dinosaurs and Their Extinction.* New York: William Morrow.

———. 1992. "Inside the Head of a Tiny *T. rex.*" *Discover,* Vol. 13 (March 1992).

Bakker, Robert T., and Peter M. Galton. 1974. "Dinosaur Monophyly and a New Class of Vertebrates." *Nature,* Vol. 248 (March 8, 1974).

Barrick, Reese E., and William J. Showers. 1994. "Thermophysiology of *Tyran-*

nosaurus rex: Evidence from Oxygen Isotopes." *Science,* Vol. 265 (July 8, 1994).

Bennett, Albert F. 1974. "A Final Word." *Evolution,* Vol. 28.

Bennett, Albert F., and Bonnie Dalzell. 1973. "Dinosaur Physiology: A Critique." *Evolution,* Vol. 27.

Brown, Barnum. 1915. "Tyrannosaurus, a Cretaceous Carnivorous Dinosaur." *Scientific American,* Vol. 113, No. 15.

Carpenter, Kenneth, and Philip J. Currie. 1990. *Dinosaur Systematics: Approaches and Perspectives.* Cambridge: Cambridge University Press.

Charig, Alan. 1979. *A New Look at the Dinosaurs.* New York: Facts on File Publications.

Colbert, Edwin H. 1968. *Men and Dinosaurs.* Harmondsworth, Middlesex, England: Penguin.

Desmond, Adrian J. 1977. *The Hot-Blooded Dinosaurs: A Revolution in Paleontology.* New York: Warner Books.

Dodson, Peter. 1974. "Dinosaurs as Dinosaurs." *Evolution,* Vol. 28.

Feduccia, Alan. 1973. "Dinosaurs as Reptiles." *Evolution,* Vol. 27.

———. 1974. "Endothermy, Dinosaurs, and *Archaeopteryx*." *Evolution,* Vol. 28.

Glut, Donald F. 1982. *The New Dinosaur Dictionary.* Secaucus, N.J.: Citadel Press.

Horner, John R., and James Gorman. 1988. *Digging Dinosaurs.* New York: Workman Publishing.

Horner, John R., and Don Lessem. 1993. *The Complete T. Rex.* New York: Simon & Schuster.

Lambert, David, and the Diagram Group. 1990. *The Dinosaur Data Book.* New York: Avon Books.

Morell, Virginia. 1994. "Warm-Blooded Dino Debate Blows Hot and Cold." *Science,* Vol. 265 (July 8, 1994).

Myers, Rex C., and Norma B. Ashby. 1989. *Symbols of Montana.* Helena: Montana Historical Society Foundation.

Osborn, Henry Fairfield. 1905. "Tyrannosaurus and Other Cretaceous Carnivorous Dinosaurs." *Bulletin of the American Museum of Natural History,* Vol. 21, Article 14.

———. 1906. "Tyrannosaurus, Upper Cretaceous Carnivorous Dinosaur (Second Communication)." *Bulletin of the American Museum of Natural History,* Vol. 22, Article 16.

———. 1915. "Tyrannosaurus, Restoration and Model of the Skeleton." *Bulletin of the American Museum of Natural History,* Vol. 32, Article 4.

Ostrom, J. H. 1973. "The Ancestry of Birds." *Nature,* Vol. 242 (March 9, 1973).

———. 1974. "Reply to 'Dinosaurs as Reptiles.'" *Evolution,* Vol. 28.

Turner, Craig. 1994. "Scientists Find Rare Tyrannosaurus Skeleton in Canada." *Los Angeles Times* (June 30, 1994).

Wallace, Joseph. 1987. *The Rise and Fall of the Dinosaur.* New York: W. H. Smith Publishers.

Wilford, John Noble. 1985. *The Riddle of the Dinosaur.* New York: Alfred A. Knopf.

ONE MAN'S MEAT

Wiles, Gary J. 1987. "Current Research and Future Management of Malians Fruit Bats (Chiroptera: Pteropodidae) on Guam." *Australian Mammalogy,* Vol. 10.

———. 1987. "The Status of Fruit Bats on Guam." *Pacific Science,* Vol. 41.

———. 1987. "The Trade in Fruit Bats in the Malians and Other Pacific Islands." *Ples,* Vol. 3.

Wiles, Gary J., Thomas O. Lemke, and Nicholas H. Payne. 1989. "Population Estimates of Fruit Bats (*Pteropus mariannus*) in the Mariana Islands." *Conservation Biology,* Vol. 3, No. 1.

Wiles, Gary J., and Nicholas H. Payne. 1986. "The Trade in Fruit Bats *Pteropus* spp. on Guam and Other Pacific Islands." *Biological Conservation,* Vol. 38.

EITHER OR NEITHER

Bonner, John T. 1944. "A Descriptive Study of the Development of the Slime Mold *Dictyostelium discoideum.*" *American Journal of Botany,* Vol. 31.

———. 1959. *The Cellular Slime Molds.* Princeton, N.J.: Princeton University Press.

———. 1969. "Hormones in Social Amoebae and Mammals." *Scientific American,* Vol. 220, No. 6.

———. 1982. "Evolutionary Strategies and Developmental Constraints in the Cellular Slime Molds." *American Naturalist,* Vol. 119, No. 4.

———. 1983. "Chemical Signals of Social Amoebae." *Scientific American,* Vol. 248, No. 4.

———. 1993. *Life Cycles: Reflections of an Evolutionary Biologist.* Princeton, N.J.: Princeton University Press.

Bonner, John Tyler, A. Chiang, J. Lee, and H. B. Suthers. 1988. "The Possible Role of Ammonia in Phototaxis of Migrating Slugs of *Dictyostelium discoideum.*" *Proceedings of the National Academy of Sciences,* Vol. 85.

Bonner, John Tyler, William Wight Clarke, Jr., Charles Lea Neely, Jr., and Miriam Kresses Slifkin. 1950. "The Orientation to Light and the Extremely Sensitive Orientation to Temperature Gradients in the Slime Mold *Dictyostelium discoideum.*" *Journal of Cellular and Comparative Physiology,* Vol. 36.

Bonner, John Tyler, and Marya R. Dodd. 1962. "Evidence for Gas-Induced Orientation in the Cellular Slime Molds." *Developmental Biology,* Vol. 5.

Bonner, John Tyler, and Marcia J. Shaw. 1957. "The Role of Humidity in the Differentiation of the Cellular Slime Molds." *Journal of Cellular and Comparative Physiology,* Vol. 50.

Hodges, Andrew. 1983. *Alan Turing: The Enigma.* New York: Simon and Schuster.

Margulis, Lynn, and Karlene V. Schwartz. 1988. *Five Kingdoms: An Illustrated Guide to the Phyla of Life on Earth.* New York: W. H. Freeman.

Turing, A. M. 1952. "The Chemical Basis of Morphogenesis." *Philosophical Transactions of the Royal Society of London,* Ser. B, Vol. 237, No. 641.

Whittaker, R. H. 1959. "On the Broad Classification of Organisms." *The Quarterly Review of Biology,* Vol. 34, No. 3.

BEAST IN THE MIRROR

Ankle-Simons, Friderun. 1983. *A Survey of Living Primates and Their Anatomy.* New York: Macmillan Publishing.

Balog, James. 1993. *Anima.* Boulder, Colo.: Arts Alternative Press.

Caccione, Adalgisa, and Jeffrey R. Powell. 1989. "DNA Divergence Among Hominoids." *Evolution,* Vol. 43, No. 5.

Cavalieri, Paola, and Peter Singer, eds. 1993. *The Great Ape Project: Equality Beyond Humanity.* London: Fourth Estate.

Diamond, Jared. 1991. *The Rise and Fall of the Third Chimpanzee.* London: Radius.

Gallup, Gordon G., Jr. 1970. "Chimpanzees: Self-Recognition." *Science,* Vol. 167 (January 2, 1970).

————. 1977. "Self-Recognition in Primates." *American Psychologist,* Vol. 32.

Goodall, Jane. 1986. *The Chimpanzees of Gombe: Patterns of Behavior.* Cambridge, Mass.: The Belknap Press of Harvard University Press.

Goodman, Morris, Ben F. Koop, John Czelusniak, David H. A. Fitch, Danilo A. Tagle, and Jerry L. Slightom. 1989. "Molecular Phylogeny of the Family of Apes and Humans." *Genome,* Vol. 31.

Goodman, Morris, Danilo A. Tagle, David H. A. Fitch, Wendy Bailey, John Czelusniak, Ben F. Koop, Philip Benson, and Jerry L. Slightom. 1990. "Primate Evolution at the DNA Level and a Classification of Hominoids." *Journal of Molecular Evolution,* Vol. 30.

King, Mary-Claire, and A. C. Wilson. 1975. "Evolution at Two Levels in Humans and Chimpanzees." *Science,* Vol. 188 (April 11, 1975).

Kingdon, Jonathan. 1971. *East African Mammals: An Atlas of Evolution in Africa,* Vol. 1. London: Academic Press.

Marks, Jon, Carl W. Schmid, and Vincent M. Sarich. 1988. "DNA Hybridization as a Guide to Phylogeny: Relations of the Hominoidea." *Journal of Human Evolution,* Vol. 17.

Miyamoto, Michael M., Jerry L. Slightom, and Morris Goodman. 1987. "Phylogenetic Relations of Humans and Africa Apes from DNA Sequences in the ψη-Globin Region." *Science,* Vol. 238 (October 16, 1987).

Morris, Ramona, and Desmond Morris. 1966. *Men and Apes.* New York: McGraw-Hill Book Company.

Nichols, Michael. 1993. *The Great Apes: Between Two Worlds.* Washington, D.C.: National Geographic Society.

Nichols, Michael, and Jane Goodall. 1999. *Brutal Kinship.* New York: Aperture.

Peterson, Dale, and Jane Goodall. 1993. *Visions of Caliban: On Chimpanzees and People.* Boston: Houghton Mifflin.

Ritvo, Harriet. 1987. *The Animal Estate: The English and Other Creatures in the Victorian Age.* Cambridge, Mass.: Harvard University Press.

Sibley, Charles G., and Jon E. Ahlquist. 1983. "Phylogeny and Classification of Birds Based on the Data of DNA-DNA Hybridization." In *Current Ornithology*, Vol. 1. Edited by Richard F. Johnston. New York: Plenum Press.

Sibley, Charles G., Jon E. Ahlquist, and Burt L. Monroe, Jr. 1988. "A Classification of the Living Birds of the World Based on DNA-DNA Hybridization Studies." *The Auk*, Vol. 105.

Sibley, Charles G., John A. Comstock, and Jon E. Ahlquist. 1990. "DNA Hybridization Evidence of Hominoid Phylogeny: A Reanalysis of the Data." *Journal of Molecular Evolution*, Vol. 30. (The two earlier studies of hominoid phylogeny by Sibley and Ahlquist were "The Phylogeny of the Hominoid Primates, as Indicated by DNA-DNA Hybridization," *Journal of Molecular Evolution*, Vol. 20 [1984], and "DNA Hybridization Evidence of Hominoid Phylogeny: Results from an Expanded Data Set," *Journal of Molecular Evolution*, Vol. 26 [1987]. These two were unavailable to me, but were well summarized in Diamond's *The Rise and Fall of The Third Chimpanzee*.)

Szalay, Frederick S., and Eric Delson. 1979. *Evolutionary History of the Primates*. New York: Academic Press.

Walker, Ernest P., ed. 1964. *Mammals of the World*, Vol. 1. Baltimore: The Johns Hopkins University Press.

Wolfheim, Jaclyn H. 1983. *Primates of the World: Distribution, Abundance, and Conservation*. Seattle: University of Washington Press.

World Conservation Monitoring Centre. 1990. *1990 IUCN Red List of Threatened Animals*. Gland, Switzerland: IUCN.

PALPATING THE TUMOR

Currie, Graham, and Angela Currie. 1982. *Cancer: The Biology of Malignant Disease*. London: Edward Arnold.

Franks, Arthur. 1991. *At the Will of the Body*. Boston: Houghton Mifflin.

Hall, J. M., M. K. Lee, B. Newman, J. E. Morrow, L. A. Anderson, B. Huey, and M. C. King. 1990. "Linkage of Early-Onset Familial Breast Cancer to Chromosome 17q21." *Science,* Vol. 250 (December 21, 1990).

Iggo, R., K. Gatter, J. Bartek, D. Lane, and A. L. Harris. 1990. "Increased Expression of Mutant Forms of p53 Oncogene in Primary Lung Cancer." *Lancet,* Vol. 335.

Malkin, D., F. P. Li, L. C. Strong, J. F. Fraumeni, Jr., C. E. Nelson, D. H. Kim, J. Kassel, M. A. Gryka, F. Z. Bischoff, M. A. Tainsky, and S. H. Friend. 1990. "Germ Line p53 Mutations in a Familial Syndrome of Breast Cancer, Sarcomas, and Other Neoplasms." *Science,* Vol. 250 (November 30, 1990).

Marshall, Eliot. 1990. "Experts Clash Over Cancer Data." *Science,* Vol. 250 (November 16, 1990).

Nigro, J. M., S. J. Baker, A. C. Preisinger, J. M. Jessup, R. Hostetter, K. Cleary, S. H. Bigner, N. Davidson, S. Baylin, P. Devilee, T. Glover, F. S. Collins, A. Weston, R. Modali, C. C. Harris, and B. Vogelstein. 1989. "Mutations in the p53 Gene Occur in Diverse Human Tumour Types." *Nature,* Vol. 342 (December 7, 1989).

Sontag, Susan. 1990. *Illness as Metaphor.* New York: Anchor Books.

Williams, Terry Tempest. 1992. *Refuge: An Unnatural History of Family and Place.* New York: Vintage Books.

Young, Robert C., Dan L. Longo, Robert F. Ozols, Joseph V. Simone, Glenn D. Steele, Jr., and Ralph R. Weichselbaum. 1991. *The Yearbook of Oncology— 1991.* St. Louis: Mosby.

RETHINKING THE LAWN

Appleton, Jay. 1975. *The Experience of Landscape.* London: John Wiley & Sons.

Balling, John D., and John H. Falk. 1982. "Development of Visual Preference for Natural Environments." *Environment and Behavior,* Vol. 14, No. 1.

Bormann, F. Herbert, Diane Balmori, and Gordon T. Geballe. 1993. *Redesigning the American Lawn: A Search for Environmental Harmony.* New Haven: Yale University Press.

Butzer, Karl W. 1977. "Environment, Culture, and Human Evolution." *American Scientist,* Vol. 65.

Heerwagen, Judith H., and Gordon H. Orians. 1993. "Humans, Habitats, and Aesthetics." In *The Biophilia Hypothesis.* Edited by Stephen R. Kellert and Edward O. Wilson. Washington, D.C.: Island Press.

Jackson, Kenneth T. 1985. *Crabgrass Frontier: The Suburbanization of the United States.* New York: Oxford University Press.

Jones, Malcolm, Jr. 1993. "The New Turf Wars." *Newsweek,* June 21, 1993.

Kellert, Stephen R., and Edward O. Wilson, eds. 1993. *The Biophilia Hypothesis.* Washington, D.C.: Island Press.

Orians, Gordon H. 1986. "An Ecological and Evolutionary Approach to Landscape Aesthetics." In *Landscape Meanings and Values.* Edited by Edmund C. Penning-Rowsell and David Lowenthal. London: Unwin Hyman.

Orians, Gordon H., and Judith H. Heerwagen. 1992. "Evolved Responses to Landscapes." In *The Adapted Mind: Evolutionary Psychology and the Generation of Culture.* Edited by Jerome H. Barkow, Leda Cosmides, and John Tooby. New York: Oxford University Press.

Pollan, Michael. 1991. *Second Nature: A Gardener's Education.* New York: Atlantic Monthly Press.

Rayner, R. J., B. P. Moon, and J. C. Masters. 1993. "The Makapansgat Australopithecine Environment." *Journal of Human Evolution,* Vol. 24.

Tobey, George B., Jr. 1973. *A History of Landscape Architecture: The Relationship of People to Environment.* New York: American Elsevier Publishing Company.

Ulrich, Roger S. 1986. "Human Responses to Vegetation and Landscapes." *Landscape and Urban Planning,* Vol. 13.

———. 1993. "Biophilia, Biophobia, and Natural Landscapes." In *The Biophilia Hypothesis,* edited by Stephen R. Kelert and Edward O. Wilson. Washington, D.C.: Island Press.

HALF-BLINDED POETS AND BIRDS

Clark, Eleanor. 1977. *Eyes, Etc.* New York: Pantheon.

Ellison, Ralph, and Eugene Walter. 1958. "Robert Penn Warren," an interview. In *Writers at Work: The Paris Review Interviews.* Edited with an introduction by Malcolm Cowley. New York: The Viking Press.

Harrison, Jim. 1989. *The Theory & Practice of Rivers and New Poems.* Livingston, Mont.: Clark City Press.

Tucker, Carll. 1981. "Creators on Creating: Robert Penn Warren," an interview. *Saturday Review*, July 1981.

Warren, Robert Penn. 1968. *Incarnations: Poems 1966–1968.* New York: Random House.

———. 1969. *Audubon: A Vision.* New York: Random House.

———. 1983. *Chief Joseph of the Nez Perce.* New York: Random House.

———. 1985. *New and Selected Poems 1923–1985.* New York: Random House.

TIME-AND-MOTION STUDY

Heinrich, Bernd. 1979. *Bumblebee Economics.* Cambridge, Mass.: Harvard University Press.

Mayr, Ernst. 1982. *The Growth of Biological Thought: Diversity, Evolution, and Inheritance.* Cambridge, Mass.: The Belknap Press of Harvard University Press.

THE BOILERPLATE RHINO

Gesner, Konrad. 1971. *Curious Woodcuts of Fanciful and Real Beasts: A Selection of 190 Sixteenth-Century Woodcuts from Gesner's and Topsell's Natural Histories.* New York: Dover Publications, Inc.

Hind, Arthur M. 1963. *An Introduction to a History of Woodcut.* New York: Dover Publications, Inc.

Kurth, Willi, ed. N.d. *The Complete Woodcuts of Albrecht Dürer.* Privately printed.

Musper, H. T. N.d. *Albrecht Dürer.* New York: The Library of Great Painters/Harry N. Abrams.

Nowak, Ronald M. 1991. *Walker's Mammals of the World,* Vol. II. Baltimore: The Johns Hopkins University Press.

Panofsky, Erwin. 1955. *The Life and Art of Albrecht Dürer.* Princeton, N.J.: Princeton University Press.

Pinault, Madeleine. 1991. *The Painter as Naturalist: From Dürer to Redouté.* Translated by Philip Sturgess. Paris: Flammarion.

Russell, Frances, and the editors of Time-Life Books. 1967. *The World of Dürer.* New York: Time Inc.

Siebert, Charles. 1993. "The Artifice of the Natural." *Harper's*, February 1993.

Strauss, Walter L., ed. 1980. *Albrecht Dürer: Woodcuts and Wood Blocks.* New York: Abaris Books.

Tudge, Colin. 1991. "Time to Save Rhinoceroses." *New Scientist*, September 28, 1991.

Younger, R. M. 1988. *Kangaroo: Images Through the Ages*. Melbourne: Century Hutchinson Australia.

LIMELIGHT

Altman, J. S. 1971. "Control of Accept and Reject Reflexes in the Octopus." *Nature*, Vol. 229, No. 5281 (January 15, 1971).

Ballard, Robert D., and J. Frederick Grassle. 1979. "Return to the Oases of the Deep." *National Geographic*, Vol. 156, No. 5 (November 1979).

Cone, Joseph. 1991. *Fire Under the Sea*. New York: William Morrow.

Corliss, John B., and Robert D. Ballard. 1977. "Oases of Life in the Cold Abyss." *National Geographic*, Vol. 152, No. 4 (October 1977).

Edmond, John M., and Karen Von Damm. 1983. "Hot Springs on the Ocean Floor." *Scientific American*, Vol. 248, No. 4.

Gunther, Klaus, and Kurt Deckert. 1956. *Creatures of the Deep Sea*. Translated by E. W. Dickes. New York: Charles Scribner's Sons.

Hamilton-Paterson, James. 1992. *The Great Deep: The Sea and Its Thresholds*. New York: Henry Holt and Company.

Idyll, C. P. 1976. *Abyss: The Deep Sea and the Creatures that Live in It*. New York: Thomas Y. Crowell Company.

Lane, Frank W. 1960. *Kingdom of the Octopus: The Life History of the Cephalopoda*. New York: Sheridan House.

Lutz, Richard A., and Rachel M. Haymon. 1994. "Rebirth of a Deep-Sea Vent." *National Geographic*, Vol. 186, No. 5 (November 1994).

Lutz, Richard A., and Janet R. Voight. 1994. "Close Encounter in the Deep." *Nature*, Vol. 371 (October 13, 1994).

Newman, William A. 1985. "The Abyssal Hydrothermal Vent Invertebrate Fauna: A Glimpse of Antiquity?" In *Hydrothermal Vents of the Eastern Pacific: An Overview*. Edited by Meredith L. Jones. *Bulletin of the Biological Society of Washington*, No. 6 (December 30, 1985).

Packard, Andrew. 1961. "Sucker Display of *Octopus*." *Nature*, Vol. 190 (May 20, 1961).

Purchon, R. D. 1968. *The Biology of the Mollusca*. Oxford: Pergamon Press.

Salvini-Plawen, L. V. 1974. "The Cephalopods." In *Grzimek's Animal Life Encyclopedia*. Edited by Bernhard Grzimek et al. New York: Van Nostrand Reinhold Company.

Voight, Janet R. 1991a. "Ligula Length and Courtship in *Octopus digueti*: A Potential Mechanism of Mate Choice." *Evolution*, Vol. 45, No. 7.

————. 1991b. "Enlarged Suckers as an Indicator of Male Maturity in *Octopus*." *Bulletin of Marine Science*, Vol. 49, Nos. 1–2.

————. 1991c. "Morphological Variation in Octopod Specimens: Reassessing the Assumption of Preservation-Induced Deformation." *Malacologia*, Vol. 33, Nos. 1–2.

————. 1992. "Movement, Injuries and Growth of Members of a Natural Population of the Pacific Pygmy Octopus, *Octopus digueti.*" *Journal of Zoology,* Vol. 228.

———. 1993a. "The Association Between Distribution and Octopodid Morphology: Implications for Classification." *Zoological Journal of the Linnean Society,* Vol. 108.

———. 1993b. "The Arrangement of Suckers on Octopodid Arms as a Continuous Character." *Malacologia,* Vol. 35, No. 2.

———. 1993c. "A Cladistic Reassessment of Octopodid Classification." *Malacologia,* Vol. 35, No. 2.

———. 1994. "Morphological Variation in Shallow-Water Octopuses (Mollusca: Cephalopoda)." *Journal of Zoology,* Vol. 232.

Wells, M. J., and J. Wells. 1972. "Sexual Displays and Mating of *Octopus vulgaris* Cuvier and *O. cyanea* Gray and Attempts to Alter Performance by Manipulating the Glandular Condition of the Animals." *Animal Behaviour,* Vol. 20.

Wells, Morris M. 1928. "Breeding Habits of Octopus." *Science,* Vol. 68 (November 16, 1928).

Young, J. Z. 1962. "Courtship and Mating by a Coral Reef Octopus *(O. horridus).*" *Proceedings of the Zoological Society of London,* Vol. 138, No. 1.

GARDENING ON MARS

Baker, Victor R. 1982. *The Channels of Mars.* Austin: University of Texas Press.

Beish, Jeff. 1988. "A Mars Observer's Guide." *Sky & Telescope,* Vol. 75, No. 5.

Beish, Jeff D., and Donald C. Parker. 1988. "Exploring Mars in 1988." *Sky & Telescope,* Vol. 75, No. 4.

Bradbury, Ray, Arthur C. Clarke, Bruce Murray, Carl Sagan, and Walter Sullivan. 1973. *Mars and the Mind of Man.* New York: Harper & Row.

Burgess, Eric. 1978. *To the Red Planet.* New York: Columbia University Press.

Carr, Michael H. 1981. *The Surface of Mars.* New Haven: Yale University Press.

Carroll, Michael. 1988. "Digging Deeper for Life on Mars." *Astronomy,* Vol. 16, No. 4.

Evans, David S. 1976. "A Fancier of Mars." *Science,* Vol. 193 (August 27, 1976).

Gifford, F. A., Jr. 1964. "The Martian Canals According to a Purely Aeolian Hypothesis." *Icarus,* Vol. 3.

Gordon, Rodger. 1988. "Martian Canals: Is Lowell Vindicated?" *Sky & Telescope,* Vol. 75, No. 4.

Haberle, Robert M. 1986. "The Climate of Mars." *Scientific American,* Vol. 254, No. 5.

Hoagland, Richard C. 1986. "The Curious Case of the Humanoid Face . . . on Mars." *Analog Science Fiction/Science Fact.*

Kaplan, Justine. 1988. "Of Mars and Men." *Omni,* July 1988.

Lowell, Percival. 1895. "Mars." An article in four installments ("I. Atmosphere," "II. The Water Problem," "III. Canals," "IV. Oases"). *The Atlantic Monthly,* May, June, July, August 1895.

Pittendrigh, Colin S., Wolf Vishniac, and J. P. T. Pearman, eds. 1966. *Biology and*

the Exploration of Mars. Washington, D.C.: National Academy of Sciences/
National Research Council.

Sagan, Carl, and Paul Fox. 1975. "The Canals of Mars: An Assessment after
Mariner 9." *Icarus,* Vol. 25.

Sagan, Carl, and Joshua Lederberg. 1976. "The Prospects for Life on Mars: A Pre-
Viking Assessment." *Icarus,* Vol. 28.

Sagan, Carl, and James B. Pollack. 1966. "On the Nature of the Canals of Mars."
Nature, Vol. 212 (October 8, 1966).

Salisbury, John W. 1966. "The Light and Dark Areas of Mars." *Icarus,* Vol. 5.

Schmidt, Stanley. 1986. "Cold Feet." *Analog Science Fiction/Science Fact.*

Soffen, G. A., and C. W. Snyder. 1976. "The First Viking Mission to Mars." *Science,* Vol. 193 (August 27, 1976).

Trefil, James. 1988. "Phenomena, Comment and Notes." *Smithsonian,* Vol. 18,
No. 10.

Webb, Wells Alan. 1956. *Mars, the New Frontier: Lowell's Hypothesis.* San Francisco: Fearon Publishers.

IMPERSONATING HENRY THOREAU

Edel, Leon. 1982. "The Mystery of Walden Pond." From *Stuff of Sleep and
Dreams: Experiments in Literary Psychology.* New York: Harper & Row.

Harding, Walter. 1970. *The Days of Henry Thoreau.* New York: Alfred A. Knopf.

———, ed. 1954. *Thoreau: A Century of Criticism.* Dallas: Southern Methodist
University Press.

Meltzer, Milton, and Walter Harding. 1962. *A Thoreau Profile.* New York:
Thomas Y. Crowell Company.

Shanley, J. Lyndon. 1957. *The Making of "Walden."* Chicago: The University of
Chicago Press.

Thoreau, Henry David. 1965. *Walden, and Other Writings of Henry David
Thoreau.* Edited and with an introduction by Brooks Atkinson. New York:
The Modern Library.

———. 1965. *Walden, or, Life in the Woods and On the Duty of Civil Disobedi-
ence.* With an introduction by Harvey Curtis Webster. New York: Harper &
Row.

———. 1962. *The Journal of Henry David Thoreau.* In fourteen volumes bound
as two. Edited by Bradford Torrey and Francis H. Allen. With a foreword by
Walter Harding. New York: Dover Publications, Inc.

———. 1987. *Cape Cod.* With an introduction by Paul Theroux. New York: Penguin Books.

GOD'S WEAKNESS FOR BEETLES

Borror, Donald J., and Dwight M. DeLong. 1971. *An Introduction to the Study of
Insects.* New York: Holt, Rinehart and Winston.

Colinvaux, Paul. 1979. *Why Big Fierce Animals Are Rare: An Ecologist's Perspective.* Princeton, N.J.: Princeton University Press.

Connell, Joseph H. 1978. "Diversity in Tropical Rain Forests and Coral Reefs." *Science,* Vol. 199 (March 24, 1978).

Conniff, Richard. 1986. "Inventorying Life in a 'Biotic Frontier' Before It Disappears." *Smithsonian,* Vol. 17, No. 6 (September 1986).

Coope, G. R. 1979. "Late Cenozoic Fossil Coleoptera: Evolution, Biogeography, and Ecology." *Annual Review of Ecology and Systematics,* Vol. 10.

Dial, Kenneth P., and John M. Marzluff. 1988. "Are the Smallest Organisms the Most Diverse?" *Ecology,* Vol. 69, No. 5.

Emsley, Michael. 1975. "Nature's Most Successful Design May Be Beetles." *Smithsonian,* Vol. 6 (December 1975).

Erwin, Terry L. 1982. "Tropical Forests: Their Richness in Coleoptera and Other Arthropod Species." *The Coleopterists Bulletin,* Vol. 36, No. 1.

———. 1986. "*Agra,* Arboreal Beetles of Neotropical Forests: *mixta* Group, *virgata* Group, and *ohausi* Group Systematics (Carabidae)." *Systematic Entomology,* Vol. 11.

Erwin, Terry L., and Janice C. Scott. 1982. "Seasonal and Size Patterns, Trophic Structure, and Richness of Coleoptera in the Tropical Arboreal Ecosystem: The Fauna of the Tree *Luehea seemannii* Triana and Planch in the Canal Zone of Panama." *The Coleopterists Bulletin,* Vol. 34, No. 3.

Gould, Stephen Jay. 1995. "A Special Fondness for Beetles." In *Dinosaur in a Haystack: Reflections in Natural History.* New York: Harmony Books.

Hutchinson, G. E. 1959. "Homage to Santa Rosalia or Why Are There So Many Kinds of Animals?" *American Naturalist,* Vol. 93, No. 870.

Klausnitzer, Bernhard. 1983. *Beetles.* Translated from the German by Sylvia Furness. New York: Exeter Books (Simon and Schuster).

Lewin, Roger. 1983. "Santa Rosalia Was a Goat." *Science,* Vol. 221 (August 12, 1983).

———. 1986. "Damage to Tropical Forests, or Why Were There So Many Kinds of Animals?" *Science,* Vol. 234 (October 10, 1986).

Mayr, Ernst. 1963. *Animal Species and Evolution.* Cambridge, Mass.: The Belknap Press of Harvard University Press.

Miller, Julie Ann. 1984. "Entomologist's Paradise." *Science News,* Vol. 125 (June 2, 1984).

Park, Thomas. 1962. "Beetles, Competition, and Populations." *Science,* Vol. 138, No. 3548 (December 28, 1962).

Sanders, Howard L. 1968. "Marine Benthic Diversity: A Comparative Study." *American Naturalist,* Vol. 102, No. 925.

Simberloff, Daniel, and William Boecklen. 1981. "Santa Rosalia Reconsidered: Size Ratios and Competition." *Evolution,* Vol. 35, No. 6.

Stanley, Steven M. 1975. "A Theory of Evolution Above the Species Level." *Proceedings of the National Academy of Sciences,* Vol. 72, No. 2.

Wolf, Edward C. 1987. "On the Brink of Extinction: Conserving the Diversity of Life." Worldwatch Paper 78. Washington, D.C.: Worldwatch Institute.

LIMITS OF VISION

Bartusiak, Marcia. 1988. "Wanted: Dark Matter." *Discover,* Vol. 9 (December 1988).

Chester, Michael. 1980. *Particles: An Introduction to Particle Physics.* New York: New American Library.

Horgan, John. 1990. "Universal Truths." *Scientific American,* Vol. 263, No. 4.

Lightman, Alan. 1991. *Ancient Light: Our Changing View of the Universe.* Cambridge, Mass.: Harvard University Press.

Lightman, Alan, and Roberta Brawer. 1990. *Origins: The Lives and Worlds of Modern Cosmologists.* Cambridge, Mass.: Harvard University Press.

Menzel, Donald H., and Jay M. Pasachoff. 1983. *Peterson Field Guides: Stars and Planets.* Boston: Houghton Mifflin.

Riordan, Michael, and David N. Schramm. 1991. *The Shadows of Creation: Dark Matter and the Structure of the Universe.* New York: W. H. Freeman.

Rowan-Robinson, Michael. 1991. "Dark Doubts for Cosmology." *New Scientist,* March 9, 1991.

Rubin, Vera C. 1983. "The Rotation of Spiral Galaxies." *Science,* Vol. 220, No. 4604 (June 24, 1983).

———. 1983. "Dark Matter in Spiral Galaxies." *Scientific American,* Vol. 248, No. 6.

Sandage, Alan, and John Bedke. 1988. *Atlas of Galaxies.* Washington, D.C.: NASA.

Trefil, James. 1988. *The Dark Side of the Universe: A Scientist Explores the Mysteries of the Cosmos.* New York: Anchor Books.

Tucker, Wallace, and Karen Tucker. 1988. *The Dark Matter.* New York: William Morrow.

Index

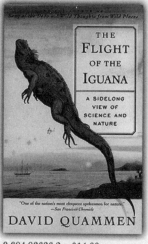
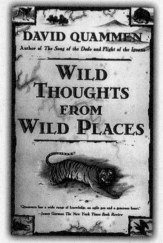